D0904125

Charles-Louis Clérisseau

The Architectural History Foundation, Inc.
New York, New York

•

The MIT Press
Cambridge, Massachusetts,
and
London, England

Charles-Louis Clérisseau

and the Genesis of Neo-Classicism

Thomas J. McCormick

© 1990 by The Architectural History Foundation and The Massachusetts Institute of Technology

Printed and bound in the United States of America.

All rights reserved. No parts of this book may be reproduced in any form or by any means, electronic or mechanical, including photocopying, recording, or by any information storage and retrieval system, without permission in writing from the publishers.

Library of Congress Cataloging-in-Publication Data

McCormick, Thomas.
    Charles-Louis Clérisseau and the Genesis of Neo-Classicism / Thomas McCormick.
        p.   cm.
      ISBN 0-262-13262-1
      1. Clérisseau, Charles-Louis, 1721–1820. 2. Architects—France-Biography. 3. Neoclassicism (Architecture)—France. I. Title.
NA1053.C58M38   1990
720'.92—dc20
[B]   90-31145
                       CIP

The Architectural History Foundation is a publicly supported, not-for-profit foundation. Directors: William Butler, Colin Eisler, Agnes Gund, Elizabeth G. Miller, Victoria Newhouse, Annalee Newman, Adolf K. Placzek. Editorial Board: George R. Collins, Emeritus; Christoph L. Frommel, Bibliotheca Hertziana, Rome; William H. Jordy, Brown University, Emeritus; Spiro Kostof, University of California, Berkeley; Barbara Miller Lane, Bryn Mawr College; Henry A. Millon, CASVA, National Gallery of Art, Washington, D.C.; John Summerson, Sir John Soane's Museum, London

Thomas J. McCormick is Professor of Art at Wheaton College, Norton, Massachusetts.

Designed by Sylvia Steiner

Frontispiece. J. Fischer (?), "Charles Louis Clérisseau," Private Collection

Contents

Cal
NA
1053
C58
m38
1990

In Memory of
Donald Drew Egbert
M. A. Gukovski

Preface and Acknowledgments

The origins and diffusion of Neo-Classicism in architecture during the eighteenth century are far from clear. Numerous people — French, Italian, and English — have been credited with its invention and thought of as seminal figures in its genesis. One of these is the French architect Charles-Louis Clérisseau (1721 – 1820), an archaeologist and artist whose exact role in the creation and spread of the style has been the subject of considerable controversy. This first book-length study was undertaken to examine and shed light on his part in the creation of Neo-Classicism in Italy and its diffusion throughout Europe and America. It is a study of his entire career.

Clérisseau's relationship to such key figures as Giovanni Battista Piranesi, Robert Adam, Johann Joachim Winckelmann, and Thomas Jefferson has been debated. On the one hand, some scholars, notably Louis Hautecoeur and Louis Réau, have described the salon of the Hôtel Grimod de la Reynière, decorated by Clérisseau, as one of the first examples of the Pompeian style in France, suggesting further that Clérisseau was also one of the precursors of the Empire style, yet this salon has been dated anywhere from 1769 – 82. Fiske Kimball and English writers on Robert Adam, on the other hand, have discounted Clérisseau's contribution to the formation of what they call the *style Louis XVI* or the Adam style, maintaining that he was merely a draftsman for the Adam brothers. Kimball and other American scholars have also been dubious about Clérisseau's part in the design of the Virginia State Capitol, chauvinistically crediting the entire conception and design to Thomas Jefferson. This lack of clarity as to Clérisseau's role and significance in history has caused others to refer to him variously as "the mysterious Clérisseau"

(John Harris), "that fount of so much neo-classic inspiration" (Sir John Summerson), "that confusing figure in the history of the eighteenth century" (James Lees-Milne), and "one of the greatest boffins of art history" (Sir Ellis Waterhouse).

There has also been considerable confusion about his drawings, many of which have been assigned to Gian Paolo Panini or Hubert Robert. On the other hand, works that have been falsely attributed to him have, during my investigations, turned out to be by such diverse figures as Louis Ducros, Jean Lallemand, Carlo Bonavia, Charles Michel-Ange Challe, J. M. Gandy, Giovanni Battista Piranesi, and Joseph-Marie Vien.

During the course of my study I have necessarily become indebted to a great many people. My greatest debts are to Professor Donald Drew Egbert of Princeton University, who first made me aware of Clérisseau and encouraged me over the years, and to Professor M. A. Gukovski of the Department of Western Art at the Hermitage Museum, Leningrad, who facilitated my study of the museum's great collection of Clérisseau drawings; without his help this work would not have been possible. This book is gratefully dedicated to their memory.

I must also acknowledge with gratitude the help I received from: Professor Rudolf Wittkower and John Fleming for allowing me to borrow transcripts of the Adam letters, discovered by Fleming, before they were in the public domain. This was the beginning of a happy and mutually beneficial relationship. My predecessors in the exploration of various aspects of Clérisseau's own career not only provided much of the groundwork but also gave advice: Professor Louis Hautecoeur, Fiske Kimball, Jeanne Lejeaux, and Professor Louis Réau.

My debt to those specializing in various aspects of eighteenth-century art is especially great: Basil Skinner, Jean Cailleux, Anthony Clark, Sir Brinsley Ford, Dr. Burkhard Gäbler, Michel Gallet, John Harris, Lesley Lewis, Professor Robin Middleton, Marianne Roland Michel, Professor Peter Murray, Professor Pierre du Prey, Andrew Robison, Pierre Rosenberg, Professor Alistair Rowan, Udo van der Sant, Professor Damie Stillman, Sir Francis J. B. Watson, Professor Edgar Wind. During my visits to Yugoslavia, Duško Kečkemet and Tomislav and Jerko Marasović provided invaluable help with the numerous problems relating to Diocletian's Palace at Spalato. Attilio Krismanić was equally helpful on the monuments of Pola.

Other scholars have helped in numerous ways: Jan Bialostocki, Professor Anthony Blunt, Professor David Coffin, John Dixon Hunt, Professor Karl Lehmann, Professor Frederick Nichols, Professor Sir Nikolaus Pevsner, Professor Nancy Ramage, Professor Walther Rehn, J. Byam Shaw, Warren Hunting Smith, Professor Wolfgang Stechow, Professor Hylton Thomas, and Professor Mark Weil.

Throughout the time of my study I have always met with considerate cooperation from the officials of museums and libraries. My greatest debt is to those at the State Hermitage Museum, Leningrad, particularly Tatiana Kamenskaya, Assja Kantor-Gukovskaya, A. N. Voronkina, and Larissa Salmina-Haskell. The following were particularly helpful: Edward Croft-Murray, Keeper of Prints and Drawings of the British Museum; the Honorable Jane Roberts of the Royal Library, Windsor; James Palmes and Prunella Frazier of The Royal Institute of British Architects Library; Sir John Summerson, Dorothy Stroud, and Margaret Richardson of Sir John Soane's Museum; Professor Michael Jaffé, Director, and Malcolm Cormack and Carlos van Hassalt, both formerly of the Fitzwilliam Museum; Iain Brown of the National Library of Scotland; Phyllis Lambert of the Canadian Centre for Architecture; Keith Andrews, Keeper of Drawings of the National Gallery of Scotland; Peter Schatborn, Rijksprentenkabinet, Ryksmuseum, Amsterdam; Peter Ward-Jackson, formerly Deputy Keeper of Prints and Drawings at the Victoria and Albert Museum; Elaine Dee of the Cooper-Hewitt Museum, New York; Stanislova Sawicki, former Keeper, and Teresa Sulerzyska, Keeper of Prints and Drawings, University of Warsaw Library, and Stephen Riley of the Massachusetts Historical Society. Those in charge of the following drawing collections were also helpful: The Albertina, Vienna; the Kunstbibliothek, Berlin; Musée des Beaux-Arts, Besançon; the Henry E. Huntington Art Gallery and Library; Musée Atger, Montpellier; the Musée du Louvre; Palais de Justice, Metz; the Galleria degli Uffizi; The Whitworth Art Gallery, University of Manchester; the Witt Collection of the Courtauld Institute of Art, University of London; the Pierpont Morgan Library; and the Staatliche Schlösser und Gärten, Wörlitz.

Numerous private collectors kindly allowed me to study their works by Clérisseau: the Duke and Duchess of Buccleuch and Queensberry, the Marquess of Linlithgow, Sir John Clerk of Penicuik, Major Percy Hope-Johnstone, Charles Adam of Blair Adam, James Knapp-Fisher, Daniel and Diane de Belder, Marjorie Clare, and Peter Pröschel. The Most Reverend Mother Superior of the Convento Istituto delle Dame de S. Cuòre (Convent of S. Trinità dei Monti) Rome graciously permitted me to study Clérisseau's Ruin Room. The Istituto per il Catalogo et la Documentazione provided detailed photographs.

I am especially indebted to Andrew Anderson, Curator of Historical Records, Scottish Record Office, General Register House, Edinburgh, for his unfailing assistance in connection with the Adam letters now in his care and for permission to quote extensively from them. The staffs of both the Virginia State Library and of the Papers of Thomas Jefferson provided invaluable help in connection with Jefferson's letters. The Haus-, Hof- und Staatsarchiv, Vienna, and the Bibliothèque Nationale and the Archives Nationales, Paris, kindly arranged for me to study relevant documents.

The libraries of Princeton University, the University of Vermont, Wells College, Vassar College, and Wheaton College, the Bibliotheca Hertziana, the British Museum, were helpful in a variety of ways. The Witt Library of the Courtauld Institute of Art, University of London, and the Frick Art Reference Library both generously shared their visual material with me.

I am grateful to the following for assistance with problems of translation: Professor Janet Letts, Professor Robert Marshall, Elizabeth K. MacCormick, Professor Helen Muchnic of Smith College, and Innis Shoemaker.

My research has been much facilitated by the award of Senior Fulbright Research Fellowships to the Courtauld Institute of the University of London (U.S.-U.K. Commission) and to the Town Planning Institute of Dalmatia, Yugoslavia. Grants from Wheaton College made possible much of my travel and the purchase of photographs and microfilm. Professor Lena L. Mandell, Professor John C. Riely, and Fannia Weingartner have read the entire manuscript critically and I am indebted to them for their comments.

Over the years, Annette Blood, Kathie Francis, Erna Huber, and Joan Silva typed numerous drafts. I appreciate their devoted and careful work.

I will always remember Professor Henry-Russell Hitchcock, who followed my work with interest and first mentioned it to Victoria Newhouse. It has been a pleasure working with her and the staff at the Architectural History Foundation, particularly Karen Banks and Jo Ellen Ackerman.

I cannot adequately thank my wife, Margaret Dorkey McCormick.

Charles-Louis Clérisseau

I

Early Life and Studies:

1721–54

The date of Charles-Louis Clérisseau's birth has long been debated.[1]

Although all contemporary sources give Clérisseau's Christian name as "Charles-Louis," Mariette calls him Jacques-Louis, a name which has been perpetuated by other writers, including Bénézit.[2]

Nothing is known of Clérisseau's youth. The earliest existing reference to him, other than his baptism, is on December 13, 1745, when he was listed at the Académie Royale d'Architecture as a pupil of "M. de Boffrand."[3] He was then twenty-four, a relatively advanced age, which would seem to indicate that he had either been a student at the Academy for some time or had started late.[4] In any case, he was advanced enough to compete with eight others for the Prix de Rome in May 1746.[5] In September he won the gold medal, entitling him to study at the French Academy in Rome for three years.[6] Unfortunately, Clérisseau's winning design for a "Town House without a Garden" has been lost.[7]

Although he won the gold medal, or Grand Prix, in September 1746, Clérisseau did not go to Rome immediately; in fact, he did not depart until May 1749.[8] This delay has never been satisfactorily explained.[9] Most likely Clérisseau had to wait for a vacancy, and during that period he may have attended J. F. Blondel's newly established Ecole des Arts, where he would have been exposed to some of the more advanced architectural ideas he was to encounter in Rome.

In February 1749, M. d'Isle requested M. de Tournehem to send Clérisseau, the oldest pupil at the Academy to win the prize of 1745, to Rome; on May 4, Clérisseau was sent his *Brevet*.[10] He arrived in Rome in late June 1749.[11] That city, with its great wealth of ancient remains, had become the center of archaeological and scholarly activity devoted to antiquity.

In 1749 the French Academy was housed in the Palazzo Mancini on the Corso. De Troy, the director since 1742, had, early in his tenure, devised a conservative program of having students copy works of art in the Vatican, and then sending the copies to France to serve as designs for tapestries.[12]

During the 1740s, a group of progressive French architectural students, bored by the rigid programs of the Academy, devoted most of their time and energy to festival designs and architectural fantasies. Many of these were made for the Academy masquerade, the year's great event, which was part of the Roman Carnival. It was these fantastic designs by young architects such as Charles Michel-Ange Challe (1718–78), Louis-Joseph Le Lorrain (1715–59), and perhaps Jean Laurent Le Geay (c. 1710–86), which not only set the stage, but represented in part the beginnings of the Neo-Classical style. Though John Harris may have overestimated the importance of Le Geay, he has presented a wealth of evidence about this new activity.[13] By the late 1740s, however, most of the progressive students had returned to France, and the situation in 1749 is best represented by the works of the artist-archaeologist Giovanni Battista Piranesi (1720–88). He was to play perhaps the major role in the formulation of Neo-Classicism, stamping it with his knowledge and personal vision of antiquity. Through his architectural etchings his influence was felt throughout Europe.

While we have no documented evidence of Clérisseau's work until July 1752, a small gouache in color of "Diana and her Nymphs Surprised by Actaeon" (Fig. 1), present whereabouts unknown, signed *Clérisseau fecit Romae,"* probably dates from the artist's early days at the Academy.[14] It is loosely based on the style of de Troy, as well as on the early eighteenth-century Italian painters Benedetto Luti (1666–1724) and Sebastiano Conca (1679–1764). The somewhat awkward depiction of the figure evident here would ultimately lead Clérisseau to frequently employ other artists to draw the figures in his pictures.[15]

"Diana and her Nymphs" is unique among the approximately 1,800 known works by Clérisseau. If it were not signed, one would not associate it with him. The subject and the crude technique, as well as the whole feeling, have no parallel in the other works of the artist. In sum, the resemblance to certain examples of Italian and French art of the first half of the eighteenth century suggests that this is one of Clérisseau's earliest works in Italy. The method of signing the picture and the addition of *"fecit Roma"* are unusual in his work, but the medium — gouache — a form of opaque watercolor in which the color is mixed with water and gum, was to become one of Clérisseau's favorites. It allows for precision of detail in bright, flat colors, because being thicker than freer flowing watercolor it is easier to use in depicting details. When dry, the colors are bright but flat because of the opaqueness. During the eighteenth century gouache was also known in England as "body colour."[16]

Another drawing by Clérisseau, in ink and wash, probably of his own costume as Pulchinello (Fig. 2),[17] undoubtedly dates from his years at the Academy and was probably done for the festivities of the Roman Carnival between 1750 and 1753.

Figure 1. C.-L. Clérisseau, "Diana and her Nymphs Surprised
by Actaeon," present whereabouts unknown

Figure 2. C.-L. Clérisseau,
"Pulchinello," Rijksmuseum

This particular character from the Italian Commedia was a popular one, a fact attested to by the existence of numerous drawings and paintings of the character by French artists in Rome. Clérisseau's drawing is interesting primarily as an early and unusual example of his work.[18]

Despite the rather circumscribed program of the Academy, Clérisseau, already trained in architecture and stimulated by the new interest in antiquity, began to draw the Roman ruins. The artist who had the greatest immediate influence on him was Giovanni Paolo Panini (1692–1765/68), the Italian *vedute* painter who was Professor of Perspective at the Academy. He was also the leading eighteenth-century Roman painter of ruin scenes. During the Renaissance, artists depicted ruins in the background of pictures, but, more than anyone before him, Panini made them the main subject.[19] His influence must have been strong by 1752, because in July of that year Charles Natoire, the new director of the Academy, wrote that Clérisseau was given to making works in Panini's style.[20]

The earliest dated visual evidence of Clérisseau's work is a drawing by Allan Ramsay of the Aqua Vergine inscribed as "after a Clérisseau of 1755" (see Fig. 26)[21] and an engraving of the Campo Vaccino and Temple of Jupiter by M. Morin after Clérisseau published in London in 1756 (Fig. 3).[22] Both of these resemble works of Panini. This early dependence on Panini can best be seen in the collection of 1,170 drawings which Clérisseau sold to Catherine the Great in 1779,[23] many of which apparently date from his early association with Panini. One of these is a very delicate pen-and-wash drawing of the Colosseum and the Arch of Constantine (Fig. 4).[24] The composition of this drawing is very similar to that of an oil painting of 1735 by Panini, now in Detroit (Fig. 5).[25] Both depict the building from the same viewpoint, opening up and distorting it in order to show more of the interior. In each case the conception is the same: The main subject, a ruined building, is carefully arranged in a landscape. The clear light and soft shade, the delicacy typical of Panini, can also be seen to a lesser extent in the Clérisseau. While both artists show the Colosseum on the same scale, Panini reduced the size of the foreground wall and pruned the vegetation around the arch so that the main objects dominate. Clérisseau, on the other hand, did not bring in other ancient objects for a more interesting composition; rather, perhaps because of his interest in architecture, he moved the ruins of the Temple of Venus and Rome forward so they assume greater importance. Already Clérisseau seemed to be following his later practice of showing each monument in its most picturesque position,[26] thus anticipating the Romantic point of view. Under Panini's influence, Clérisseau carries on the long tradition of *vedute* art by depicting actual scenes often rearranged in an artistic but frequently undramatic way. Ferdinardo Arisi, in his monograph on Panini, speaks of a collaboration between the two artists on oil painting from 1749–54 and later.[27] But our present knowledge of Clérisseau's oil paintings (none of which has been positively identified)[28] makes his assertion doubtful. While there is no doubt that Clérisseau was greatly influenced by his predecessor and may have copied his drawings,[29] one cannot say more with any assurance.

Clérisseau probably met Giovanni Battista Piranesi, whose etching shop was opposite the Palazzo Mancini, shortly after his arrival in Rome. The two artists became close friends, and remained so during the almost twenty years Clérisseau

Figure 3. Morin after Clérisseau, "Temple of Jupiter Capitolinus
in the Campo Vacino at Rome," 1756, McCormick Collection

Figure 4. C.-L. Clérisseau, "The Colosseum," Hermitage

Figure 5. Gian Paolo Panini, "The Colosseum," 1735, oil, Detroit Institute of Arts

spent in Italy.[30] From Piranesi's biography, compiled from his sons' notes by J. G. Legrand, Clérisseau's son-in-law, we learn that Clérisseau and other students at the French Academy such as the Challe brothers were often present with Piranesi at the ruins.[31]

> [When] a new excavation opened, they ran there, one found them united often without having notified each other and moved by the same curiosity, their domain became wider, for all that they taxed each other with unbounded ambition . . . and when the workers in marble came to search the debris for something to make a base, a bust, a vase, and disarranged the picturesque disorder of the fragments, our two antiquarians called these *barbarian incursions into their realm.* This union gave birth to the beautiful work of Piranesi entitled, *Della Magnificenza ed Architectura de Romani.* . . .[32]

Clérisseau was in Italy from 1749–67, and we do not know exactly when these trips with Piranesi occurred. The *Della magnificenza* appeared in 1761. Legrand, however, wrote in 1799 that Clérisseau and Piranesi, in the company of Claude-Joseph Vernet (1714–89), went to Tivoli to draw the ancient remains.[33] Inasmuch as Vernet was in Italy only from 1734 to 1753, this trip to Tivoli must have taken place during Clérisseau's early student years. The intimate relationship and constant interchange between Clérisseau and Piranesi over the years make the discernment of influence and style difficult,[34] but Piranesi was probably the greatest single influence on Clérisseau throughout his years in Rome.

In all probability the first works of Piranesi that Clérisseau saw were the fantastic piled-up compositions of dramatically lighted and juxtaposed columns, arches, pyramids, sarcophagi, and obelisks — for example, "Parte di ampio magnifico Porto all'uso degli antichi Romani" from *Opere varie di architettura, prospettive, groteschi, antichità,* published in 1750 (Fig. 6).[35] Somewhat similar in feeling, but more conservative, are the drawings of the progressive French architectural students of the 1740s, notably those of C. M. Challe.[36] Challe's "Roman Temple" of 1746 (Fig. 7)[37] has some of the same irrational juxtaposition of architectural elements and the same interest in dramatically lighted archways and grand staircases, possibly inspired by Baroque stage designs. Clérisseau must have seen or heard about this and similar drawings at the Academy, because many of them were Roman festival designs. Clérisseau may even have met C. M. Challe, who did not leave Rome until September 1749,[38] two months after Clérisseau's arrival.

Clérisseau's "Antique Fantasy" (Fig. 8)[39] in the Hermitage, while far more restrained than either the Piranesi or Challe, has some of their same sense of grandeur and irrationality. His bridge and boat pale by comparison with those of Challe, but the grand staircase leading up from the landing stage, the truncated pyramid, the sharp contrasts of light and dark, and the fantastic combination of sculpture and architecture from various periods demonstrate Clérisseau's awareness of works by both Piranesi and Challe.

Even closer to Challe is an unsigned pen, ink, and wash drawing in the Louvre ascribed to Clérisseau,[40] the authenticity of which has not been questioned until

Figure 6. Giovanni Battista Piranesi, "Parte di ampio magnifico Porto all´uso degli antichi Romani," 1750, F 122, Pl. 22, *Opere varie d´architecttura prospettive grotteschi, antichità*

Figure 7. Charles Michel-Ange Challe, "Roman Temple,"
1746, Montreal, Canadian Centre for Architecture

Figure 8. C.-L. Clérisseau, "Antique Fantasy," Hermitage

recently. The irrational massing of elements, the obelisks on the elaborately decorated bridge, and the monsterlike boat all seem very close to Challe, as well as
strongly influenced by Piranesi. Although the finer pen technique in the Louvre
drawing differs from the much broader handling of any comparable work by
Challe, the general feeling and nearly every motif are paralleled in the Challe
drawing in Montreal (see Fig. 7). The pen-and-ink medium of the scene in the
Louvre can be found in drawings known to be by Clérisseau, which are similar in
detail but very different in effect. The drawing must be by Challe.[41]

Clérisseau was attracted not only by Piranesi's early fantasies but also by his
stagelike Bibienesque recreations of the Classical world such as the "Campidoglio
antico," first published in the *Prima Parte* in 1743 and in the *Opere varie* of 1750
(Fig. 9), which can be compared with a Clérisseau drawing in the Hermitage made
up of very similar elements (Fig. 10).[42] Clérisseau also looked at Piranesi's scenes of
actual Roman monuments. In 1748 Piranesi published some of these in a small
format (by comparison with his later large-scale etchings) in a series entitled *Antichità romane de' tempi della repubblica*. Clérisseau's drawing of the "Forum of
Nerva" in the Hermitage (Fig. 11)[43] shows some of the same dramatic quality, a
similar viewpoint, and a related vision of antiquity when compared with Piranesi's
etching of the subject (Fig. 12) from this series.[44] Both depict the ruin from the
same point, emphasizing the architectural and sculptural detail, but the Piranesi is
far more spectacular in its contrast of light and dark, the addition of figures, and
the dramatic handling of detail. Clérisseau, though looking at antiquity from
Piranesi's point of view, does not have the powerful imagination of the Italian
artist. The same comparison and contrast of quality can be seen in two views of the
Forum of Augustus by Clérisseau and Piranesi (Figs. 13, 14).[45] Clérisseau convincingly depicts what he sees, while Piranesi gives rein to his imagination, adding
vegetation and sharp contrasts of light and dark. In addition, Piranesi's use of black
ink for his prints provides a more dramatic contrast than the brown and gray used
by Clérisseau in his drawing.

The close relationship between the two artists, as seen in the etchings of 1748
by Piranesi and undated Clérisseau drawings, is undeniable. Undoubtedly, these
were among the Piranesi prints that Clérisseau saw shortly after his arrival in Rome
in 1749 and soon imitated. However, Legrand's biography of Clérisseau states that

> Clérisseau's studies, constantly directed towards the antique, made Piranesi
> change his style and abandon the bad Neapolitan-style cartouches which he
> had used for his first frontispieces and substitute the beautiful antique
> fragments . . . which enriched them thereafter.[46]

Impressive as this sounds, one must not forget that Legrand was Clérisseau's
son-in-law. So, since Piranesi's ruin scenes of 1748 precede Clérisseau's arrival in
Rome, it follows that Clérisseau could not possibly have influenced these early
works. The cartouches which Legrand refers to must be the *Grotteschi* of
1747–48.

Piranesi and Panini played the most important roles in the formation of Clérisseau's pictorial style, but one cannot overlook the new approach of the French

Figure 9. Giovanni Battista Piranesi "Campidoglio antico,"
1743, F 9, Pl. VII, *Prima Parte*

Figure 10. C.-L. Clérisseau, "Fantasy," Hermitage

Figure 11. C.-L. Clérisseau, "Forum of Nerva," Hermitage

Figure 12. Giovanni Battista Piranesi, "Parte di Foro di Nerva," 1748,
F. 46, *Antichità romane de' tempi della repubblica*

Figure 13. C.-L. Clérisseau, "Forum of Augustus," Hermitage

Figure 14. Giovanni Battista Piranesi, "Il Foro de Augusto," 1748,
F. 56 *Antichità romane de' tempi della repubblica*

Academy in Rome. After Natoire's appointment as director on January 26, 1752, the teaching of the Academy was revitalized by a greater emphasis on drawing from nature, and also on copying the great works of antiquity and the Renaissance, particularly those of Raphael.[47] It is quite possible that many of Clérisseau's pure landscape studies now in the Hermitage were made at this time. Even the scenes of Roman monuments by Clérisseau already discussed show a close study of nature, although his view of these ruins has clearly been inspired by Panini and Piranesi.

We have already mentioned that, in July 1752, Natoire wrote favorably to Vandières, the Surintendant des Bâtiments, about Clérisseau's drawings in the style of Panini, adding that he was pleased with Clérisseau's conduct and requested an extension for the artist.[48] Natoire later sent Vandières one of Clérisseau's drawings and the extension was granted.[49] In addition to Panini and Piranesi, Clérisseau's close friends at this time were mostly fellow students, like J. D. Le Roy, who arrived in 1751[50] and, somewhat later, joined Clérisseau and others in refusing to sign the required certificate of Easter communion.[51] Le Roy's subsequent career and his famous publication, *Les Ruines des plus beaux monuments de la Grèce* (1759), demonstrate that he and Clérisseau had much in common. M. J. Peyre, who arrived in Rome in 1753, towards the end of Clérisseau's term, and who later became an architect of great originality, may well have become a close friend.[52] There is little doubt that Charles Bellicard (1726–86), the architect who came to the Academy at the same time as Clérisseau and who was later employed by Cochin to draw the illustrations for *Observation sur les antiquités d'Herculaneum,* was also a close associate.

The earliest surviving portrait of Clérisseau is a caricature made in Rome by Pier Leone Ghezzi (1674–1755) on December 26, 1751 (Fig. 15).[53] Like many of Ghezzi's portrait drawings with exaggerated noses and protruding lips, it could be almost anyone, except for the inscription identifying the sitter as "M. Clérisseau, a French architectural student, an excellent man who posed on December 26, 1751."[54] Later portraits of the architect, made towards the end of his life, depict him in more conventional terms but with a slightly large nose and much less protruding lips.[55]

Apart from the references in the French Academy records of the director's correspondence, the most important documentary evidence for Clérisseau and his activities before 1753 is contained in a second caricature by Ghezzi dated August 26, 1752, now in the British Museum (Fig. 16).[56] In it, Clérisseau is shown seated at a table drawing a plan. His face is again depicted with Ghezzi's unflattering exaggeration of features. The petulant open mouth and rather complaining expression suggest that Clérisseau was not the most placid of souls or the easiest person to get along with. Subsequent events at the Academy, as well as Clérisseau's later encounters with the Adam brothers and with Catherine the Great substantiate this. The chief importance of this caricature, however, is not the drawing itself but the text underneath. Although it contains Ghezzi's usual superlatives, it is revealing because it mentions an architectural project by Clérisseau.

Monsieur Clérisseau, a Frenchman, pensionnaire at the French Academy. De Troy being the director of the same. The aforesaid pensionnaire is a fine

Figure 15. Pier Leone Ghezzi, "Caricature
of Clérisseau," Dec. 26, 1751, Rome,
Gabinetto della Stampe, Farnesina

Figure 16. Pier Leone Ghezzi, "Caricature of Clérisseau,"
Aug. 26, 1752, London, British Museum

architect, as such he came to Camaldoli..the Hermitage at Frascati of his Eminence Cardinal Domenico Passionei who ordered a drawing..to make a kind of Arcadia to be used as a Folly in the clearing which is in the woods in the aforementioned Hermitage, which he did marvelously well in the presence of his Eminence. Made by me Cavalier Ghezzi the 26 of August 1752 in my 78th year.[57]

In 1738, the Cardinal Domenico Passionei (1682–1761), the most important eighteenth-century protector of the Jansenists, began transforming his country estate at Camaldoli, near Frascati, into a hermitage to house his important collection of antique works of art and ancient inscriptions.[58] The estate is often mentioned in travelers' accounts and, after 1755, in the letters of Winckelmann, the noted archaeologist and a close friend of the Cardinal.[59] These accounts speak of the inscriptions, the gardens, aviaries, etc., but do not mention this particular structure. This is surprising in Winckelmann's case, as he was an intimate of Clérisseau during the 1760s.[60]

A possible explanation for this omission is that the structure was never built, but remained only a design that had been made on the spot for the Cardinal. After the Cardinal's death in 1761 Clérisseau took James Adam to Camaldoli to see the house and collection, which was then being dispersed. Adam and Clérisseau were investigating possible purchases, and Clérisseau may have also wanted to show Adam his first work.[61] In any case, the design was for a small garden pavilion, possibly a porticoed Roman temple, if the plan held by Clérisseau in the second Ghezzi portrait (1752) is a true or even partial representation. Clérisseau's interest in creating representations of picturesque ancient ruins and the Cardinal's own preoccupation with nature and antiquity might explain why Clérisseau had been invited in the first place.

Clérisseau continued his study at the Academy during the rest of 1752 and early 1753. Natoire's letter to Vandières of May 15, 1753, states that Clérisseau was "working with much ardor, and composing ruin pieces with great facility."[62] In July, however, Vandières wrote Natoire, asking him to remove Clérisseau's name from the list of *pensionnaires* because he and others had refused to sign the required certificate of Easter communion. It is possible that Clérisseau's refusal was an expression of eighteenth-century rationalism or, as now appears more likely, Jansenism. And, as Clérisseau was the oldest student, he was thought to be the leader and was noted as one of the most rebellious.[63] Natoire replied in August, agreeing that Clérisseau should leave, citing his many bad qualities, among them the fact that he associated with the English travelers and had great success in selling them his drawings.[64] Clérisseau wrote to Vandières, refusing to apologize to Natoire on the grounds that he had done nothing wrong.[65] The difficulty continued until Natoire accepted a private apology after the intercession of his sister, Madame Vleughels, wife of a previous director. Clérisseau was returned to grace in October 1753.[66]

Later that year, probably in early December, Clérisseau met the young French painter Laurent Pécheux (1729–1821), who had come to Rome to study, and who had letters of introduction to Clérisseau, to Bartolommeo Guilol (a pupil of Anton Raphael Mengs), and to Natoire.[67] In his "Autobiography," Pécheux describes the meeting, refers to Clérisseau as a "born artist," and adds that Clérisseau found him lodgings and advised him to avoid Clérisseau's friends (presumably the students at the French Academy) because they were dissipated and worked very little.[68] Pécheux became a leading painter of historical subjects, but his few surviving drawings of Roman scenes, such as "A View of the Roman Forum" (in the Canenano Collection at Genoa), show the influence of Clérisseau.[69]

Later in December Clérisseau was taken gravely ill with a high fever, possibly the result of his difficulty over the communion incident.[70] Mariette described him as being at death's door.[71] After his recovery he worked with more fervor than ever,[72] even though the Abbé Bouret had failed to obtain another extension of his fellowship.[73] Bouret, in his plea on Clérisseau's behalf, mentioned that he had accomplished the unusual feat of making friends with the English and that they had bought his drawings.[74] After the fellowship ended, Natoire, as director, arranged for Clérisseau's return to France. He left Rome early in May 1754.[75] Afterwards, Natoire wrote that Clérisseau had departed without speaking to him and that the Academy was well rid of this student.[76]

Clérisseau did not, however, return to France. According to Mariette:

> . . . not satisfied with having drawn in Rome all the antiquities which it contained, he was determined to make the same research in all parts of Italy. He went to Naples and there was not a corner of the environs that he did not investigate.[77]

While this is possible, it seems unlikely that Clérisseau would have been able to afford such investigations. Quite possibly he did some traveling, but his main travels were from 1755 to 1757, in the company of Robert Adam.

It may have been at this time that Clérisseau made some of the many archaeological studies now in the Hermitage. Most of these drawings are of ancient Roman and Renaissance buildings. Among them are also elaborate, tinted designs of ceilings and decorations from Roman buildings, particularly palaces and baths. The majority of the decorative drawings are of arabesques copied from both ancient and Renaissance monuments. Among the sculptural representations are drawings of reliefs from antique sarcophagi, many of which remain unidentified. One portfolio is devoted to drawings of vases and candelabra, the latter showing the influence of Piranesi.[78] There are also drawings of furniture and of architectural details.[79] Many of these works were probably done either during Clérisseau's stay at the Academy, or after 1754 and before his departure from Italy in 1767. Even though it seems highly likely that some of these drawings come from the earlier period, the earliest dated study in the Hermitage is that of a ceiling, made in 1766.[80]

The most valuable source of information for the time after May 1754 is a letter written on September 26 by Clérisseau to a friend in France ("Monsieur et tres cher ami"), in which he addresses a variety of matters. He mentions some silver and a complete set of Piranesi's works that he has bought for this friend, three Piranesi drawings, "two of which he would be willing to sell at high prices as he had great difficulty in obtaining them," and various other prints and books. Clérisseau discusses other available works of art, and this suggests that he may have been working as a small-scale dealer or at least purchasing things for friends in France.[81] Further, he writes that he expects to remain in Florence until the following spring, at which time he will return to France. Of greater interest is his mention of being shown Robert Wood's book on Palmyra by Sir Horace Mann[82] and his reference to an English "Milord" with whom he is planning to travel to Greece and Egypt.[83] The identity of this person is not revealed in the letter but it may possibly be Sir William Chambers or, less likely, the sculptor Joseph Wilton.

When Joseph Wilton (1722–1803) introduced Robert Adam to Clérisseau, who had been living at Ignazio Enrico Hugford's house in Florence, in January 1755, he mentioned that "William Chambers . . . owes all his hints and notions to this man with whom he differed and to whom he behaved ungratefully."[84] We do not know when or where Clérisseau and Chambers (1723–96) met. Thomas Hardwick, in his biographical sketch of Chambers attached to Gwilt's edition of Chambers's *Treatise on Civil Architecture* of 1825, was the first to state that it was in Paris that Chambers "studied under the celebrated Clérisseau and acquired from him a freedom of pencil in which few excelled him."[85] This is impossible, because Chambers arrived in Paris only in the autumn of 1749, and Clérisseau had left for Rome the previous June.[86] It is assumed that Chambers studied at this time in Paris with J. F. Blondel, because he later referred to the latter as his "ancient master."[87]

Chambers was in Italy from late 1750 to March or April 1755,[88] so the two artists could have known each other at any time during those years. Edward Edwards, in his dictionary of British painters published in 1808, states that Clérisseau "studied long at Rome and resided there at the same time with Sir William Chambers and J. Wilton."[89] Wilton may have spent the last four years of his Italian stay in Florence before returning to London in 1755, and probably left Rome in 1751 or 1752 after having been there since 1747.[90] Chambers could have met and studied with Clérisseau in Rome either between January 1751 and the summer of 1752 or between 1753 and January 1755.[91]

It has been suggested that the imaginary landscape setting of Chambers's design for the Mausoleum for the Prince of Wales owes something to Clérisseau.[92] There is no doubt that the drawing of the cross-section of the domed mausoleum (dating from February 1752), which depicts it as a ruin overgrown with vegetation (Fig. 17),[93] resembles Clérisseau's drawings not only in conception but also in technique. This would imply that the two artists had met by early 1752 at the latest. The convention of portraying a modern building in a picturesque setting or as a ruin, perhaps first done by Oppenord in his design for a garden pavilion, became standard practice.[94] This design suggests that Chambers's approach to antiquity may have been partly formed by Clérisseau. Certainly Chambers's later designs, such as the "Ruined Triumphal Arch for Kew" of 1759 (Fig. 18),[95] based on the Arch of Constantine, show the same decorative possibilities of ruins that we see in Clérisseau's drawings.[96] Chambers wrote about the Kew design: "My intention

Figure 17. William Chambers, "Cross Section of Mausoleum design for the Prince of Wales," Feb. 1752, London, Victoria and Albert Museum

Figure 18. William Chambers, "A View of the South Side of the Ruins at Kew," 1759, *Plans, Elevations, Sections and Perspective Views of the Gardens and Building at Kew, in Surrey The Seat of Her Royal Highness The Princess, Dowager of Wales*, London, 1763, Pl. 42

was to imitate a Roman antiquity built of brick with an incrustation of stone."[97] The so-called Franco-Italian album of sketches, most of which were done by Chambers during his European years, includes a great variety of drawings of modern and antique monuments, ground plans, and decorative details.[98] In scope, if not in style, number, or originality, the contents of this album resemble the great collection of Clérisseau drawings in the Hermitage. Clérisseau made Chambers aware of the rich remains of ancient Rome as a source for contemporary architecture and taught him how to depict them so as to heighten their ruined qualities. Finally, it should be mentioned that among Chambers's effects in the inventory of 1790 was a Chambers drawing finished by Clérisseau.[99] Chambers also owned a copy of Clérisseau's book on Nîmes which was included in Chambers's sale of 1796.[100] Nonetheless, Clérisseau's influence on Chambers was limited. Nothing is known about the cause of the falling out between Chambers and Clérisseau mentioned by Wilton.

Although Clérisseau was to remain in Italy for thirteen more years, his break with the Academy marked the end of his formal student days. The training he had received from teachers such as Panini, and his continuing association with Piranesi, who, like Panini, imparted his own personal view of antiquity, became the foundation of Clérisseau's career as an artist and teacher. Equally important was his association with fellow architectural students, among whom were probably M. J. Peyre, later the author of the influential *Oeuvres d'architecture* (1765), and Soufflot, who would both become leading Neo-Classical architects. In addition to Clérisseau's relationship with such advanced artists and architects was his friendship with the new collectors of antiquities, including Cardinal Passionei and various traveling Englishmen.[101]

Perhaps most important of all, Clérisseau had been introduced to and had immersed himself in a study of the monuments of antiquity and the Renaissance, which were to be the main sources of inspiration throughout his long life. His technical facility, acquired during his thorough academic training, combined with his knowledge of antiquity and his connections with other progenitors of the new movement, had prepared him for the future. Nevertheless, Clérisseau's clashes with the authorities of the Academy and his troubles with Chambers foreshadowed the frequent personal conflicts that were to mark — and hamper — his entire career.

II

In Italy with Robert Adam:

1755-57

Early in 1755 Clérisseau was staying at Ignazio Enrico Hugford's house in Florence, where he first met Robert Adam (1728-92).[1] Adam's diary and letters to his family from this period describe this encounter in detail.[2]

The following descriptions by Adam of this first meeting are the first indications of what the relationship between the two men was to be. Furthermore, they shed a most revealing light on Adam's character, giving a clear picture of the Clérisseau-Adam problem and the encounter which was to change the course of Adam's "grand tour," and of his life.[3]

> Mr. Wilton introduced me to a most valuable and ingenious creature called Clérisseau who draws ruins in Architecture to perfection, He stays in this house with Mr. Hugford the painter, to whom I delivered my letter from Mr. Hamilton the painter in London.[4]

On January 31 he wrote more specifically to his brother William:

> I have also got acquaintance with one Clérisseau who draws in architecture delightfully in the free manner I wanted. Chambers, whom Jamie knows of, owes all hints and notions to this man with whom he differed and to whom he behaved ungratefully. This Wilton tells one.[5]

The two accounts are illuminating not only because they conclusively disprove that Clérisseau was merely Adam's draftsman, as has been generally assumed, but also because of the mention of the relationship with Chambers discussed earlier.[6]

Adam may therefore have exaggerated the break between the two men, perhaps recognizing that Chambers would become his greatest rival in England. The general tone of Adam's letters reveals him as an intensely ambitious person, both professionally and socially. Anxious to make the proper connections for the future, Adam was devoted to gossip, the more malicious the better.[7]

A further description of the meeting with Clérisseau and subsequent arrangements are included in a letter from Robert Adam to his brother James written on February 19.

> I found out Clérisseau A Nathaniel in whom tho' there is no guile, Yet there is the utmost knowledge of Architecture, of perspective, and of Designing and Colouring I ever Saw, or had any conception of; He rais'd my Ideas, He created emulation and fire in my Breast. I wish'd above all to learn his manner, to have him with me at Rome, to Study close with him and to purchase of his works. What I wish'd for I obtain'd; He took a liking to me, He engag'd in doing what drawings I pleas'd. He engag'd to go with me to Rome and if it suited my Conveniency wou'd Stay in the Same House with me, wou'd Serve me as an Antiquarian, wou'd teach me perspective and Drawing, wou'd give me Copys of all his Studys of the Antique Basrelievos and other ornaments, in Short he sets out the day after me in order to be at my Command as Soon as I arrive at Rome, And I shall furnish him a Chamber and pay his Meltiths, And think it is one of the luckyest circumstances cou'd have happen'd.[8]

This letter indicates what the arrangement between the two men would become: Not only would Clérisseau instruct Adam in drawing but he would also introduce him to the wonders of ancient art and architecture. After giving Adam some preliminary instruction in Florence, Clérisseau went to Rome first, as planned, and Adam arrived later, on February 24.[9] Letters dating from Adam's first months in Rome have been lost, but subsequent ones tell about the activity at this time, both in regard to Clérisseau and the program of study. The July letter to James shows that Robert's trip would be no ordinary grand tour. Other letters make clear that he was preparing himself to assume the leadership of English architecture. Clérisseau, who could instruct him in the techniques of architectural drawing as taught at the French Academy and who could convey his vision of ancient architecture formulated under the influence of Panini and Piranesi, was the ideal teacher of the architectural and decorative possibilities of ancient Roman art and architecture. As a friend of men such as Piranesi and Raphael Mengs (1729–79),[10] Clérisseau could introduce Adam to their circle. All this Clérisseau evidently was willing to do. Because his relations with the French Academy were strained, he had no desire to return to France. Instead, he had decided to remain in Italy where he could continue to study and draw the ancient ruins in the company of the wealthy young Scotsman. Unlike most French students, Clérisseau, from his early days in Rome, had been friendly with foreigners, particularly the English, and had already sold them many drawings.

Clérisseau became Adam's most important teacher, but there were others. Among them was Laurent Pécheux, whom Adam could have known through Clérisseau, and who gave instruction in figure drawing. Adam referred also to an unnamed artist who tutored him in landscape.[11] Although the painter Hubert

Robert was living in Rome during these years, there is no evidence that he and Adam met, although Clérisseau presumably knew him. This was all part of a carefully planned program designed to outdo Chambers, as the following letter to James in July of that year attests.

> These considerations made me determine to go to the bottom of things, to outdo Chambers in Figures in Bas relieve and in ornaments. . . . My progress as yet is very trivial, Though Pecheux, my instructor, gives me great encouragement, and assures me in 3 or 4 Months I shall do infinitely better than Chambers ever did or ever will do.[12]

The same letter describes his daily activity with Clérisseau.

> Ornaments come of themselves as I see and coppy every day and have made some progress in Sketching them; Whilst I find my Idea of Architecture are a good deal inlarged and my principles of the grand more fixt than ever they were before; Clerisseau preaches to me everyday to forbear inventing or composing either plans or Elevations till I have a greater fund. That is, till I have made more progress in seeing things and my head more filled with propper ornaments and my hand able to draw to purpose what I woud incline, as he very justly says that inventing indifferently, and drawing So So ornaments is to fix these in your head and to prevent Your getting into the taste of better ones. In spite of these admonitions I must still be Scrawling a plan of a temple, or a bit of Front now and then makes its appearance. . . . I am surprized you have never said one word about poor Clerisseau who is not only the most ingenious but the best of Mortals, we live in the greatest Harmony together. . . .[13]

As for Clérisseau, many of his numerous drawings of ancient Roman and Renaissance decorative details of cornices, friezes, ceilings, wall paintings, statues, and vases, as well as the more usual scenes of architectural ruins and Renaissance palaces now in the Hermitage, date from this period. A delicately drawn "Arabesque after the Antique" (Fig. 19) showing a detail of a stucco or painting, a beautiful drawing of a garland and bucranium in relief (Fig. 20), and a sensitive drawing of a molding (Fig. 21),[14] all from the Hermitage collection, illustrate Clérisseau's skill and sensitivity in depicting antique forms. One can understand why Adam was so enthusiastic about having Clérisseau instruct him. Antique details, such as those selected by Clérisseau, were to be a major source of inspiration for the architecture and decoration of Neo-Classicism, including Robert Adam's own work.

During their first few months in Rome, Adam and Clérisseau not only sketched and drew ancient baths, forums, and villas, with their decorative details, but also Renaissance buildings such as the Villa Madama, the Farnese Palace, and perhaps the Vatican Loggia. On May 1, Clérisseau wrote Huquier that he was in Naples and had made great quantities of drawings of Herculaneum.[15] One can surmise that Adam accompanied him.

Besides acting as Adam's tutor and cicerone, Clérisseau introduced the young man to his archaeologically minded friends, the most important being Piranesi,

Figure 19. C.-L. Clérisseau, "Arabesque
after the Antique," Hermitage

Figure 20. C.-L. Clérisseau, "Garland from the Ara Pacis," Hermitage

Figure 21. C.-L. Clérisseau, "Architectural moulding," Hermitage

with whom Adam quickly became friends. Adam's comments on his new friendship with Piranesi shed light on his calendar and on his study under Clérisseau.

> Piranesi of whom I have wrote You often having seen some of these
> Sketches was so satisfy'd with them and with the collection of Antique
> things I have got casts of, That he has absolutely changed his resolution of
> Dedicating his plan of ancient Rome to one of the Cardinals here and has
> dedicated it to me, with the title of Friend and Architect Dilectantissimo
> nella Antichita. . . . This fancy of Piranesi's of dedicating his plan to me in
> preference of all the nobility here and of all the English and of Mr. Wood So
> famous for his Palmyra, I have considered in every light and cant find any
> bad affect from it, on the contrary every body tells me it cannot faill to have
> good effects in making me the object of every bodys attention as one so
> beloved and priz'd by Piranesi, a man of so much genious and invention,
> who never was known to praise one he did not admire nor admire those he
> did not think ingenious. It will however cost me some Sous in purchasing
> 80 or 100 coppys of it, which I propose sending to England and Scotland to
> be resold. . . . Chambers who courted Piranesi's friendship with all the
> Assiduity of a Lover never cou'd bring him even to do him a Sketch of any
> one thing, and told me I would never be able to get any thing from him, So
> much is he out of his Calculations that he has told me that whatsoever I
> want of him he will do for me with pleasure, and is just now doing Two
> Drawings for me which will be both Singular and Clever. When he sees this
> dedication what must he then think. Either that I am extremely Clever, or
> that I have bribed him to do it as thinking it woud raise my reputation: The
> first I am conscous cannot be the Case as yet and the last I am sure is not the
> Case, as I never was so surprized as when Clerisseau told me that Piranesi
> had such regard for me that he was determin'd to dedicate his plan of Rome
> as it was antiently to me, and to none else and he was determin'd he woud
> take no refusal.[16]

The next day Adam wrote to his sister Jenny about Piranesi:

> As his Character is extremely high amongst all Connoisseurs, it cannot miss
> to give all of them in England and Scotland a vast notion of me, as one
> deserving so much regard and Such Compliment from Piranesi who never
> flatter'd nor never prais'd unless when the Person deserv'd it . . . [17]

Clérisseau's close friendship with Piranesi doubtless encouraged the latter's admiration for Adam and his drawings. It may further explain the Italian's almost
unheard-of generosity. Piranesi dedicated a plate to Adam without charge, and
willingly executed drawings for him. But Adam's burning desire to surpass all of his
rivals makes one suspect that he may have exaggerated the degree of his own
intimacy with Piranesi and may even have paid him, as others did, although Adam
denies this in the letter previously quoted.

Letters written to his sisters Jenny and Nelly at this time describe expeditions in
search of antiquities with Piranesi, Clérisseau, and Pécheux, to whom he refers as
his "three friends cronys and Instructors,"[18] and dinners and visits with "Signor

Piranesi and mon/r Clerisseau Seeing the ancient Thermae or Baths of Caracalla the Ruins of which are most magnificent."[19] Clearly Adam was receiving the same training from Piranesi as Clérisseau had earlier.

From these references to Clérisseau in Adam's letters to his family, one gathers some idea of their relationship. It was not one of social and intellectual equals, and yet neither was it one of master and servant. One can best describe it as a student-tutor relationship. They were living and eating together; Clérisseau was included when Adam entertained, and Adam's friend, Lord Huntingdon, invited Clérisseau to dinner "out of compliment" to Adam.[20] Adam also enjoyed playing patron to Clérisseau, whom he not only supported but further assisted by persuading his English friends to purchase Clérisseau's drawings.[21]

In addition to being tutored in the study and drawing of ancient architecture and decorative arts, as well as in their Renaissance offspring, Adam planned an archaeological publication which would "make a great puff conducive to raising all at once one's name and character."[22] Clérisseau, of course, was to do much of the work; one suspects that Adam would supervise. Adam's publication *Ruins of the Palace of the Emperor Diocletian at Spalatro in Dalmatia*, begun in 1757 and published in 1764, certainly established Adam as an authority, but there were several earlier projects that were never finished. One of the first of these is mentioned in a July 4 letter to James.

I have another scheme in view which if it takes place woud be no less conducive to raising all at once ones name and character then it would be profitable to me and useful to every body. It is shortly this. Degodets book is almost intirely out of print neither in England, France or Italy can one get a copy of it under double price, severals have thought of reprinting it but neither had the talents the money nor the Courage, As I am on the Spot where these Antiquitys are, Have Clerisseau's assistance and other conveniences, In course of Conversation with Wood and Ramsay the thought struck me that it woud be good Skeme for me. I communicated my thoughts to Clerisseau who approved so much that he said if he had money he woud do it himself, And to augment the value of it, I not only proposed taking the measure so as to prove if they were just, but intended to add perpective views of these Buildings as they appear at present a work which Clerisseau will undertake for me with infinite satisfaction and will execute with thorough beauty and justness. Where any of my measures differed from Degodets these I show by a red line, which lets them know the error and this with a Smart preface, a Clever print of the Author's head, an Alligorical print in the way of palladic, and Some remarks added to these of Degodets in different Characters coud not faill to be of great authority and introduce me into England with uncommon splendour. They coud not miss to admire one who knew all the Antiquitys to an Inch and coud have nothing to Object not having any of My own designs to object to. I have filled my paper to have your opinion fully, mention not a word of any of My projects as that woud spoil every thing. I forgot to tell You that before

I leave Rome I shall draw Landscape tollerably having a good master for that branch likewise.²³

The project of updating Antoine Desgodetz's *Edifices antiques de Rome* was unfortunately abandoned the next year, but by then Clérisseau had made numerous drawings for it; some of these may be part of the large collection now in the Hermitage.²⁴ Clérisseau intended to publish these on his own later, according to a mention in the preface to his *Monumens de Nismes*.²⁵

Adam's training under Clérisseau included a thorough study and depiction of the ancient remains and the great Renaissance buildings throughout Italy. We can assume that Clérisseau had visited all these sites earlier. In the early fall of 1755, Clérisseau and Adam made an extensive trip along the "Hadriatick shore." Robert wrote James at length about the proposed journey.

As the weather is now becoming Moderate in this Country and that every body will in a fortnight forsake Rome, and fly to their Villiagatura I have form'd a Skeme of Making a Considerable tour through part of Italy during that time In order to see those places which woud be a great retardment to me upon leaving Rome for good and all. You may look on the Map of Italy and Youl find that what I am going to mention comprehends most of those towns betwixt Rome and Venice. I shall go first to Capriole, from that to Narni and Terni to Fuligno and Spoletto Betwixt which places is a temple which You will see in Palladio, with immense long Stairs that go up Sideways rather like a ladder than a Stair with a Small portico You enter by, I dare say You will know it by this discription. From that to Fossambrone and Fano upon the Sea Coast then I shall go to Rimini and Ravenna being the Straight Road along Coast to Venice the last within 2 days of it. But as I reserve Venice for my return home, I tack about and I return coasting it all the way back as I came from Fano then go on to Ancona and Loretto and return by another Road from Loretto to Fuligni in my way back to Rome. I shall not Stay a Night in Rome when I return no woud come near it if it was not my only road but shall go directly to Albano, Jensano Riccio, Palestrine and Marino Being places about 20 miles South of Rome where the throng of the Villiatura people go, Famous for the Summer Seats of Pope and pretender, as well as for many good painting in the Churches the Remains of the Horatian and Curiatian Tomb, with other Antiquitys. . . . Clerisseau and I make this Jaunt in a post Chaise, and shall go post all the way to lose the least time possible So that I expect in a month from my Setting out to my final conclusion of it. Donald is to be our attendant on Horseback as he can now make out as much Italian of the Clept kind as not only prevent himself from starving but to provide us Sumptously. And what more woud a man wish.²⁶

Among the great quantity of Clérisseau's drawings are several which must have been made on this trip.²⁷ These include three in the Hermitage: "The Temple of Clitumnus near Spoleto" (Fig. 22), which is the building illustrated by Palladio mentioned in the preceding letter, "The Waterfall at Terni" (Fig. 23), and "The

Figure 22. C.-L. Clérisseau, "The Temple of Clitumnus near Spoleto," Hermitage

Figure 23. C.-L. Clérisseau, "The Waterfall
at Terni," Hermitage

Arch of Augustus at Fano" (Fig. 24). A drawing of "The Arch of Augustus at Rimini," now in a private collection, is also presumably from this trip. Clérisseau depicted the unusual Temple of Clitumnus from an angle, in order to show one of the peculiar vaulted wings.[28] While every detail of the building is apparent in Clérisseau's drawing, the softness of the lighting and overall tonality of the brown ink and gouache give it a soft, warm quality relieved only by the green vegetation. The representation, while topographical, has a personal quality as well. In conception, it stands between Panini and Piranesi.

The drawings of the Arch of Augustus at Fano and the one at Rimini are accurately detailed, precise delineations of the monuments. A little dry in execution, they have some of the picturesquely ruined quality of Piranesi's drawings, but without his sense of the dramatic. If it were not for the figure, one would be inclined to suggest that the drawings were archaeological studies with the figures added later.

One of Adam's documents at Penicuik House found by John Fleming was a bound volume of sketches entitled "n. 1–192 Views of Antiquity in and about Rome and other Parts of Italy."[29] Fleming has discerned several hands in the drawings, most of which are by Adam but some of which Fleming attributes to Clérisseau.[30] Although this is not the place to argue the authorship of the various drawings, there is no doubt about their varying quality. A drawing of particular interest is "The Arch of Augustus at Fano" (Fig. 25), which Fleming attributes — I think rightly — to Adam.[31] A comparison of it with Clérisseau's drawing of the same arch (see Fig. 24) shows similarities in conception and detail. The unsure quality of the line and the overattention to detail in Adam's work show how much he still had to learn. Numerous drawings by Adam in the sketchbook, when compared with works by Clérisseau, further demonstrate the two architects' relationship.

On the other hand, "The Waterfall at Terni" (see Fig. 23), though drawn by Clérisseau on this trip, is in the freer, more delicate pen-and-ink style seen earlier in "The Colosseum and Arch of Constantine" (see Fig. 4). The choice of subject and composition resemble those of the French landscapist Claude-Joseph Vernet, whom Clérisseau had known in Rome.[32] The minute figures recall ones by Piranesi. This is one of Clérisseau's rare pure landscapes, and has a freshness lacking in many of his ruin scenes.

None of the Clérisseau drawings discussed so far is dated, but they must be from this period because of their similarity to drawings in Adam's Penicuik Album. Most of the places visited and drawn by Clérisseau and Adam were the usual ones; an exception was the journey in 1756 to Sora which included such places as S. Isola di Liri and Aquino. Drawings of these places by Adam are included in the Penicuik Album.[33]

Although it was not in Adam's nature to belittle himself or to praise Clérisseau at Adam's expense, he has provided valuable information in a letter written in October 1755 about the proposed visit of his brother John to Italy.

> To stay a couple of twelve months in Rome without a proper conductor who can point out the proper method of studying, and in a manner, by seeing his progress and works can inspire one with a taste and love for the

Figure 24. C.-L. Clérisseau, "The Arch of Augustus at Fano," Hermitage

Figure 25. Robert Adam (?), "The Arch of Augustus at Fano,"
Penicuik House, Midlothian, Sir John Clerk Collection

Grand, you will spend much time in Rome to little purpose. Without Clerisseau I shoud have spent several years without making the progress I have done in one fourth of the time. The reason is evident, the Italians have at present no manner of taste, all they do being more French than anything else. Piranesi who may be said, alone to breath the Antient Air, is of such disposition as barrs all Instruction, His Ideas in locution so ill ranged, His expressions so furious and fantastical, that a Venetian hint is all can be got from him, never any thing fixt or well digested so that a quarter of an hour makes you sick of his Company. If John travels in the first instance he comes to Rome when we have left it (as Clerisseau returns to Paris, when I return to England, as with the greatest difficulty I got him to Rome and prevail'd on him to stay in Italy till I leave it) and when he is in Rome he cannot propose studying in the extensive way, as he does not know so much of Landscape or Figures or perspective, without which he coud not better himself much of what he sees of the Antient Remains by making views of them, and there is absolutely no body here can instruct him.[34]

Robert Adam goes on to suggest that James should come to Italy before John:

You are just now of a right age, and every days delay is losing time, and of dangerous consequences, . . . you will be master of perspective in a fortnight with Clerisseau instructions which otherways woud take you a month, and never able to apply it to practice, as he has all these knacks, so necessay to us architects. . . . I will give you one instance of the many that happen in Rome every year, where from bad advice and following a bad manner the young people are intirely lost. A young Swiss came to Rome 3 days after me. He knew Clerisseau at Florence admired him, made progress being with him and wanted to associate himself with us at Rome, as neither Clerisseau nor I liked his temper and disposition we resolved to have nothing to do with him, upon which he paid court to the students of the French Academy, and herded with the young Italians in Rome and I may realy say that in proportion to my improvement he has degenerate with childish fancys and unmeaning triffles becoming every day less pure, and less knowing, and indeed its plain that unless one frequents people more knowing than themselves they never improve, on the contrary imbibe their faults.[35]

Life continued to be busy for Adam and Clérisseau in late 1755 and early 1756. The Desgodetz project was in full swing by January 1756 when Adam wrote, "I have Clerisseau constantly with me, three or four lads constantly working for me . . . ,"[36] but the project was to come to nothing. During this time it seems likely that Allan Ramsay (1713–84), the Scottish painter and friend of Adam, also studied with Clérisseau.[37] Adam's letters tell of traveling with Ramsay, and his sketching with Adam and Clérisseau.[38] Six surviving drawings by Ramsay, four of them dated 1755, show Clérisseau's influence.[39] In fact, they are the most important dated evidence we have for Clérisseau's style at this time. One, "Interior of the Aqueduct of the Fontana di Trevi" (Fig. 26), is inscribed: "After a drawing of

Clerisseau by A R 1755."⁴⁰ A comparison of it with a Clérisseau drawing in the Hermitage illustrating the same interior (Fig. 27)⁴¹ shows such a similarity of viewpoint and handling of detail with a thick brush-stroke technique that it confirms the previously presented idea of Clérisseau's style — that in which he was to work throughout his long life.

The Penicuik Sketchbook also contains two views of this same scene, both of which correspond to the Ramsay and Clérisseau works.⁴² One is reproduced in Figure 28. Fleming attributes these two views in the Penicuik Album to Adam or Clérisseau,⁴³ but my study of the originals shows that they are of such a lower level of execution and of overall quality that I believe both of them to be by the pupil, Adam, rather than the master, Clérisseau.

Ramsay's representation of "The Temple of Venus and Rome" (Fig. 29) is related to at least three Clérisseau drawings of the scene, but is closest to one in the Hermitage (Fig. 30).⁴⁴ Although the two drawings represent the same subject from the same point of view, Ramsay's seems weaker than his others, and so may be one of the first drawings that he made under Clérisseau's tutelage. The other four Ramsay drawings also represent Roman ruins, but stylistically are less close to Clérisseau. Three represent sections of the Colosseum, two of which are inscribed in Ramsay's hand as being drawn " . . . in the Coliseo 1755" and " . . . in summer 1755." The fourth represents the Round Temple at Tivoli and is dated on the back "Sept. 29, 1755."⁴⁵ This last drawing suggests that Clérisseau and Adam were in Tivoli at this time, together with Ramsay, even though their sketching there is thought to have occurred in April 1756.⁴⁶ Of course, it is very possible that Adam and Clérisseau went to Tivoli more than once. Fleming suggests that the Adam drawings depicting Hadrian's Villa, now at Blair Adam, must date from this trip.⁴⁷ In any case, Adam's drawings of Tivoli⁴⁸ resemble the work of Clérisseau in the feathery quality of the vegetation, in the ways the bricks are indicated, and in the emphasis on the ruinous aspects of the buildings. This is particularly obvious in a comparison of Adam's drawing of the vestibule of the Piazza d'Oro, now at Blair Adam (Fig. 31), with one of the same building by Clérisseau (Fig. 32),⁴⁹ now at the Hermitage. This drawing by Clérisseau can also be compared to a much poorer Adam drawing of the same building, included in a sketchbook devoted to Tivoli (now in the Library of the Royal Institute of British Architects).⁵⁰ Other drawings from this same sketchbook, including a view of a ruined building seen from a hallway (Fig. 33), seem inept in comparison with a signed Clérisseau drawing in the Fitzwilliam of exactly the same scene (Fig. 34).⁵¹

Such variation in the quality of Adam's drawings of the same views of Tivoli, presumably made while with Clérisseau, suggests that the two men may have gone to Tivoli at least twice: in 1755 with Ramsay, when the RIBA drawings were done, and in 1756 when the more accomplished Blair Adam drawings were made.

The problem of dating the Tivoli drawings underscores the greater difficulty of tracing Clérisseau's growth as an architect and his influence on the development of Adam's style. The basic problem is the lack of any dated drawings by Clérisseau and the existence of very few by Adam. It is for this reason that the Ramsay drawings of 1755 are so important. They demonstrate Clérisseau's style and its

Figure 26. Allan Ramsay, "Interior of the Aqueduct of the Fontana de Trevi," 1755, Edinburgh, National Gallery of Scotland

Figure 27. C.-L. Clérisseau, "Aqueduct of the Trevi Fountain," Hermitage

Figure 28. Robert Adam (?), "Acqua Vergine in via del Nazareno, Rome,"
Penicuik House, Midlothian, Sir John Clerk Collection

Figure 29. Allan Ramsay, "The Temple of Venus and Rome in the Forum," Edinburgh, National Gallery of Scotland

Figure 30. C.-L. Clérisseau, "Le temple de Venus et de Rome," Hermitage

Figure 31. Robert Adam, "Ruins of Hadrian´s Villa
at Tivoli," Blair Adam, Kinross

Figure 32. C.-L. Clérisseau, "Extérieur d´un temple
a la ville Adrienne proche de Rome," Hermitage

Figure 34. C.-L. Clérisseau, "Hadrian´s Villa at Tivoli," Cambridge, Fitzwilliam Museum

Figure 33. Robert Adam, "Hadrian´s Villa at Tivoli," London, Royal Institute of British Architects Library

reflection in the Adam drawings from that time. Equally valuable is a print after Clérisseau's "A Prospect of the Ruins of the Temple of Jupiter Capitolinus in the Campo Vacino at Rome," engraved by M. Morin and published by Thomas Major in London on April 19, 1756 (see Fig. 3).[52] This print clearly demonstrates Clérisseau's absorption of Panini's topographical rendition of classical monuments, with the artful addition of sculptures carefully arranged to present a pleasing view of antiquity. The original drawing, which may well have been one Clérisseau sold to an English tourist, has not been found, but he later drew views of the opposite side of the temple, which is also known as the Temple of Concord. By referring to letters, one can arrange many of the Adam and Clérisseau drawings by subject matter to obtain a reasonably clear chronology. In case of doubt the more accomplished drawings of Adam should be dated later than the poorer ones, as in the case of the Tivoli drawings.

Among such far more accomplished drawings are an "Interior of the Pantheon" by Adam in the Penicuik Sketchbook (Fig. 35) which must be contrasted with a beautiful Clérisseau from the Hermitage (Fig. 36). Fleming has suggested that the Adam is a copy of the Clérisseau, which is possible, though the difference in the lighting suggests that it was done on the spot.[53] In spite of a certain linear quality and an overattention to detail in the Adam work, the drawings are very similar, indicating that Adam was becoming more skilled.

Copying of drawings was part of an artist's training in the eighteenth century; this is not an isolated instance in the Clérisseau-Adam relationship. A comparison of the drawings by Adam in the Penicuik Sketchbook with similar ones by Clérisseau reveals many possible copies, among them: "The Arch of the Goldsmiths" after a drawing by Clérisseau of the same monument in the Hermitage;[54] "The Basilica of Maxentius," to be compared with a Clérisseau drawing in a private collection;[55] and "The Forum of Trajan," resembling another drawing by Clérisseau in the Hermitage.[56] In every case the Adam "copy" is less refined, more finicky in detail, and lacking the solidity of the Clérisseau. Sometimes the detail is misunderstood by Adam, and in the case of "The Grotto of Egeria" (Fig. 37), the general effect is crude and flat by comparison with Clérisseau's original (Fig. 38).[57] However, one should not rule out the possibility that the compared drawings may both have been done at the location depicted at the same time: They may not be copies at all. Either possibility demonstrates how closely the two men worked together.

The only dated drawing in the Penicuik Sketchbook is an interior view of "The Entry to the Farnese Palace," inscribed "Rome 1756"(Fig. 39).[58] The level of accomplishment of this drawing and the wealth of detail, despite a certain dryness, make it the finest in the sketchbook. However, these characteristics also make it the work of Adam, particularly if one compares it with Clérisseau's interior of the "Vestibule of the Palazzo Massimi" (Fig. 40),[59] which is more three-dimensional in feeling and far more skillful in the handling of light.

Besides the drawings of actual monuments produced by Adam under Clérisseau's tutelage from 1755 to 1757, there were also great numbers of imaginary and fantastic buildings set into landscapes. One of these, now in the Soane Museum in a volume called *Miscellaneous Drawings,* is dated Rome 1756 (Fig. 41).[60] This is one of several very similar drawings in the Soane Museum which have been published by Arthur Bolton as dating from 1782.[61] However, all of them must belong to this early period.[62] Besides those in the Soane Museum, there are others from this time which are also by Adam, including several in a sketchbook in the Pierpont Morgan Library.[63] They all must date from about 1756–57 — that is, during the second or third year of Adam's training. This dating is reinforced by Clérisseau's strictures to Adam, already quoted from a letter to James of July 4, 1755, against inventing or composing either plans or elevations until he had greater knowledge and had made more progress in seeing things.[64] A beautiful Clérisseau drawing of fantastic ruins, probably made at this time or earlier, shows a similar approach in its imaginative arrangement of various elements (Fig. 42).[65] There can be no doubt that drawings such as this one by Clérisseau are the source of Adam's very similar works. It can also be compared to a freely drawn design of 1757 by Adam, in the Victoria and Albert Museum, depicting a fantastic building with columns and buttresses (Fig. 43). It has the same freedom as the Clérisseau, although it lacks his solidity and sureness of line. On the verso of this Adam sketch is an elevation and floor plan for one of the imaginary palaces Adam designed at this time (Fig. 44). Above it is the fragment of an inscription which reads: "J'aprouve cette project fait à rome an de grace Mille Sept Cent Cinquante Sept — Clery." Inasmuch as "Clery" is Clérisseau, he not only saw this drawing but also approved it.[66]

Clérisseau's study and drawing of antique and later architecture and decoration were not pursued solely for antiquarian interests. He was primarily an architect, and he wished to put his knowledge to use in creating architecture in his own day. Certainly Adam too had this as his driving ambition; he ardently wished to return to England with his head so full of antiquity that he could immediately use his knowledge to surpass every other architect in England.

The raison d'être for the long years of study by Clérisseau and then by Adam can best be seen in the imaginative designs of ancient interiors — not reconstructions by re-creations of antiquity — which Clérisseau drew, with Adam following in his wake. This type of archaeological drawing may have originated with Piranesi. Clérisseau's drawing in the Hermitage entitled "Maison Antique" (Fig. 45) at first appears to be a reconstruction of an actual monument, perhaps a Roman bath, but upon closer examination one becomes aware of the fact that no single ancient building ever combined all these architectural forms and decorative motifs. Their tasteful arrangement, filling the walls, seems ancient, but obviously is not. The elaborate entrance at the right, composed of authentic elements, is clearly not Roman but strictly Clérisseau. Perhaps most striking of all is the handling of space: Is this a domed room with barrel-vaulted arms? Even more intriguing is the screen of columns at the left leading to a semicircular room beyond.

The title of another work, "Intérieur de la Chambre Sépulcral de ma Composition" (Fig. 46),[67] makes clear his intention. Here the grandeur of Rome, truly re-created in an enormous domed space inspired by the Pantheon, is plausibly ancient; yet no Roman ever used segmental arches for niches and then screened off the lower parts with columns and flat lintels. The motif of niches alternating with tabernacles is obviously derived from the Pantheon (see Fig. 36). The inset plaques of great delicacy and the arches supporting the dome are ancient forms used in new

Figure 35. Robert Adam, "Interior of the Pantheon," Penicuik
House, Midlothian, Sir John Clerk Collection

Figure 36. C.-L. Clérisseau, "Intérieur du Panthéon à Rome," Hermitage

Figure 37. Robert Adam, "Grotto of Egeria," Penicuik House,
Midlothian, Sir John Clerk Collection

Figure 38. C.-L. Clérisseau, "Vue de l'intérieur de la grotte
de la nimphe Egérie à Rome," Hermitage

Figure 39. Robert Adam, "The Entry to the Farnese Palace," 1756,
Penicuik House, Midlothian, Sir John Clerk Collection

Figure 40. C.-L. Clérisseau, "Intérieur d´un vestibule
au Palais Maxime à Rome," Hermitage

Figure 41. Robert Adam, "Imaginary Landscape," 1756,
London, Soane Museum

Figure 42. C.-L. Clérisseau, "Fantastic Buildings
in a Landscape," Florence, Uffizi

Figure 43. Robert Adam, "Fantastic Scene," recto,
London, Victoria and Albert Museum

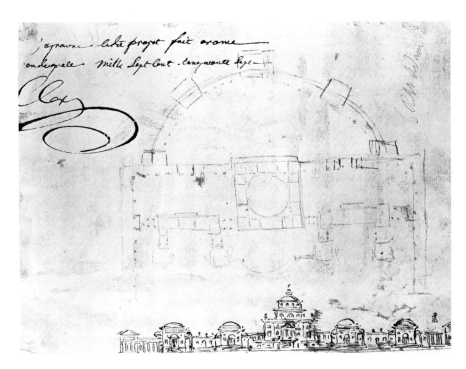

Figure 44. Robert Adam, "Plan and Façade of Palace," verso
of Fig. 43, London, Victoria and Albert Museum

Figure 45. C.-L. Clérisseau, "Maison Antique," Hermitage

Figure 46. C.-L. Clérisseau, "Intérieur de la Chambre
Sépulcral de ma Composition," Hermitage

Figure 47. Robert Adam, "Reconstruction Based
on the Roman Baths," London, Soane Museum

combinations. The great profusion of decorative friezes, roundels, and delicate
swags may suggest the work of an interior decorator, albeit a talented and sensitive one, but it is the architectural forms themselves that give the composition its
strength.

Clérisseau's influence on Adam's compositions in this vein further reveal
Adam's indebtedness to his teacher. For example, Adam's "Reconstruction Based
on the Roman Baths" (Fig. 47)[68] shows much the same view into a corner, a similar
delicacy, and a variety of ancient details, friezes, tabernacles, elaborate stucco
decorations, and coffers — all arranged in a coherent architectural form evocative
of antiquity, and of Clérisseau. Therefore, the true beginning of the Adam style,
with its wealth of delicate, ancient-inspired decorations, vaulted ceilings, screens
of columns, niches, and rooms in a great variety of shapes, derives from Clérisseau.

That Clérisseau originated this style is clear from Adam's letter of July 24,
1756, to James.

> But one night ruminating by muself on what Clerisseau had talk'd to me of
> his highest ambition in the way of settlement Viz/t 200 a year or even 150,
> it occur'd to me that supposing we travelling brothers shoud fix that upon
> him, and keep him a purpose for travelling till such time as we were well
> established in England, when I woud bring him over and give him the
> inspection of our drawing room, and to put things in perspective and make
> views of all the principal places in England, get him to oversee any thing one
> intends to publish, which woud I imagine make him quite happy: And woud
> be much for our advantage. The travelling scheme you see keeps him distant
> some years so that he can neither interfere nor eclipse the first flash of
> character and after that is over he comes secretly like a thief in the night and
> no one regards him. Tho' a French man he has no Allegria in Company, nor
> no thoughts of Eclat or Ambition Thus tho' sencible of his own Merit
> (which is Infinite) yet he may be managed like a lap dog, allow him to cross

himself and eat fish on meagre days and hear mass on Sundays and say prayers morning and evening, which may be called the compendiary of the whole duty of Catholick man, he neither desires, nor aims at more.[69]

This thought recurs in a letter written in September of the same year.

My opinions about Clerisseau I wrote some time ago and according as you write shall try to settle matters with him for the mutual interest of the travelling brothers. John in his last wishes I coud prevail with him to come with me to England, but that woud be the worst of politicks for my character, as Chambers and etc woud not be idle in saying he can do nothing by himselft it is Clerisseau that does all, whereas if any of you propose travelling only inform me how and when and I will take my measures accordingly.[70]

In spite of these cynical machinations, study and activity continued. The Desgodetz project was abandoned and one on the ancient baths begun. Details about these, and insights into the workings of the Adam team, are given in a letter to James of September 11.

. . . my Project of Degodet in the way I wrote you of formerly, I was obliged to throw up, or lay aside, which you will, it was a work of years, and I found retarded more material studys; such as that of Adrians Villa and the Baths of Caracalla and Diocletian which are in a very prosperous way and I dare say will please you take with the public; I am to show the Baths in their present ruinous condition, and from that the make other disigns of them as they were when intire and in their glory, in which project Ld Burlingtons book has been of unspeakable service as he is vastly exact in his measurements; and in Palladio's time they were much more intire so that I get great light from him; My other studys are the drawings of what good buildings are in Rome, either within or without, particularly those done from the Antients by Piero Ligorio, Algardi and Salvi; I think I have now as good as agreed with my two lads who work to me here to accompany me to England; I mean Mon/r Brunace and my Liegois. The first, bred a painter, I have converted into an architect, he does all my ornaments and all my figures vastly well. The last is my plan man and line drawer, off an active, undaunted and bustling spirit, but hithertoo much attached, honest and laborious. Besides these two I have an Italian lad who does all the drudgery business of putting things in proportions from sketches, but him I hold in no esteen but as a dayly slave at 1 shill per day. Clerisseau and I are the directors of these youths, and by means of their industry and my pay, we get more time to think, and I to apply to sketches of taste and invention which otherways I could not do. And Clerisseau to draw his ruins by which he lives. Dont you approve of this distribution of men and employment.[71]

In October 1756 Adam planned to go to Frascati for the first time. He wrote to his sister Nelly that he would carry "my Clerisseau, my Chariot, my Cook and my Valet de Chambre alongst with me."[72] The long delay in visiting Frascati suggests that Clérisseau's project for Cardinal Passionei had not been built, for, if it had,

Clérisseau surely would have shown off his first architectural commission at an earlier date.[73]

Adam informed James in July that he planned to stay abroad until the spring of 1757 traveling with Clérisseau.

> Clerisseau and I being together will continue so on the road homewards as long as we can, at Venice, Vicenza, at Pola in Istria, and at many other places, which will consume the next spring, to the best of purposes. If I return thro' Germany he will continue to go with me perhaps into Holland from which I come to England and send him to Paris.[74]

In October he wrote to Nelly:

> I rejoice much at My Lord Hopetouns approving my stay this winter at Rome, but if he had not it woud not have changed me as I in a manner lost the intention of being at Rome without staying to finish my interprising projects which go on with success. At Venice and Vicenza I shall have more time that I expected, for my jaunt into Dalmatia and Pola in Istria. If you knew with what a sad heart I return without seeing Greece expecially to be on the very coast of it.[75]

During the next few months, Adam, having had to forego a trip to Greece, was involved in many other travel projects. He was intent on preparing a publication, and, because the Desgodetz project had been abandoned and the one on the Roman baths was evidently slowed down, he decided to undertake the Spalato project, which he referred to in a letter to Jenny as "Domitians Palace at Spalatro."[76] The project seems to have been selected because it was the one large, unpublished site nearby. Accordingly, Adam and Clérisseau left Rome with the Ramsays, stopping at Viterbo on May 9, then going to Florence.[77] Journeying on to Bologna, they met Count Algarotti, who admired Adam's and Clérisseau's works and "came a second time to see Clerisseau's drawings with which he was also astonished."[78] Algarotti gave Adam a letter of introduction to Consul Joseph Smith. They proceeded to Padua and then to Venice, arriving on July 1. In Venice they made preparations for the trip to Spalato, and applied for permission to excavate. Adam, Clérisseau, and two draftsmen sailed on July 11,[79] making their way to the ruins at Pola and then on to the ultimate goal, Diocletian's Palace at Spalato.

Clérisseau's days as Adam's teacher were now over. At Spalato, more than ever before, he became Adam's employee, thereby further complicating the relationship between them and adding to the potential for future conflicts.

III

Clérisseau and the Adam Brothers:

1757–64

The first stop on the voyage to Spalato in 1757 was presumably at Piram (now Poreć, in Yugoslavia) on the west coast of Istria, where Clérisseau drew the famous church.[1] While the drawing could date from Clérisseau's visit to Istria in September 1760 with James Adam, it was probably done at this time as it is one of a group of views of Istria and Dalmatia which Clérisseau included in one of the portfolios he sold to Catherine the Great. They proceeded south to Pola (now Pula), which Robert Adam had earlier proposed to explore.[2]

The two artists made drawings of the Roman monuments, and three rapid but measured drawings by Robert Adam have been preserved. These are on-the-spot drawings of major Roman monuments: the amphitheater, the triumphal arch (Fig. 48), and the Temple of Augustus, which he titled the Temple of Diana.[3] The drawings have little artistic merit, but do show Adam's careful observation of ancient monuments and his awareness of the importance of plans. Twenty-five drawings by Clérisseau of the ancient and medieval monuments of Pola and two related engravings exist.[4] All were made during this trip or were based on drawings done then. They cannot date from Clérisseau's later stay at Pola with James Adam because the architects did not receive permission to make drawings during that visit.[5] Although four of the drawings are dated 1760,[6] I believe them to be based on earlier sketches. In August 1760 (a month before the unsuccessful second visit to Pola), James mentions in a letter to Robert that the proposed size of some engravings was to be based on the size of the drawings of Pola.[7] Among the twenty-five drawings are two in the Hermitage, representing the Temple of Augustus (Fig. 49) and the Arch of the Sergie,[8] which served not only as the basis for later engravings (Fig. 50) but also for other versions of the drawings. In both, the presence of figures

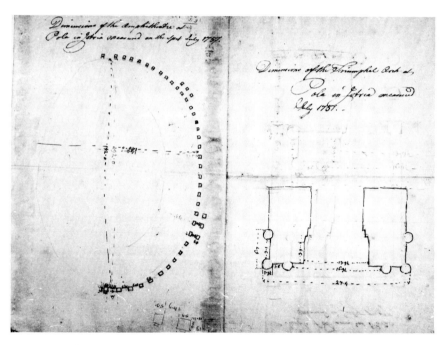

Figure 48. Robert Adam, "Dimensions of the Amphitheatre and Triumphal Arch at Pola in Istria," July 1757, London, Royal Institute of British Architects Library

Figure 49. C.-L. Clérisseau, "Temple of Augustus," Hermitage

Figure 50. Cunego after C.-L. Clérisseau, "Temple of Augustus, Pola,"
London, Royal Institute of British Architects Library

close to those in the engravings made by Domenico Cunego[9] suggests they are the finished drawings for the prints made after sketches done on the spot. One such original sketch by Clérisseau done at Pola is a small pen-and-brown-wash drawing depicting the rear of the Temple of Augustus and Diana (Fig. 51).[10] It has a freshness and immediacy lacking in the other works executed on a larger scale in shades of tan and green or in bright colored gouache.[11] Two drawings in the Hermitage represent Pola's most famous monument: the amphitheater or arena (Fig. 52).[12] There is also a drawing of it in the collection of the Duke of Buccleuch.[13] Fleming suggests the Clérisseau and Robert Adam stayed only briefly in Pola, because Adam had heard that Stuart and Revett had "planned that antiquity."[14] In 1748 Piranesi had published etchings of the arch, temple, and amphitheater at Pola as part of his series, *Antichità romane de tempi della repubblica.* Clérisseau's drawings are far less dramatic and do not seem to be indebted to Piranesi's.

Besides studying and sketching the Roman monuments of Pola, Clérisseau was also attracted to those of the Middle Ages. He made at least two drawings of a group of three joined Byzantine churches, S. Maria Formosa o del Canneto, which consisted of the ruins of an apse flanked by two cruciform religious buildings (Fig. 53).[15] These drawings have particular value, as only one of the cruciform structures remains (Fig. 54). Undoubtedly, the geometric clarity of the buildings appealed to Clérisseau. He also drew the Byzantine fortress.

After leaving Pola, they made their way down the Dalmatian coast. Adam instructed the Captain to "coast it all the way and lie ashore every night."[16] Two handsome drawings by Clérisseau, now in the Hermitage, record visits beyond Pola. The first represents the Cathedral of Zebenigo (now Sibonik; Fig. 55). One of Clérisseau's finest works, it is a beautiful, delicate drawing with soft washes and figures.[17] Obviously done on the spot, even perhaps from the ship, it shows the building before the removal in the late nineteenth century of the bell tower, granary, and Church of St. Roch,[18] and reveals the artist's considerable skill in capturing the salient features of a building.

In the other drawing, Clérisseau depicted the town hall of Trau (now Trogir), the Church of S. Maria della Piazza, the clock tower, and the loggia (Fig. 56).[19] This drawing is the only pictorial record of the church, which was destroyed in the nineteenth century, and confirms the findings of recent archaeological investigations.[20] Despite the value of the drawing for its depiction of a lost church, it is not a completely accurate representation of the entire scene. Clérisseau, ever the artist, took many liberties. First, he drew the angled facade of the town hall on the left, as well as depicting the church, tower, and loggia slightly from the left; these cannot all be seen from this point of view. In addition, Clérisseau lowered the clock tower for a better compositional effect and expanded the bays of the loggia from five to seven. Finally, the decorative plaques on the town hall are, for the most part, imaginary.

The travelers arrived at Spalato on July 22, 1757. Surprisingly little is known about their activity there as most of Robert's correspondence between July and November 1757 has been lost. However, from two letters written to James on

Figure 51. C.-L. Clérisseau, "Rear of the Temples of Augustus
and Diana," present whereabouts unknown

Figure 52. C.-L. Clérisseau, "View of
the Amphitheater," Hermitage

Figure 53. C.-L. Clérisseau, "Three Byzantine Churches Pola," Hermitage

Figure 54. S. Maria Formosa o del Canneto, Pola

Figure 55. C.-L. Clérisseau, "Vue de Zebenigo en Dalmatie," Hermitage

Figure 56. C.-L. Clérisseau, "Vue de Trau en Dalmatie," Hermitage

August 6 and November 1, and from the "Introduction" to the Adam work entitled *The Ruins of the Palace of the Emperor Diocletian at Spalatro,* published in 1764, we get an inkling of his problems. On August 6 Robert wrote his brother:

> I arrived the 22d in good health, as were also my fellow travellers. Since that time till this day I have been employed in considereing the antiquities of this place, which I hope will prove a work very acceptable to the public as it is different from all other things yet published.[21]

In the published "Introduction" he describes certain difficulties he had encountered, namely, the inhabitants had destroyed parts of the palace for building materials, they had built houses upon the old foundations, and the ancient and modern foundations were so intermingled as to be indistinguishable. Without any reference to Clérisseau, he adds, as if he were the only observer,

> . . . assiduity, however, and repeated observation, enabled me to surmount these difficulties. Attention to such parts of the palace as were entire, conducted me with certainty to the knowledge of those which were more ruinous.[22]

Both Robert Adam's letter of August 6 and the "Introduction" mention other troubles — or, as he called them, "stoppages" — that he encountered. The local authorities thought he was a spy surveying the fortifications. Furthermore, the excavation permit he had applied for had not arrived from Venice. It was only through the intervention of General Graeme, who "took my part with great warmth," that he was able to surmount these obstacles. Adam wrote to his brother, "now all difficulties are removed and . . . in 8, 10, or at most a fortnight I shall be ready to depart for Venice with all my operations in my pocket."[23] Adam's "Introduction" describes the work:

> . . . fear of a second interruption added to my industry, and the unwearied application during five weeks we compleated, with an accuracy that afforded me great satisfaction, those parts of our work which it was necessary to execute on the spot.[24]

On November 1, long after the expedition was over, Robert wrote James:

> We left Venice on the 11th of July and arrived at Spalatro the 22d of July. The 28th of August left Spalatro and the 11th of September arrived at Venice so that you see we were just 5 weeks at Spalatro — and that 4 people were constantly at work which is the equal of 20 weeks of one person. Mr. Wood was but 15 days at Palmyra and had not one man to work for him — judge then the accuracy of such a work![25]

In the manuscript version of the "Introduction" Adam wrote:

> For that purpose I prevailed with Mr. Clérisseau a very particular friend of mine to accompany me on this expedition whose taste and long experience in the study of architecture and antiquity, I hope to keep as much assistance in the prosecution of this work as I should receive pleasure from his company and conversation at the same time.[26]

In the published version, personal feelings were omitted and Clérisseau is not described as a "very particular friend," nor is there reference to any pleasure to be gained from his company or conversation.

> Having prevailed on Mr. Clérisseau, a French artist, from whose taste and knowledge of antiquities I was certain of receiving a great assistance in the execution of my scheme, to accompany me in this expedition, and having engaged two draughtsmen, of whose skill and accuracy I had long experience, we set sail from Venice on the 11th of July, 1757, and on the 22nd of that month arrived at Spalatro.[27]

The only other reference to Clérisseau is equally impersonal: He is listed among the foreign subscribers to the volume. Not one of the plates bears the name of Clérisseau to show that he was the author of the original drawing or plan, although there can be little doubt that he made most, if not all, of such drawings. However, Clérisseau included his name in an inscription—ICED IACET CARUS CLERISSU PICTOR—on a sarcophagus in Plate XXVIII, perhaps in retaliation, as Alistair Rowan suggests in one of his Slade Lectures.[28]

Clérisseau's role in the Spalato expedition and in the subsequent preparation and publication of the book about it is complex and unclear. I propose to describe it in two parts, beginning with the history of the preparation of the publication over a period of five years from the Adam family point of view, using letters and other documents as source material. The correspondence between James and Robert concerning other projects and travels with Clérisseau during this same period will explain why Clérisseau's role has hitherto not been clear. Secondly, I propose to examine Clérisseau's part in the expedition, and the production of the publication with the help of the surviving drawings and engravings as primary source material, and, as secondary material, recent studies of the palace. The period of time involved in the preparation of the publication was long, for the book was not ready to be printed until 1762 and was further delayed until 1764.[29]

After the return to Venice and Adam's subsequent departure for Germany in October 1757, Clérisseau stayed in Venice to finish the drawings for the plates and to supervise the engraving of those which were not to be engraved in other countries.[30] This work must have occupied the greater part of his time for the next few months.

Clérisseau also continued to work on the drawings for the new edition of Desgodetz that he and Robert Adam had started and abandoned earlier. James Adam, aware of this, wrote Robert suggesting that the two of them publish the work after Clérisseau had made the final drawings for the engravings. Robert replied to James as follows on June 17, 1758:

> . . . I think you might go half and half with him in the profits of the Books, or if you was to take me in alongst with you two then 1/3d to each woud be better for us and I think sufficient for him considering that the whole outlay of money falls heavy on us, but what I cannot fall on a way to cure is the disagreeableness of publishing it under his name join'd to yours alone, or to

yours and mine together I think the only method to prevent that is this, after the work is ready for the press tell him that a French name woud spoil the sale in England and as he is not known there it woud do him no honour and in order to made amends for that offer him 50 more than his ½ or ⅓ part to desist from it.[31]

To this James answered:

From what you have frequently tole me about C-au's manner and his want of ambition and a desire of fame, I did not imagine that he wou'd insist upon giving his name to the copy of the book and I think by the giving him a small consideration he wou'd be very ready to yield the name and it wou'd be worth our while to have it.[32]

The project eventually was pursued by James, but it never came to anything. Much later, when Clérisseau was on his own, he announced that he was preparing a new edition of Desgodetz, but this, too, was never published.[33]

Work on the Spalato volume proceeded, however. By September, some plates were being engraved in London; others, under Clérisseau's supervision, were engraved in Venice. Proofs were sent to Robert in London and to James in Edinburgh.[34] By November, Francesco Bartolozzi, who probably added the figures to Clérisseau's finished drawings for the engravings, was demanding more money.[35] Clérisseau, too, was having money problems. He needed fifteen pounds to have his belongings shipped from Lyons, and offered Robert drawings to sell in England in exchange. Robert wrote James an account of this:

. . . my answer was this: That I allowed him to take that money and that I woud endeavour to put it to my eldest brothers account in this way. That as he was to have 100 yearly from him even when he was maintaining him in his travells, that he found that sum too small when he had to hyre a house servant and c., on his own sum, but that he might send his effects and that I woud either take or dispose of them and allow him the value of them in accot; This I told him to keep intirely secret. . . . But I have no notion when you join him that you shou'd continue the 100. I know that you can make that easy, by entering into another bargain and giving him the hopes of profits from publishing which will please him more than any fixt salary you can give him a hint is not conveni[ent] for you to give, but rather make him a present now and then as I did.[36]

Once again the Adam brothers were taking advantage of Clérisseau.

Nothing seems to have progressed further on the Spalato volume until James Adam's visit to Italy in the summer of 1760. On reaching Venice about June 25, he wrote Robert that Clérisseau expected to have "all finish'd in about 3 months time."[37]

This was the first meeting of Clérisseau and James Adam, who had come to Venice not only to see about the book, but also to spend several years traveling in Italy. Clérisseau was to look after James, to be his guide and mentor, and to earn that elusive Adam retainer. On first meeting Clérisseau, James wrote to Robert.

I see from Clérisseau how usefull he will be to me in every respect, he is one of the most obliging creatures I ever saw. . . . I knew him immediately from your description, but he is infinitely younger looking than I imag'd.

The letter went on to say that the two men had obtained lodgings with seven great rooms. Clérisseau added a footnote to James's letter:

tres cher ami je vous embrase Etoute le plenitude de mon Coeur lallegresse me transporte mes sens sont troublés l'embaras de notre maison-me fait remettre a vour ecrire Samedi adieu tres cher ami Cler.[38]

With Clérisseau as cicerone, James saw churches and palaces and studied the language.[39] From London on July 24, Robert wrote to James the following letter.

I dont know if any of our people write to you that I had a letter from Mr. [Joseph] Smith in which he pays the highest flummery you can imagine first of me then of Clerisseau and then of your great character and how he longs for you. I am sorry at several of his impressions which shows how little precaution your messmate has taken to conceal his having drawn the view of Spalatro. As Smith terms them those very fine drawings done by Mr. C - under your eye. This he I mean C - has out of vanity I find told to all the English he coud lay his hands on, by which means they spread it in England and Mr. Chams [i. e. William Chambers] and Mr. Milns [i. e. Robert Mylne] and all of them may and I dont doubt but do give it out that all the drawings are Cl - 's and how can it be otherwise when he wishes it should be known. This only leads me to ask you a question, how can I put R. A. delint. at the bottom of the plates when Cl - has told the contrary, I really should be glad of your advice concerning this point. Besides his drawing the views of Pola and sending them to Lord Brudenel and others was stupid as it makes these things common should we ever need to add these ruins to any work. Stuart you see will never publish more Le Roy has done no justice, why then might no we have taken up the cudgils and why woud he out of a piece of idle vanity prostitute these antiquitys to people who are fixt friends to Mr. Blackfriars [i. e. Mylne] and who never chuse to look me in the face nor show not the smallest enclinations to see me or subscribe or any thing else. I mention these things to you that you may be upon your guard, as really things of that nature are hurtful and vexatious that after you carry one about with you pay him handsomely and as a friend, that he should out of mere vanity do so unfriendly an action. At the same time that I love the body and his good qualitys I cannot help being enraged at the inconsistency of his actions. . . . [40]

James spoke to Clérisseau about his actions and wrote Robert about them in August.

As to C - 's indiscretion in point of vanity I cannot answer for it, I dont doubt but he has been foolish enough to say things to the English that he shou'd not have said on that subject, but he says nothing of that kind to me, I dont know how to check him. I was angry at his giving Ld. B - l [Brudenell] the views of P - a [Pola], which he excuses by a long history of Mr. Wrights having drawn him into agree to it after his having refus'd and that he agreed only on having my Lords promise of having no copy taken because he did not look upon them as his property only, you and I having an after intention to publish them. Whither he had ever talk'd to Smith of the Spalatro drawings I dont know, but I see they are friends only from the teeth foreward.[41]

James went on to write about the business of the names on the plates.

Notwithstanding all this, I can't see you shou'd be at any loss to put your name to the prints, these being things understood; as you had so many draughtsmen there, as you mention in your preface, tis not to be suppos'd that they were idle while you drew all, neither can it be supposed that you did all the views while Clerisseau was carried there by you a purpose, but as tis the form for the Archt. who publishes a work to put his name as the drawer, I cant see why you shou'd not, especially as 3 fourths of the people who ever see the book will imagine that you did the whole, and the remaining fourth, cannot know but that you did some of them. As for what Ch - rs and M - n's say that I hold for nothing and shou'd at any rate expect the worst from that quarter.[42]

James changed his mind about this, however, because in September he wrote to his sister Betty as follows:

In this I have upon reflection chang'd my opinion, and am convinc'd it wou'd be better to put Clerisseau's name to all the perspective views. My reasons are these, first that it is known to the world by his own preface that C - u was carried there by him, and those English who know C - au must guess the reason, and must be sensible that most of these views were done by him; Bob confessing of this, is much more honest and much more candid than to seem to desire the reputation which is due to another. Besides if all the regular architecture is mark'd of Bob's doing, he is no less master of the whole performance than if the views had likewise been done by him, and his improvement as an Architect is the same, the other being rather the work of a painter in which still we must take care to have C - au allways appear in England, and which will be no great difficulty to mannadge. Another argument is, that when the prints are publish'd seperately from the work, it will be better to see Clerisseau's name to them than Bob's, and serves to retain a propper dignity. These reasons have so far weigh'd with myself, that determin'd in anything I do, to follow the plan, rather than submit to the above inconveniencys. I shall be glad to hear Bob's opinion of this, or if he has any material objections.[43]

In the end, all names except those of the engravers were omitted from the plates.

At about this time James wrote Robert concerning his other activities and publication projects with Clérisseau, remarking that they would be "a real source of profit, and wou'd at the same time extend our names as travellors to the uttermost ends of the earth." [44] Long before James had come to Italy, he had suggested as a joint project with Clérisseau the publication of the Desgodetz volume begun by Robert and Clérisseau;[45] he now proposed a different one.

Clérisseau had particular pleasure in sending you the plan of the Thermes of Agrippa, which I hope you wou'd receive safe and dare say you wil reckon it a cheap acquisition at ½ sequin, which I paid with great pleasure to the hump back'd voleur. You may be sure I long to hear your opinion of our sceme for the Thermes, which I still continue to think will be a magnificent work, tho' not a profitable one; because I forsee they will be very expensive and the sale not general, that is not like Palmyra and *ca.* To answer to this, I think they wou'd bring reputation, and we behoov'd to trust to our other works for profit, which we propose drawing in this manner. Clerisseau's views of Pola, we determin'd the size of other views, and wou'd engrave them of two different dimensions, the greatest 23 in by 15 in the smaller 16 in by 11 in. In the former we are regulated by Piranezi, in the latter by Le Roi. These views thus reduc'd to two sizes we propose to publish, in a book along with the detail journey, and description *ca.* that whoever chooses the work compleat may find it in that book and may purchase it if he pleases; but for those whose taste does not extend so far, we wou'd at the same time publish our views by themselves, which we propose shou'd be very clever and very interesting *ca.* whi. distant name engrav'd under them, might induce the publick to prefer them to all other ornamental prints, Strange only excepted. . . . What do you say to this? I am so fond of this reconciling fame and fortune.[46]

Clérisseau, having at last become aware that he might not be given any credit for his projects with the Adams, apparently had retained a complete copy of the plans, because James wrote home: "Bob thinks he has the only copy of the plans of the Thermae. I know Clérisseau has an exact copy of all." This is confirmed by the 1820 catalogue of the sale of Clérisseau's library.[47]

In his letter to James of July 24, Robert expressed his displeasure with Clérisseau showing the Split drawings as his own, as this implied a certain disloyalty to the Adam brothers. The letter ended with a complaint about Clérisseau's work as an archaeologist on the Spalato project.

By Clerisseau's last letter I see he wants to do something to the inside of the Imperial appartments but I am affraid that is pushing the joke too far. In a ground plan the smallest bitt above ground gives hints but where no walls remain except in one spot it woud be absurd to suppose they were all remaining besides I do think the publick have enough for their money. . . .[48]

Adam's dissatisfaction touched on the liberties Clérisseau took with the restoration, though it should be noted that Clérisseau's original plan for Spalato, including the imperial apartment, was more accurate in many ways than the one published by Adam. In August, James wrote to Robert about the problem of the exterior windows in Diocletian's bedchamber, which were impossible to reconcile with the rest of the restoration. James suggests, perhaps on Clérisseau's advice, that they be eliminated and that skylights be inserted.[49] This suggestion was followed in the publication. In the next month, further discrepancies were noted, and James again wrote about the corrections proposed by Clérisseau. The mention of the

Venetian window raises the question of accuracy on the part of Adam, suggesting that the complaints about Clérisseau were based on other grounds.

> I send inclos'd half of the Geometrical Ruin of the Marine wall, which Clerisseau and I have fully consider'd and are of the opinion that any alteration that is made on it might be done on this plate and not the view it being a pity to alter it, whereas this can't suffer; some corrections are made on it by Clerisseau, and the arches are made a little more compleat to answer to those of the view. The columns of the Venetian window are also restor'd, which can have no very bad effect, because if they are not there now, they have been there, and shou'd future travellers ever criticise tis easy to suppose they were there in Bob's time.[50]

It is apparent that Clérisseau was considered an employee, not a colleague or equal. Robert had discovered him and subsidized his work, which had been of invaluable help to Clérisseau in the past as it now was to James. Robert had proposed financial arrangements many times, and suggested an arrangement for James to follow. What actually happened is made clear in James's letter of early September:

> . . . inform Bob, that I have fix'd with C - au in the way he advis'd, that is, for no certain sum but rather a supply from time to time, but as he pled his necessity of having something to trust to, in case of his eyes failling, and likewise as a reward for his fatigues, I complied with a request which I thought so reasonable and agreed to give him $1/_3$ of the profit on the Degodetz after paying all expence and the interest of the money laid out. I shou'd be glad to have Bob's opinion of this agreement because without his concurrence it comes to be void and null, and I think by this scheme I have plac'd his profits at such a distance, that it can be no great inconveniency our sparing a third at that time.[51]

In the fall of 1760, James Adam and Clérisseau began their travels together through Italy. Most of the letters from this time are lost, but portions of a diary, supposedly by Robert Adam but actually by James, were published in fragments in 1831. The original is now lost and the following account is a summary of it insofar as it relates to Clérisseau.[52] On October 1 and 2, Adam, with Clérisseau and Antonio Zucchi, went to Sala to visit Abbé Farsetti; they missed him but visited the garden described by James. They went on to Padua, Vicenza, Verona, and Ravenna. In Verona they noted that the measurements of the amphitheater differed from those of Desgodetz, so they measured it carefully. On October 20, Clérisseau and James returned to Venice, and there dealt with engravers.[53] In November, they went to Ravenna, Ponte de Lago, Oscuno, Ferrara, Argente Faienza, and Bologna, where Clérisseau made drawings of the towers. The next stop was Florence, where they stayed a month[54] before moving on to Pisa and Livorno, where they inquired about going to the Levant and Egypt. They then returned to Pisa and visited the Campanile, the Campo Santo, and the Duomo Baptistry, where Clérisseau and James drew the antique inscriptions. On January 4, 1761, they returned to Florence, and James reported that Clérisseau had made a drawing of the Fountain of

Venus in the Villa Reale de Petraia. James was impressed by the grotesque style of the Villa Castello:

> . . . many of the rooms painted in the grotesque taste and with spirit and invention. . . . Here and there are ornaments, also in the grotesque style worth more perfect attention at another time.[55]

They went by way of Siena to Rome, where they settled down. Little is known of their activity there, but Hayward remarked in his comments on the English travelers in Rome in 1760 that "Adams the Architect's Bro^r wh. his Director Monsr Clérisseau set up a Manufactory of Virtu employing painters Engrav^rs Architects etc." [56] Their lifestyle is described in James's letter to Robert, which mentions that his Roman staff included "Clerisseau, segretario al Cavaliere"; five draftsmen: George Richardson, Domenico Cunego, Antonio Zucchi, Giuseppe Sacco, and Agostino Scara; and four servants: a footman, cook, valet, and coachman.[57]

In July and August they made excursions to Frascati, where they visited the Belvedere and the villa of Cardinal Passionei, whose antiquities they looked at. Because the Cardinal had died, the villa was about to be torn down. No reference was made to Clérisseau's work there. In September, without Clérisseau, James set out for Naples, Veletri, Terracina, Mora de Cayeta, and Capua. After arriving in Naples, he visited Pompeii, where he saw "a room which seemed to have been painted with arabesques." Clérisseau joined him in Naples and the two went to the Temple of Serapis. James described what they saw:

> . . . also at Cumae some ancient sepulchres where the stuccos are remaining vastly entire: they are of excellent workmanship, and the lowest relief I ever beheld: but their being close upon the eye made that more necessary.[58]

Perhaps it was at this time that Clérisseau made the drawing of a sepulchral interior with stucco decorations near Pozzuoli that was in the collection of Major Percy Hope-Johnstone (Fig. 57).[59] They returned to Pozzuoli, and then went to Baia to see the Temple of Apollo and Grotto of the Sibyl.[60] Then they went to the Sepulcher of Agrippina and to Caserta. With Clérisseau, Zucchi, and his servant George, Adam went to Beneventum, where he drew the arch. Back in Naples, he discovered that his request to go to Sicily and dig there had been refused; he considered going nonetheless. He proposed taking only one draftsman and two servants, namely Clérisseau, George, and Joseph, and having Clérisseau take a servant with him. Instead, they all returned to Pozzuoli, where:

> . . . with Clérisseau I examined with great care the Temple of Serapis, which in forming the plan has its own difficulties, particularly this; that besides the columns of the great or inner portico, there are a great many fragments of other two diameters, the lesser of which we could find no use for, because by the fragments of circular and straight architraves, one must determine that the order of the circular building in the centre and the portico round the cortile have formerly been of the same diameter.[61]

They went on to the Temple of Neptune and the amphitheater. The next day they proceeded to Baia, where they examined the temples of Venus, Diana, and

Figure 57. C.-L. Clérisseau, "Ancient Sepulchre near Pozzuoli,"
Lockerbie, Dumfriesshire, Hope-Johnstone Collection

Mercury, and the unusual baths that were part of them. Drawings were made on the spot of the stucco ceiling's elegant workmanship. I connect one of these drawings with a Clérisseau drawing in the Hermitage entitled "Bath at Baia (Temple of Mercury)" (Fig. 58).[62]

On November 1, they went again to Pozzuoli and looked over what James termed Clérisseau's "Operation."[63] Saturday, November 14, saw them setting off for Paestum, with a stop at Salerno on the way. On the following Tuesday, James wrote:

> Clérisseau took this opportunity to talk to me of his situation and seemed to dread the uncertainty of his share in the designs; when to make sure at all events. I agreed to give from the end of those months he had received at Venice, one hundred and fifty zechini per annum to the time I left him, and afterwards two hundred zechini per annum, and to take twelve designs per annum at twelve zechini each, for which he is to answer all my commissions, direct the engravings, and deliver the original drawings.[64]

At Paestum they made views of the two basilicas that the Journal notes can "enter into the work," presumably for one of the volumes proposed by James. "The Ruins of the Temple of Poseidon at Paestum," now in the Hermitage (Fig. 59), may be one of these drawings.[65] While there, they also made some general measurements of the buildings. After stopping in Sorrento, they finally arrived back in Rome on December 13, 1761. Here James remained most of the time until his return to England in May 1763.

It is not known whether Clérisseau remained with James throughout this period or whether he returned to Venice. It was probably in 1762, if not at the time of James's first visit to Rome in 1761, that Clérisseau introduced him to Cardinal Alessandro Albani, whom Clérisseau had met in 1755. In any case, Adam knew Albani in 1762. Clérisseau possibly also introduced James to Raphael Mengs before that painter's departure for Spain in 1761.[66]

While James and Clérisseau were traveling in Italy, work was progressing on the Spalato volume. Without James there, the engravers in Venice worked slowly, and the plates were not forwarded to him in Rome until May 1761.[67] The book was completed by early 1762. On February 8, 1762, Robert expressed his dissatisfaction to James, who was still in Italy:

> Clerisseau has been very thoughtless in his views if you look at the steps of the Temple of Esculapius you will see that are so large and so high that in place of 15 steps he could not have 10, Then he says it was Bricks incrusted with marble, whereas it really is of stone, like jupiters, both out side and inside and no brick about it, you will also observe that in view of the out side of Jupiters Temple He has made columns remaining in the sides of the octagon that do not remain, and are markt faint in the Plane.[68]

These comments are indeed true, as can be noted by a comparison of Plate XLII of the Spalato book, which has nine steps, and Plate XLIV, which has fifteen. When finally published, the text referring to this temple was changed to read, "the walls of the Temple are built of Freestone."[69] Plate XXVI and XXVII of the

Figure 58. C.-L. Clérisseau, "Baja terme (Temple de Mercure)," Hermitage

Figure 59. C.-L. Clérisseau, "The Ruins of the Temple of
Poseidon at Paestum," Hermitage

so-called Temple of Jupiter do not agree. According to Robert Adam, all of these differences are due to mistakes on Clérisseau's part.

In the same letter Robert wrote:

> I have read over the preface and introduction you returned to me, I see the few alterations you have made, and that one with regard to Clerisseau, who Henry told me has complained to him at Rome about his situation, I told him that was owing to mad fits he was seized with at times which made him complain against his best friends for that you were living in the greatest harmony, and that he complained against me as much at time as he did againest you. . . . [70]

Robert's statements referring to Clérisseau's fits of madness and complaints against his best friends are mentioned in a long letter written by James from Rome on August 14 of the preceding year.

> I see by yours of the 5th of July that Clerisseau has wrote to you in a complaining stile of my behavior to him. I believe I shall easily convince you that I had some reason to change my behavior to one, who an offer no excuse for his, but that vein of madness, which he still seems to me to have strongly at times. . . . You know when I first arriv'd there I knew next to nothing of the language, which made me not think of frequenting any of the company of that place, but only the few Engligh that were there this made me be very much with Clerisseau who I found extremely entertaiining on all subjects concerning our own Art *c.* but extremely insipid on all others. My want of the language, and my desire of applying myself to study, made me also leave to him, the manadgement of all affairs of every kind, with which he seem'd extremely happy, as it flattered his taste for importance, which you know he has very strong, so that in treating with any body about any of my affairs, he never so much as mention'd my name, or spoke in the plural number a piece of vanity, which tho' I observ'd, I was far from being angry at or taking any notice of it, to him. During this time it was that he took many occasions of telling me how contented he was with my behavior to him, and how ill pleas'd he had been with yours on many occasions, which I will not here repeat to you. My general reply to him on these subjects was, that one cou'd not judge without knowing all the circumstances, and that it was impossible to know, without having heard you. Thus we departed from Venice excellent good friends and continued just in the same way at Bologna and Florence from the same reasons. When I got forward to this place I was become much more frank in the language, and had a strong desire of mixing with some of the better sort of people in the country. . . . I communicated my inclination to Abbe Grant who told me if I had that desire, he shou'd take care to have me properly introduc'd and accordingly where he was not accustom'd to go himself he had me presented by means of a nobleman of this place, to whom he had introduc'd me a purpose, in going through this career of the Beaux Monde, I us'd to pass the evening from abt. 6 o'clock till 12, a period of time when you know there is no such thing as daring to study here after a day spent in applications. C - au took an

opportunity one day to mention this to me, and alledg'd that my life was much chang'd, that now we liv'd no longer together, that I seem'd to have no pleasure in conversation, that it was from friendship and pleasure of my conversation, that he had consented to make this journey with me, and not from any motives of self interest, and that unless we cou'd be more together he cou'd not think of passing his time with one who was not attach'd to him as a friend; I was surpris'd at this complaint but calmly heard it to an end, tho very long, and attended with many formal circumstances in his stile, and then I answere'd him with the same composure, assuring him that my friendship for him was not in the smallest degree diminish'd, but gave him my reasons for acting so, as I have given them to you, and added that I cou'd not reckon it a breach of friendship, the being seperate a few hours an evening from a person who I breakfasted and din'd with every day and who cou'd see one another when they wou'd by stepping from room to another, but says I, if you are vex'd at this, it will soon be over, for when the weather becomes good we shall go every other night and visit antiquitys and palaces together. . . . For sometime after this I imagin'd I had by this conversation quieted C- au's mind and consequently all complaints, but this was not the case, for Abbe Grant told me soon after, that he had been making complaint to him, and when he came upon the subject of my allways being seperate from him of an evening the Abbe gave him my reasons for wishing to see a little of the good company here. . . . But one night upon coming home I found a letter from George upon my table opn'd and read it. After an apology for venturing to take that step . . . he then proceeds to inform me that he in the name of the other young folks and his own was to inform me, of what greatly displeas'd and shok'd them in Mr. C - au's behavior Vizt. his manner of talking of me to them. In the first place he desir'd them to attach themselves to him and to regard him as their master, for says he, were Jacques Adam to dy tomorrow I wou'd just continue to carry on the same works and in that case I wou'd dismiss those that were not firmly attach'd to me, besides, says he, you see he does not much interest himself about what is going on, he is so much engag'd with his visits and intrigues; he leaves all to me, and not only these affairs but the manadgement of the house and money . . . after all this Jacques thinks to have the honor of all these works, but I shall take care of that, he will find himself mistaken there. . . . [Here, James quotes George's letter verbatim] 'As for Robert he is wholly directed by me in everything, he never did one thing without taking my advice, tis true he was very ignorant of Architecture when he came to me, except the Gothick, but I put him off that; and gave him some taste for the Antique.' If you can imagine this and twenty more such speeches to be spoke by any but a vein french madman, than you have a better opinion of C - au than I have. . . . I therefor determin'd to curb this manner of talking and found a good opportunity and told him as a friend to take care of his way of talking of me and you behind backs, because he never utter'd a word, nay scarcely a thought, but what I knew all, I wou'd however give him no particulars that he might not guess my intelligencer, he was at first extremely astonish'd at this attack, but as I dar'd not to cite instances he pluck'd up courage to defend himself. the defence however was but lame, tis impossible to repeat all that pass'd in this conversation. which concluded with my dersiring him to be for his own sake, more cautious for time to come. I cannot admit mention one thing among many others, that pass'd in order to show you the man's present ideas of himself. Indeed, says he, I never consider'd any difference betweixt you and I, but that you had more money than I have. . . . Thus ended a long conversation since when he has been more reserv'd with the boys and I resum'd my usewal behavior to him, which is just as easy and polit as any person can be that is on so familier a footing with another. Tis true, I am persuaded, he is still discontented and far from having any sentiments of friendship, which never seem to have been strong, and tother day I had a new prooff of his resentment by his telling one of the lads who he thinks he can trust, to come to him when he had any complaints to make and not to me, for says he I can redress you, as well as he, the only difference betwixt us is that he has more sechins, I have greater talents.[71]

This letter reveals some of the complexities of the relationship between Clérisseau, who had been a devoted employee since 1754, and the two Adam brothers. Despite the fact that he had been treated shabbily in terms of money, as earlier letters attest, and was deprived of his rightful share in projects, he had been unstintingly loyal. While he had his pride, or, as Robert termed it, his "vanity," he had given much of himself and expected the same in return. As this was not always forthcoming, Clérisseau, basically honest and simple, became resentful.

The Adam correspondence makes obvious what many have long suspected, namely, that Clérisseau's role in the Spalato expedition and the resulting publication was far greater than Adam was willing to admit in his book. Even without the corroborating evidence, it is apparent that the presence of Clérisseau, who was "one of the most original architectural draftsmen in Europe,"[72] would be of crucial importance in an expedition undertaken by the young Scottish architect, who, for all his talent, training, and ambition, was still an amateur.

Clérisseau played a major role in studying and drawing the ruins, in making reconstructions of the palace, in training the two draftsmen, and in preparing the drawings for publication. The letters of Robert and James Adam indicate Clérisseau's role in the drawing of the plates, his part in various reconstructions, and in the descriptions which accompanied the plates.

At the most, there are only sixteen drawings by Clérisseau, a drawing by Canaletto after what is presumed to be a lost Clérisseau, and an engraving after a plan, now lost, that can be connected with the Spalato project.[73] A great number of drawings was either destroyed by the Adam brothers or disappeared over the years. Of those remaining, twelve are in the Hermitage among the vast collection Clérisseau sold to Catherine the Great, so they must be his. Two others may be copies by draftsmen, and another, if it is by him, is a *capriccio* based on one of the palace gates.

Clérisseau's plan, entitled "Plan Exact de ce qui existe de Palais de Diocletian à Spalatro," is known only from the engraving published in L. F. Cassas and

J. Lavallée's *Voyage pittoresque et historique de l'Istrie et de la Dalmatie rédigé d'après l'intinéraire de L. F. Cassas* of 1802 (Fig. 60).[74] It shows the fourth-century Emperor's fortified residence with two major arcaded streets intersecting in the center. After the intersection, the north-south street, the *cardo,* widens into a peristyle. This terminates at the entrance to the palace living quarters, which are entered through a portico and domed vestibule. Facing the Adriatic, on the south side, is an arcaded cryptoporticus. The peristyle separates two other major structures: the octagonal mausoleum (called the Temple of Jupiter in the eighteenth century and now used as the cathedral) and the small Temple of Jupiter (known then as the Temple of Aesculapius and today as the Baptistry). This plan is our most valuable piece of evidence, as it is clearly stated as being by Clérisseau. He wrote below this plan that "the black indicates parts which remain visible and the gray parts destroyed but of which there are definite traces." [75]

A comparison of Clérisseau's plan with the one published as the "General Plan of the Palace as it now Remains," Plate IV of the Adam volume (Fig. 61), shows differences. Clérisseau's plan indicated that nothing of the residential floor or palace proper on the south side remained except the round entrance vestibule with niches, the outer walls, and parts of the cryptoporticus. Adam, on the other hand, depicted the central part of the residential quarters as a series of rectangular rooms and halls. Furthermore, the Adam plan shows both corners of this residential section as groups of rooms of various shapes: some square or rectangular, others terminating in semicircular apses, and tri-lobed forms which eventually play a major role in Adam's own architecture. Clérisseau's plan indicated rooms of these shapes similar to those in the publication in the southwest corner, but he clearly stated that they are basement rooms. Adam's plan does not make this clear and suggests the rooms are on the main floor.

It is apparent that Clérisseau, Adam, and the draftsmen entered some of the corner underground rooms, which were the only accessible sections of this lower part.[76] Clérisseau showed them correctly as underground rooms, whereas Adam assumed they were identical in form with the part of the palace above them, which he proceeded to show as following the same plan. Adam's assumption was correct, although he lacked the evidence.[77] There are differences even in their drawings of the plans of this corner, whether aboveground or belowground. For example, Adam inserts a corridor between the outside wall and the tri-lobed room (now known as 1D); Clérisseau does not. Recent studies show Clérisseau was correct (Fig. 62).[78] Just north of rooms 4B and 3D is the basement of an eighteenth-century private house, now the Hotel Slavija, which incorporates sections of the western thermae foundations. If Clérisseau entered this area, he did not draw the walls correctly and added an extra wall (see Figs. 60, 62). He did not seem to realize that the walls were part of the Emperor's private thermae. Adam's regular spacing of these walls is equally wrong (see Fig. 61).[79]

The Adam plan erred in its cavalier depiction of the rest of the residential area. Since there is very little of the main floor remaining, it is clear that he based his reconstruction on what was underneath the southwest corner. The basement rooms of the southeast corner, with the possible exception of part of one of the waterfront rooms, was filled in by the late Renaissance and have become accessible only with recent excavations. These have revealed that the plan of this area, which was beneath the Emperor's Triclinium, was far from symmetrical with the southwest corner (see Fig. 62).[80]

A comparison of other parts of the two plans reveals that Adam's conjectural restorations are based on little evidence. His depiction of what remains of the northern half is very different from Clérisseau's and at variance with what remains today (see Fig. 62). Clérisseau correctly showed that the northeast corner pier, at the intersection of the *cardo* and *decumanus,* survived aboveground whereas Adam does not. On the other hand, Clérisseau neglects to show some of the remaining walls in the northeast quarter, which are shown in the Adam plan and exist today. At times the two plans agree, as in the drawing of the storage magazines along the western perimeter. The most recent investigations have revealed that the plans drawn by Adam and Clérisseau are more correct than the 1912 ones by Hébrard and Niemann.[81] The plan published by Adam was far more conjectural and daring than that by Clérisseau. While the Adam plan often ignored the evidence, he had an intuitive sense which often proved him right. The difference in the plans of these two men also may be indicative of their contrasting characters.

During the five weeks that Adam, Clérisseau, and the two draftsmen — Brunias and Dewez — were at Spalato, Clérisseau and the others made a great number of drawings of the palace from various points of view. These drawings were used not only for the plates but also for the plans and reconstructions. The style of all of the plates is coherent and is undoubtedly due to Clérisseau.

In any group effort it is difficult to identify individual hands, since sketches are often refined, enlarged, and copied by others. My discussion of the individual plates will be limited to those for which there are surviving drawings and which one can reasonably assume to be by Clérisseau. Nearly all are part of the group he sold to Catherine the Great. Fortunately, four very different drawings of the peristyle and vestibule by Clérisseau are known today and are in the Hermitage. The largest and most finished drawing of the peristyle and palace (Fig. 63)[82] depicts the entire arcade looking south from the intersection of the two streets to the palace itself. It is a very detailed work and very close to Santini's engraving, Plate XX of the Adam book (Fig. 64).

The viewpoint is identical, the sizes similar, and most of the details the same. A close comparison suggests, however, that this drawing may not have been the one Santini used. The figures are very different[83] and there are many changes in the right wall of the engraving: the addition of a balcony, the extension of the building above the cornice, and an additional bay at the right. These changes, except for the figures, are based on what was actually there in the eighteenth century and remains today, as a photograph of the scene shows (Fig. 65). One can surmise that the engraver did not put in the additions. Santini had not accompanied Adam to Spalato, so he could not have been aware of what actually existed. Thus the engraving must be based on a lost Clérisseau drawing which showed the right wall exactly as it is depicted in the engraving. Our drawing could be a near replica made by Clérisseau for his own use, a practice he had followed with the plan for Hadrian's Villa and the thermae drawings.[84]

Figure 60. C.-L. Clérisseau, "Plan Exact de ce qui existe du Palais de Dioclétian à Spalatro," engraving by Desmaisons (from L. Cassas and J. Lavallée, *Voyage pittoresque* . . . , Paris, 1802, Pl. 54 bis)

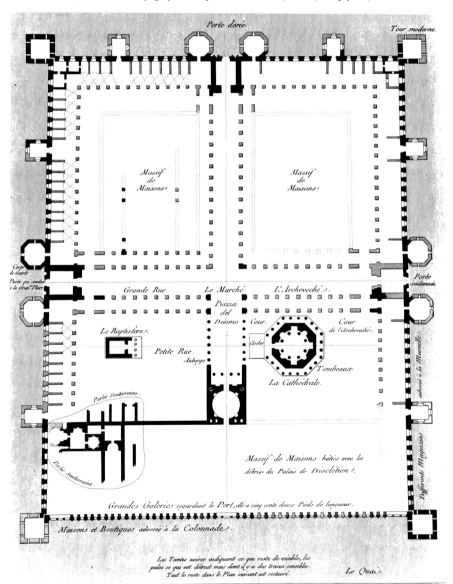

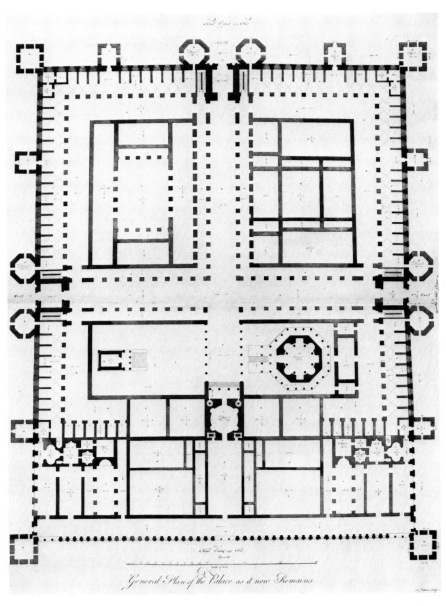

Figure 61. "General Plan of the Palace of Diocletian as it now Remains," engraving by
F. Patton, Pl. IV, R. Adam, *Ruins of the Palace of Diocletian,* London, 1764

Figure 62. Plan, Diocletian's Palace, showing underground rooms (from
T. Marosović, *Diocletian's Palace*, Belgrade, 1967, 49)

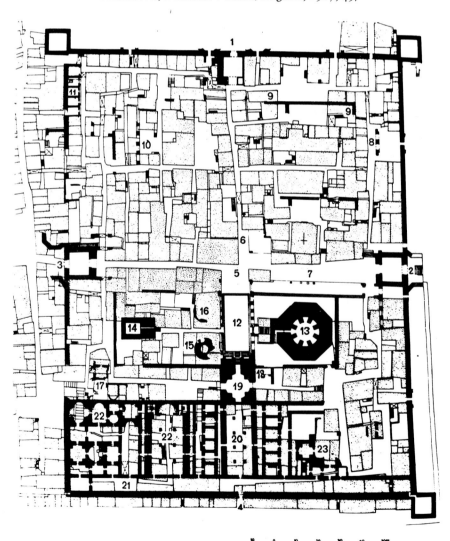

Figure 63. C.-L. Clérisseau, "Court de la Palais de Diocletian," Hermitage

Figure 64. "View of the Peristylium" engraving by Santini, Plate XX,
R. Adam, *Ruins of the Palace of Diocletian*, London, 1764

Figure 65. Peristyle, Diocletian´s Palace,
Spalato, as it is today

Figure 66. C.-L. Clérisseau, "Peristyle
Sketch," Hermitage

Figure 67. C.-L. Clérisseau, "Peristyle
Looking West," Hermitage

The next drawing is a view of the entrance to the vestibule and the east side of the peristyle (Fig. 66).[85] It is a detailed work and appears to show the palace as it existed in the eighteenth century with all the later excrescences, including the addition of one-story chapels at each side and the walled-up central opening of the portico. The depiction by Clérisseau of a Pietà in the completely filled-in upper arch of the prothyron is at variance with the large drawing and engraving already seen (see Figs. 63, 64), where the arch is partly opened. In a Cassas watercolor of 1782, engraved in 1802, the arch is completely walled up; only in recent years has it been partially opened.[86] Clérisseau used his imagination not only in opening up the wall, but also in adding the Pietà, almost certainly inspired by the sculptural group on the portal of a Benedictine convent just north of the palace.[87] Such a work may never have been in the position shown by Clérisseau. Otherwise, the drawing appears to be an accurate depiction of the scene as it existed, and probably was made at the site. The lack of figures seems to confirm this assumption.

The third representation of the scene in the Hermitage is a small ink-and-wash drawing (Fig. 67) bearing the inscription, "Composition architecturale," [88] on the verso. It obviously represents the vestibule entrance looking west to the Temple of Jupiter.[89] At first glance, it appears to be a very free sketch of the palace as Clérisseau saw it, a less finished, quicker version of the preceding drawing made from a different point of view. Upon closer examination, however, it is evident that this immediacy is misleading. The portico of the palace is not shown as it was in the eighteenth century, or even as it is today. The post-Classical additions have been removed, so the columns stand free, and the original door and one of the side niches are visible. Furthermore, the peristyle is shown in ruins, giving a clear view of the temple, proving that this is an imaginary drawing, made perhaps as a restoration study, but more likely a *capriccio* based on the palace.

Clérisseau's drawing of the interior of the domed vestibule also in the Hermitage (Fig. 68) is almost identical with Plate XXIII (Fig. 69) which has added figures.[90] This drawing, or a similar one, is surely the basis for the engraving. While the staffage has changed, all the architectural features are identical, with the exception of the addition of a tiny window above the portal to the left in the engraving. The sketchy quality of the Clérisseau and the suggestion of the individual stones gives the drawing an immediacy, indicating that it was done on the spot.

Only one of Clérisseau's drawings of the exterior of the mausoleum, which he called the Temple of Jupiter, has survived. It is in the Hermitage and is closely related to Plate XXVII (Fig. 70).[91] The figures are different, though, unusually; the Clérisseau drawing has figures, and the engraving shows more of the building, as was the case with the large print of the peristyle. These differences are slight and leave little doubt that the drawing is related to the Bartolozzi plate.

In 1975 there appeared at Christie's in London a drawing by Antonio Canaletto entitled "Venetian Capriccio" (Fig. 71) which was recognized by the present writer and by Mr. J. G. Links as based either on a now lost Clérisseau drawing of the side of Diocletian's Mausoleum or on Plate XXVII, engraved by Bartolozzi (Fig. 72).[92] Links, who confirmed the attribution to Canaletto, first noticed that Canaletto shows part of a side of the octagon not visible in the engraving or in the drawing just discussed. Inasmuch as Canaletto never visited Spalato, it seems logical to assume that he must have seen Clérisseau's original drawing in Venice in

Figure 68. C.-L. Clérisseau, "Interior of Vestibule," Hermitage

Figure 69. "View of the Inside of the Vestibule," engraving by Bartolozzi, Pl. XXIII,
R. Adam, *Ruins of the Palace of Diocletian*, London, 1764

Figure 70. C.-L. Clérisseau,
"Temple of Jupiter," (The Mausoleum), Hermitage

Figure 71. A. Canaletto after Clérisseau,
"Mausoleum," present whereabouts unknown

Figure 72. "Temple of Jupiter," engraving by
Cunego, Pl. XXVII, R. Adam, *Ruins of the
Palace of Diocletian*, London, 1764

the late 1750s or early 1760s. While Canaletto has changed many of the figures, there is no doubt that this drawing is related to the mausoleum plate.[93]

Clérisseau's pen-and-wash drawing of the interior of the mausoleum (Fig. 73)[94] is the finest of the Spalato drawings, and shows the interior of the cathedral in use. Stylistically, the sense of flickering light and delicate shading makes it resemble the two Dalmatian churches Clérisseau drew before his arrival in Spalato. This on-the-spot drawing shows the cathedral as it looked in 1757, which is still the way it looks to a great extent. Nevertheless, Clérisseau had taken certain liberties, as the frieze on the second level does not correspond in its arrangement to the original. The lower balustrade shown is not the one which existed in the eighteenth century and the upper one is imaginary, as is the pavement design. The details of the pulpit are also incorrect.[95] Plate XXXIII of the Spalato publication (Fig. 74), which is from a somewhat different point of view and therefore not based on this drawing, shows the interior without the later additions. However, the engraving resembles Clérisseau's work, so it could be based on a lost drawing by him. I would like to think that the figure shown sketching at the lower left represents Clérisseau, but it is more likely to be Robert Adam. It is interesting that in this case the later additions were removed in the engraving, whereas they were kept in the peristyle print (see Fig. 64).

The Hermitage also has several drawings of the Temple of Jupiter, which Adam called a Temple of Aesculapius. The finest is one of the largest of the Spalato drawings (Fig. 75),[96] and is identical in nearly every way with Plate XLII of the Adam book, engraved by Bartolozzi, except that it lacks figures. It is either the original drawing used by the engraver or a second copy; the only changes are the removal of the fragments at the right to make room for the figures and the addition of a second window in the house at the left. Even the vegetation is nearly the same.[97] In both cases there are nine steps leading to the temple, which disagrees with the side elevation, Plate XLIV (Fig. 76), where there are ten, as mentioned by Adam. Clérisseau's assertion that the building was made of brick encrusted with marble is more clearly reflected in the drawing than in the engraving, which evidently was changed to agree with the revised text. In Clérisseau's plan (see Fig. 60) and drawing none of the columns of the portico have remained standing. The belfry, which was added to the building in the Middle Ages, is not shown in Clérisseau's drawing nor in the print, but does appear in the Cassas drawing of 1782 published in 1802.[98] The Victoria and Albert Museum in London has a drawing identified as Robert Adam's study for Plate XLII; there are only slight differences, mainly in the vegetation, between it and the engraving.[99] The figures and nearly all details are identical with the print, including the small window at the left not present in Clérisseau's drawing. The poor quality of the drawing supports my opinion that it is by an unknown copyist after the engraving.[100]

The Hermitage also has a smaller Clérisseau drawing of the Temple of Jupiter, which is almost identical to the one discussed above.[101] The differences are those of vegetation, background buildings, and only eight steps leading to the entrance instead of the nine shown in the other drawings.

In the collection of the late Sir Albert E. Richardson there is an enigmatic drawing which at first appears to show the temple from the same point of view, that is, from the right.[102] However, there are many differences, including the placement

Figure 73. C.-L. Clérisseau, "Interior, Mausoleum," Hermitage

Figure 74. "Temple of Jupiter" (Interior, Mausoleum), engraving by Cunego,
Pl. XXXIII, R. Adam, *Ruins of the Palace of Diocletian*, London, 1764

Figure 75. C.-L. Clérisseau, "The Temple of Aesculapius" (Temple of Jupiter), Hermitage

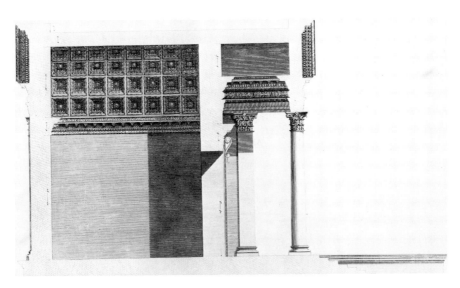

Figure 76. "Section of Temple of Aesculapius" (Temple of Jupiter), engraving by F. Patton,
Pl. XLIV, R. Adam, *Ruins of the Palace of Diocletian*, London, 1764

of a plain, sarcophaguslike box to the left of the entrance and changes to the building at the left. If one compares it with the engravings of the building in the Adam volume, it becomes clear that it is the reverse of Plate XLI, engraved by Bartolozzi, with the figures eliminated. The general weakness of the drawing and lack of sureness suggests that it could be by one of the two draftsmen, Brunias or Dewez. It could possibly be the work of a copyist who traced the engraving and reversed it, for the dimensions are almost identical with those of the engraving (the drawing is 11 × 15½ inches and the engraving is 10⅛ × 14⅝ inches). Ordinarily, drawings are reversed when they are engraved, but this is not the case with the Spalato drawings, such as those of the peristyle (see Fig. 63), the Temple of Jupiter (see Fig. 75), and the Porta Ferrea (see Fig. 78). One should also note that the large, covered sarcophagus, seen in the Hermitage drawing and in the engraving, has been moved away from the entrance door when the temple is shown from the left. This was probably done to allow more of the façade to show.

Besides the drawings by Clérisseau, which can definitely be identified with the plates for the Adam book, there are others which are *capriccios* based on parts of the palace, particularly the Temple of Jupiter. Three of these are in the Hermitage. The first (Fig. 77) shows the temple with the addition of a freestanding column supporting a small piece of entablature, which extends from the spur wall.[103] The temple has been moved to the edge of the peristyle and is shown at an oblique angle, so one can see the portico and part of the wall of the peristyle. Two other drawings depict the temple façade from the same viewpoint, with the spur wall omitted and the addition of sculptural fragments blocking the door. Variations are seen in the architectural details of the door and the sculptural reliefs.[104] These must be *capriccios* based on the Temple of Jupiter.

The large collection of seventy-nine Clérisseau drawings in the Fitzwilliam Museum includes two *capriccios* based on the temple.[105] One depicts it from the left with a column added on the right, and the addition of a fountain which blocks part of the temple.

The second Fitzwilliam drawing is more problematic. It was a separate bequest to the Fitzwilliam and not part of the major gift of seventy-four drawings from the Reverend Whittaker or of the four given by the founder. Its lack of spur walls relates it to the two similar ones in the Hermitage, but the entablature is much more detailed. The medium—pencil, pen, and sepia wash—is different as well. An attribution to Robert Adam has been suggested by David Scrase,[106] but the view is far more linear and detailed than any other Adam drawing.

Clérisseau's drawing for the Porta Ferrea (Fig. 78)[107] is exactly the same size as the first drawing of the Temple of Jupiter. It is almost identical with Bartolozzi's somewhat smaller engraving made from it, Plate XVII (Fig. 79). Aside from the figures, the main differences are the presence of the Gothic arcade at the right in the drawing and the addition of buildings at the right foreground in the engraving. A study of the buildings of eighteenth-century Spalato shows that the buildings to the left of the gate are depicted in the drawing and subsequent engraving exactly as they were, except for the Romanesque tower adjoining the left side of the gate, which actually rose higher and terminated in a bell tower.[108] The tower is still standing today (Fig. 80). Clérisseau lowered the tower in order to expose the

Figure 77. C.-L. Clérisseau, "The Temple of Aesculapius, Capriccio," Hermitage

Figure 78. C.-L. Clérisseau, "Porta Ferrea," Hermitage

Figure 79. "View of the Porta Ferrea," engraving by Bartolozzi, Pl. XVII,
R. Adam, *Ruins of the Palace of Diocletian,* London, 1764

Figure 80. The Porta Ferrea, Diocletian´s
Palace, as it is today

opening behind it. The depiction of the right side of the gate, however, bears less
relation to the true situation. Then, as now, the portal of this gate was built up on
both sides, so that only the opening itself and one window above were visible (see
Fig. 78). Clérisseau removed these Gothic buildings, and replaced them with a low
structure next to the gate in order to expose the niche, which he drew on the basis
of those on the Porta Aurea (Fig. 81). Beyond this niche, he designed a higher
building with a Gothic arcade.[109] Bartolozzi, however, treated the building at the
right differently.

A drawing by Clérisseau, or possibly one of the two draftsmen, of the Porta
Aurea is in the Library of the Royal Institute of British Architects in London (see
Fig. 81).[110] This gate is the best preserved of the three entrances to the palace and
the only one completely exposed in the eighteenth century, although the entrance
itself had been blocked up since the fourteenth century. Clérisseau's drawing
emphasizes the blocked-up door, the broken columns, and ruins strewn around.
He also added statues to the three top niches under the arcade. Santini's engraving
for Plate XII (Fig. 82) likewise emphasizes the ruinous aspect. However, he elimi-
nates Clérisseau's statues and the locked voussoirs of the flat arch, rearranges the
fallen fragments, adds picturesque figures, and shows more of the left side. Adam's
own proof copy of the volume contains a first state of Santini's engraving of the
plate, showing the statues and locked voussoirs as in the Clérisseau drawing (Fig.
83). Adam has written on what is called Table II, "The statues were not remaining

Figure 82. "View of the Porta Aurea" engraving
by Santini, PL. XII, as published, R. Adam,
Ruins of the Palace of Diocletian,
London, 1764

Figure 81. C.-L. Clérisseau, "The Porta Aurea,"
London, Royal Institute of British Architects Library

Figure 83. "View of the Porta Aurea" proof print,
engraving by Santini, Pl. XII, R. Adam, *Ruins
of the Palace of Diocletian*, London, 1764

Figure 84. C.-L. Clérisseau (?), "An Oblique View
of a Section of a Ruined Building," New York,
Cooper-Hewitt Museum of Design

in the niches when I was at Spalatro, but I was informed that they had been very lately removed." [111] At present the columns shown supporting the arcade are also missing.

The last drawing is also problematic (Fig. 84).[112] The drawing is signed, but the signature is unlike any other in that the first letter is so small. The style of the drawing is similar to Clérisseau's, although the quality of the architectural drawing is weak. Second, does it represent Spalato, and, if so, what part of the palace? The association with Spalato is based on the unusual architectural features already described. For instance, the flat, arched door with locked voussoirs and carved keystone surmounted by an open lunette, actually a relieving arch, flanked by an architecturally framed niche or window, are features seen in the Porta Ferrea and Porta Aurea (see Figs. 79 and 82). The drawing cannot represent the third of the gates, the east or Porta Aenea, as this was completely walled up in the eighteenth century. Only in 1946 was it exposed and restored.[113] The carved keystone recalls the Porta Ferrea, not visible in the Clérisseau drawing (see Fig. 78), and only barely seen in the Bartolozzi engraving (see Fig. 79). However, the keystone on the Porta Ferrea originally contained a Winged Victory-like figure, which was transformed into a cross in the fifth century. The pedimented niches have no parallels in the palace. I believe this drawing is a *capriccio* based on the palace. If it is not by Clérisseau, I might attribute it to one of the two draftsmen, as does Jerko Maraso-vić.[114]

The various types of drawings by Clérisseau define his role in the Spalato expedition. They were essential to the production of Adam's book. The correspondence of Robert and James Adam reveals Clérisseau's instrumental role in the success of the project. The book was one of the pioneering archaeological studies, but with its publication, Clérisseau's involvement with the Adam brothers was ended.

IV

Clérisseau on His Own in Italy:

1755-67

It was not until James Adam left Italy for England in May 1763 that Clérisseau resumed his life in Rome with friends, new and old, including Piranesi, Cardinal Alessandro Albani, and Johann Joachim Winckelmann. The friendship with Piranesi, as we know, dated from his earliest years in Rome.[1] Clérisseau's friendship with Cardinal Albani started as early as February 20, 1755, when Clérisseau delivered a group of Alexander Gordon's engravings of Egypt and a letter of recommendation from Horace Mann, British envoy to the Tuscan Court from 1740 to 1786.[2] As a result, the Cardinal offered to help Clérisseau in any way he could.[3] Nevertheless, concerning Clérisseau's work for the Adam brothers in the late 1750s, his only known connection with the Cardinal is revealed in the Cardinal's correspondence with Horace Mann in 1757. On September 27 of that year, Mann asked the Cardinal for help in securing passports for Robert Adam, Clérisseau, and a servant.[4] Though Cardinal Albani wrote of the high regard he had for both Adam and Clérisseau, he refused to help them obtain a visa on the grounds that it was unsafe to go to Germany.[5]

It was probably through Albani that Clérisseau met Winckelmann, who had arrived in Rome from Dresden in November 1755, and was to become the Cardinal's librarian in 1759. In a letter dated January 29, 1757, Winckelmann wrote to a friend named Berendis that "a French architect is my good friend but he has disassociated himself from his nation in order not to feel ridiculous."[6] From what we have learned earlier, it is not hard to identify the French architect as Clérisseau.[7] Winckelmann's protector and close friend was Cardinal Passionei, for whom Clérisseau had drawn the design for a folly at Camaldoli in 1752.[8] Winckelmann visited Passionei at Camaldoli on numerous occasions, and it is conceivable that he admired Clérisseau's design, either executed or on paper. There is no evidence to support Locquin's claim that Clérisseau accompanied Winckelmann to Paestum in 1758;[9] it seems unlikely as Clérisseau was then employed elsewhere by the Adam brothers. In any case, Clérisseau probably met Winckelmann as early as 1757. In 1762 the German scholar referred to him in the introduction of his *Remarques sur l'architecture des ancienes* as an architect well versed in the science of antiquity and as an expert architect in relation to the Spalato project.[10] In 1763, when Winckelmann recommended that students should study with "the best architect," [11] he was again referring to Clérisseau. This friendship not only brought Clérisseau into the Roman archaeological circle during the 1760s, but also played a crucial part in securing architectural commissions: the decoration of the coffeehouse of the Villa Albani, the Ruin Room for Père Le Sueur and Père Jacquier, and the ancient garden for Filippo Farsetti (Farcetti) at Sala.

Winckelmann's influence and his confidence in Clérisseau are shown in a letter of September 22, 1764, to Caspar Füssli: "I have persuaded Cardinal Albani to leave the decoration and arrangement of one of the rooms of his villa to Clérisseau, whom the Cardinal had visited twice in my company and the last time in the company also of the Princess Albani. It is to be begun during the coming months and is 60 palms in length." [12] This room was the coffeehouse or café. On December 7 Winckelmann wrote to Phillip von Stosch:

> . . . all beautiful pictures of Antiquity are being sought for it and most of them will be painted on copper. M. Clérisseau who is known to us all will guide the work, and will paint the large landscapes and antiquities in Dalmatia and near Baja.[13]

The coffeehouse was built as part of a semicircle with an arched loggia opposite the main part of the villa. Originally decorated in the 1760s, it has undergone various trials and, during the plundering of the Napoleonic era, many of the best statues were sent to Paris. The coffeehouse was in poor condition when the Torlonia family purchased it in 1866 and remained so until they restored it in 1871.[14] Consequently, its condition today may not give a true picture of the original, for which one must rely on early descriptions. The eighteenth-century accounts of the room say very little about the decoration, and most of those from the nineteenth century add little more.[15] Morcelli, Fea, and Visconti's description of 1870 goes into more detail, though the authorship implies it was derived from Morcelli's putative 1785 description, with some modifications.[16] The room was described in 1870 as follows:

> This beautiful gallery is decorated with sixteen composite Ionic pilasters. On each of them, in the middle of elegant arabesques, are tiny bas-reliefs in white on lacquer background or exquisite subjects derived from antique reliefs known at the time. On the vault the painter Lapiccola has painted, in perfect proportion, a lovely work derived from a drawing by the celebrated Giulio Romano which is also a part of the collection of the Villa. The side

panels are also by Lapiccola. One must also remark on the small paintings, beautifully done, on four of the pilasters by Paolo Anesi.[17]

Justi, writing at the time of the Torlonia restoration, quotes the Winckelmann letter of December 7, 1764, in which he states that Clérisseau will direct the work and paint the large landscapes. To this comment Justi adds:

Anesi executed the landscape and seascapes and in the same room Niccola Lapiccola of Calabria painted the Bacchanal of Giulio Romano on the ceiling, following the small colored drawing in the Albani Gallery. Otherwise Anton Bicchierari, almost the last fresco painter who was still decorating Roman churches in the old manner, was in charge of decorating the room with views, landscapes with ruins, ancient villa scenes and chiaroscuro reliefs.[18]

Twentieth-century writers have added little to this. Luigi Callari, for example, describes the sculpture and the paintings by Lapiccola and Anesi. Pecchiai's "La Villa delle Rose" adds nothing, and the virtue of Jacques Veysset's "Les Merveilles Cachées de la Villa Albani" is the excellence of the photographic illustrations. Isa Belli Barsali's comprehensive *Villa di Roma* simply quotes Winckelmann.[19] Anthony Clark, however, noticed that the two frescoes by Lapiccola reproduce specific ancient mosaics.[20] Only in Veysset's article is there any mention of Clérisseau.[21] Noack, writing in 1912, mentions arabesques by Clérisseau, but this apparently is based on the letters of Winckelmann.[22]

The Clérisseau scenes of the antiquities and landscapes of Dalmatia and Baia (Baja) are not in the villa now, and the omissions noted in the nineteenth- and twentieth-century comments make one wonder if Clérisseau's work was ever executed.[23] Was it destroyed during the Napoleonic occupation? Or could it be that the paintings, if they did exist, were removed during the 1871 restoration?[24] Justi indicates that they were executed by Anesi. Yet even though Clérisseau's two large paintings might not have been executed, he might have been in charge of the decoration, arrangement, and supervision of the work, as Winckelmann indicates in the letter already quoted and in another of 1767.[25] Even as the room exists today, with its colored pilasters, some with raised figures and oval and rectangular plaques with small, painted ancient scenes, Clérisseau's ideas and planning are still in evidence.

A much later Clérisseau project of 1773 for a Roman house commissioned by Catherine the Great shows just such a room with scenes set into the walls and with arabesques (Fig. 85).[26] Here, Clérisseau divided the wall into a series of panels of various sizes, some square, some rectangular, with two large horizontal rectangles containing ruin scenes between the doors. The one at the left is the Temple of Augustus at Pola in Istria, based on a drawing already discussed (see Fig. 49). The other large picture is very similar to a signed and dated Italian view of 1759, which could be a scene near Baia (see Fig. 96). In the smaller square and rectangular panels are additional ruin scenes and, in the overdoor panels, Classic scenes. The remaining smaller panels are devoted to arabesques and other Classical motifs of the type seen in the Clérisseau drawings now in the Hermitage, some of which were used as

Figure 85. C.-L. Clérisseau, "Project for Roman House," 1773, Hermitage

sources for the Russian project.²⁷ I believe that Clérisseau's plans for the decoration of the Villa Albani, executed or not, resembled this design.

Another connection with Winckelmann should be mentioned. I pointed out in Chapter II that perhaps Clérisseau had introduced James Adam to Raphael Mengs before the painter's departure for Spain, after the completion of the "Parnassus" ceiling of the salon of the Villa Albani in 1761. However, there is no documentary evidence that Clérisseau actually knew Mengs, though this acquaintance has always been assumed. Mengs may have already left Rome by the time of Clérisseau's arrival there in June 1749, but Mengs returned in 1752 and stayed until 1761.²⁸ It seems probable that Clérisseau met him either before 1754 while he himself was still at the French Academy, or about 1761 through Winckelmann. It was probably due to Winckelmann's influence that Clérisseau obtained the commission for the Ruin Room he decorated for the mathematician Père Thomas Le Sueur (1703–70) and his associate, Père François Jacquier (1711–88), at the Convent of S. Trinità dei Monti.²⁹ There are numerous references to the two mathematicians in Winckelmann's letters of 1760 and 1763.³⁰ The exact date of the room is not known; the earliest mention of it is in a 1767 Winckelmann letter to Clérisseau: "We meet in the lovely room you painted for Père Le Sueur, lived in now by Père Jacquier. You can imagine that we have talked of you much of the time."³¹

When Janson first published this letter in his 1781 edition of the *Lettres familières de M. Winckelmann,* he noted: "This room, which is one of the curiosities of Rome, represents the interior of a ruined antique temple in which one imagines that a hermit lived. Clérisseau did not work here [in Rome] in this style little known in France."³¹

J. J. Lalande did not refer to the room in his report on his Italian travels during 1765 and 1766, although he visited the cloister of the convent of S. Trinità dei Monti and mentioned Le Sueur and Jacquier. This might mean that the room had not yet been completed.³² When Casanova visited Père Jacquier in Rome in 1771, he did not mention the room;³³ nor did Goethe, who visited Père Jacquier at the convent in 1787, describe the room.³⁴ We must therefore rely on the description found in J. G. Legrand's biography of Piranesi.

> Clérisseau had just transformed into a picturesque ruin the cell of Père Le Sueur, his friend, the celebrated mathematician at the convent of Trinità dei Monti. Père Jacquier Minime, no less knowledgable, succeeded him in this singular habitation, one of the curiosities of Rome.
>
> On entering you think you are seeing the cella of a temple adorned with antique fragments that have escaped the ravages of time; the vault and several parts of the wall have fallen apart and are held up by a rotting scaffolding which seems to allow the sun to shine through. These effects are rendered with skill and truth and create a perfect illusion. This effect is enhanced by the furniture which is in character. The bed was a richly decorated vessel, the fireplace a mixture of diverse fragments, the desk a damaged antique sarcophagus, the table and the chairs a piece of cornice and inverted capital. Even the dog, faithful guardian of this new style of furniture, is shown lodged in the debris of an arched niche.³⁵

Figure 86. C.-L. Clérisseau, "Ruin Room, window wall," c. 1766, Hermitage

Figure 87. C.-L. Clérisseau, "Ruin Room, entrance wall," c. 1766, Hermitage

Figure 88. C.-L. Clérisseau, Ruin Room, c. 1766, Convent
of S. Trinità dei Monti, Rome, entrance wall as executed

Among the eight drawings published in an article appearing in *Starye Gody* in 1913,[36] one was immediately recognizable as representing the Ruin Room (Fig. 86). The Hermitage provided a photograph which showed the inscription, "Vue de la même chambre faisant voir des autres côtes." [37] Later, when examining the Clérisseau drawings in the Hermitage, I discovered one of the other end of the room (Fig. 87) with the following valuable inscription:

> View of the room designed and painted in Rome by Clérisseau for Père Le Sueur the mathematician, now occupied by Père Jacquier. This room represents the ruin of an antique temple where one imagines a Hermit wished to live. The seats are in the shape of different fragments. The desk appears as a sarcophagus, and so forth for the other furniture.[38]

Although the drawings and the various descriptions give a clear idea of the Ruin Room, there is no substitute for the original, which was presumably destroyed. However, John Fleming, acting upon information given him by the present writer, had the good fortune to discover the room still intact at the Convent of S. Trinità dei Monti. He arranged to have it photographed, and we collaborated on an article about it.

The room, located in the convent between the church of S. Trinità dei Monti and the Villa Medici, was until recently a dormitory room in the convent school. The room (Figs. 88–90) was executed almost exactly as planned in Clérisseau's drawings. The overall effect is of a room in ruins with illusionistically painted detail. The colors are bright and flat, resembling Clérisseau's gouache pictures, with bright blues and a soft green, which are dominated by various shades of brown in the crumbly stone. The coffers of the ceiling are painted in yellow-brown and gray, with some red. There are other red accents, the most prominent being the parrot perched on the beam on the long south wall. This bird gives the room its present name, "La Chambre du perroquet." [39] Like the ruin pictures by Clérisseau already noted, there is the same careful depiction of crumbling ancient details overgrown with vegetation. Although the various details are visible in the drawings and in photographs, the illusionism of the vines and floral still lifes, undoubtedly derived from Pompeian wall paintings, is not readily apparent. This is particularly true of the vase of flowers on the east (entrance) wall, which does not appear in the drawings, and of another on the north wall, behind the door.

The shape of the room is rectangular except for the bookcase niches in the south wall, which contain the original painted books, including one entitled *Newton*. On the opposite wall is a second niche to the left of the colonnade.

A comparison of the drawings with the actual room shows only minor changes. The niche to the right of the walled-up arch on the east wall has become a walled-up door, presumably matching the original entrance door on the other side, which has been replaced. The garland and patera panels above the windows, doors, and niches have been replaced by bucrania. Minor variations exist in the broken details, but the general effect is the same. Although it was not possible to photograph the west wall, it has remained as planned, with the fireplace niche, a relief of Meleager in the apse over it, and a dog in a niche. Unfortunately, none of the original furniture has survived.

Figure 89. C.-L. Clérisseau, Ruin Room, c. 1766, Convent of
S. Trinità dei Monti, Rome, side wall as executed

Figure 90. C.-L. Clérisseau, Ruin Room, c. 1766, Convent of
S. Trinità dei Monti, Rome, ceiling as executed

In 1772, Louis-Gabriel Blanchet (1705–72) painted a portrait of the two patrons, Le Sueur and Jacquier, commissioned by Jacquier after Le Sueur's death (Fig. 91).⁴⁰ In it, the two men are depicted engaged in their scientific work. At the left is a bookcase with the volume entitled *Newton,* and at the right a window. This arrangement is similar to the placement of the bookcase with a painted volume also labeled *Newton* and to the window of the ruin room. However, the architectural setting in the painting does not seem to represent the S. Trinità dei Monti cell.⁴¹

It is not surprising that mathematicians of the caliber of Le Sueur and Jacquier should have commissioned Clérisseau to paint such a room for them. Their interest in mathematics and in architecture led Jacquier to measure the Colosseum, and both to collaborate on a study of the dome of St. Peter's.⁴² So Clérisseau's plausible re-creation of the architecture of an ancient temple would appeal to them as it did to Winckelmann.⁴³

The idea of a Ruin Room has had a long history, going back at least to the one in Giulio Romano's Palazzo del Tè at Mantua of 1534, where the building appears to be in the process of falling down, and to Gregorio de Ferrari's (1644–1726) Sala della Ruine in the Palazzo Balbi Gruppello, Genoa. Clérisseau's design is closely related to his general interest in Classical ruins and his concern with archaeological detail, and falls into the tradition of the Ruin Room. The painting of the ceiling as a crumbling vault supported by wooden beams (see Fig. 90) is a continuation of the hermitage ruin tradition where a real or self-styled monk could meditate. Prince-Bishop Damian Hugo von Schonborn of Speyer had such a structure built in 1730 at Waghäusel, near his palace at Bruchsal. The ceiling done by Manchini was painted as a dilapidated wood structure seemingly resting on collapsing Classical columns. Damian wrote it was painted "in hermit fashion" (Fig. 92).⁴⁴

As I have stated elsewhere,⁴⁵ Clérisseau may have been inspired by the engravings of the Chapelle des Enfants Trouvés in Paris. In 1750 this elegant room had been decorated with scenes of the Nativity by Charles Natoire, but with the ceiling painted in ruins by the Brunetti Brothers.⁴⁶ These were executed shortly before Natoire went to Rome as director of the French Academy. In October 1752, Natoire was working on the drawings for the engravings of this room, and Clérisseau could well have seen those drawings or the resulting prints. Furthermore, the chapel itself had been designed by Germain Boffrand,⁴⁷ Clérisseau's professor at the Académie Royale d'Architecture. In addition, Boffrand had worked for the brother of Prince-Bishop Damian von Schonborn at Wurzburg.⁴⁸ Perhaps Clérisseau had seen drawings of the hermitage ceiling at Waghäusel as well. Clérisseau's Ruin Room not only continues this tradition but represents its culmination in archaeological terms.

Unlike examples from the sixteenth century or even the early eighteenth century, such as the room at Pommersfelden, Clérisseau's design did not show the building in the process of collapse. Instead, he selected a calmer mood, stressing the ruinous aspects of the scene. Piranesi admired the room and intended to make engravings after it,⁴⁹ even though it lacked his dramatic chiaroscuro quality.

Closest to Clérisseau's designs for the Ruin Room are the designs Robert Adam made while working with Clérisseau in the mid-1750s. These are labeled "Une coté du Temple Ruiné, et restoré avec les fragmens antiques" and "Un autre temple frequenté par un Hermit et par [ou il est converté a] Chappelle." These two

Figure 91. Louis-Gabriel Blanchet,
"Portrait of Père Lesueur and Père
Jacquier," 1772, Nantes, Musée des Beaux-Arts

Figure 92. Painted Ceiling, Waghäusel, after
1730 (from M. Gothein, *A History of
Garden Art,* London, 1928, II, 235)

drawings were later adapted for the design of an artificial ruin to be erected at Kedleston (Fig. 93).[50]

However, Clérisseau's design had its greatest influence in Italy. After describing the room, Legrand says:

> This fantasy of the artist was a success; Judge de Breteuil, the French ambassador of Malta to Rome, wished to decorate his house in a pictur-esque style, and several years later employed the talents of the painters Lavalleé Poussin and Robert, so renowned in France for the grace of his compositions, the richness of his imagination, and his astonishing rapidity of execution. The Roman architect Barberi, currently in Paris, directed the work. Piranesi's advice was very useful to them and the result this collabo-ration was a most agreeable place which foreigners hastened to visit and which is still known as the Garden of Malta. The Marquise Boccapaduli Gentili followed this example and had town and country houses decorated similarly. . . .[51]

The room commissioned by de Breteuil was in the Villa de Malta and not at S. Maria del Priorato, as Focillon suggested.[52] Neither it nor those in the Palazzo and Villa Boccapadula still exist. M. J. Ballot, writing in the twentieth century, states that

> Piranesi directed the work for the Priory of Malta; Clérisseau designed the gardens and made the ruins. Piranesi, with the help of la Vallé Poussin, Hubert Robert and the architect Barbier, decorated the interior.[53]

Aside from this reference, which I suspect is a garbled version of Legrand, there is no evidence that Clérisseau had anything to do with the villa.

Another room in Rome may have been inspired by Clérisseau's Ruin Room or, if not, is a further example of painted hermitage decoration. This room is in the villa built between 1763 and 1766 by Cardinal Flavio Chigi (1711–71) in a vineyard near the Via Salaria. The pictorial decorations survive today and include on the first floor the Stanza della Tebarde adjoining the chapel. This *stanza,* painted by Francesco Nubale, is a trompe l'oeil hermitage complete with cavelike stone walls, arched openings, broken wooden beams, and crumbling wooden doors. The decoration repeats many of the same details and creates the same feelings of Clérisseau's Ruin Room. To complete the picture, two monks are shown seated in the middle of the room.[54]

One of Winckelmann's letters to Clérisseau in 1767 is the source for our knowl-edge of another commission that Clérisseau received. The letter was written after Clérisseau left Rome for France, and Winckelmann mentions that many of his friends missed him.

> . . . M. Abbé Farsetti; he is afraid that you will abandon the magnificent project which he commissioned you to do. He thinks that only in Rome is it possible to compose in the true antique style which he says that you have stolen from the ancients. On that I am strongly of his opinion; and the superb drawing which you delivered to him of the *Spina antica,* which is part of his project, seemed to me the portrait of an antique monument

Figure 93. Robert Adam, "Ruin for Kedleston"
London, Victoria and Albert Museum

rather than a composition in the same manner. I very much hope for you and for him that the noxious modern air that you are going to breathe does not invade your new productions . . . I see again always with new pleasure and even with illusion the large model of the ruin which will be at the end of the vista from his house. It has a perfect truthfulness, and your Neapolitan Polichinelle has put into his execution admirable precision and spirit. Abbé Farsetti is delighted with it. He charges me to instruct you again to continue a project so well begun, and to send to him as soon as possible the consular road and the triumphal bridge that lead to it. You have no doubt received the general plan of his territory which he sent you. He can't wait to start the whole thing and you cannot avoid supervising it yourself; he is counting on that.[55]

Fortunately, Janson, the first editor of Winckelmann's letters, provided a footnote which gives a fuller description of the project.

This project was to have been carried out at Sala in the vicinity of Venice. M. l'Abbé Farsetti wanted an extensive garden which would represent the ruins of a Roman imperial residence in the style of Hadrian's Villa near Rome. The main road, which crossed approximately the middle of his property, was to have represented the remains of an Antique consular road, ornamented with all the monuments which customarily border them, such as fountains, statues, inscriptions, and a large number of tombs and sarcophagi. This road was to be bordered in part by a canal 200 *toises* long over which a triumphal bridge was to have been placed.

The Spina Antica was to be a continuous stylobate eighty *toises* long ending with two obelisks; a fountain would occupy the center, and the rest would be ornamented with statues, vases, tripods, altars, and other antique fragments.

The ruin which was to terminate the vista from his house, 280 *toises* away, and of which a fifteen foot model has been made in cork, would represent the remains of an immense triumphal monument enriched with antique fragments, figures, bas-reliefs, etc. The whole mass would be forty *toises* wide by nearly 100 feet high. At some distance from this monument were to be a Naumachy and an amphitheater. The main part of the house would be a superb museum.[56]

This complete description gives Clérisseau's plans for an antique garden which would, in effect, have been an outdoor version of the Le Sueur room on a much larger scale. The Abbé Farsetti was known for his interest in antiquity as well as for his collection of ancient art; his gardens were famous for exotic plants of all kinds. In choosing Clérisseau, this cultured antiquarian had selected the ideal person to design and carry out his plans. In March 1753, Farsetti is mentioned in the correspondence of the directors of the French Academy as being interested in the Academy, and he could have met Clérisseau at that time.[57] The Winckelmann letter, which states that the work was a plan never executed, is reinforced by Mariette.

Clérisseau, after doing considerable work for Abbé Farsetti, who had asked for building plans which, to judge by the drawings of them that Clérisseau showed me, were beyond the power of one man to execute, decided to return to France.[58]

A study of contemporary literary sources and travelers' accounts of the villa and gardens in the eighteenth century reveals no trace of Clérisseau. Emilio de Tipaldo's *Descrizione* of 1833 mentions nothing. Giuseppe Mazzotti's *Le Ville Venete* of 1954 illustrates an eighteenth-century view of the villa which shows nothing resembling a design by Clérisseau.[59]

In the letter already quoted Winckelmann admired the design for Farsetti because it "seemed to be more a portrait of an Antique monument than a composition in the Antique style." That this is so results from Clérisseau's long experience in the study and depiction of ancient ruins. Such an original and authentic conception of antiquity surely appealed to Winckelmann, who had great sympathy for Clérisseau and admiration for his work. His elaborate plans for the Farsetti garden are reminiscent not only of the ruin room, but also of his own imaginative drawings of created ruin scenes (see Fig. 42), as well as those by Robert Adam (see Fig. 43).

Another project by Clérisseau for Farsetti, perhaps related, was the plan for an academy of drawing, which also was never executed. The German architect Friedrich von Erdmannsdorff (1736–1800), who was to be one of Clérisseau's pupils, mentioned the plan in his diary of December 28, 1768, writing that "the idea is vast and discreet, the façade most noble." Von Erdmannsdorff and his patron Prince Franz of Anhalt-Dessau (1740–1817) probably first met Clérisseau in Rome in 1765–66.[60]

Although the friendship between Clérisseau and Winckelmann probably dated to 1757 and there are continued references to the Frenchman in various letters written by Winckelmann over the years, the only surviving letters between them date from 1767 and early 1768, after Clérisseau's departure from Italy. We have already seen how valuable the excerpts from the letters written between the summer and early December 1767 have been for documenting Clérisseau's activities during the 1760s. There seems to have been a falling out between the two men sometime in 1766, because Reiffenstein wrote to Mechel on October 8, 1766, that "Our friend has begun to visit him [Clérisseau] again, which pleases me because of the great respect I have for each of them."[61] However, there is no other evidence of a quarrel.

In these 1767–68 letters Winckelmann is concerned primarily with Clérisseau's archaeological studies in southern France. Winckelmann comments on the inscriptions Clérisseau sent him, looks forward to receiving the drawings of the Pont du Gard and the arch and tomb of St. Rémy, and—most important—refers to the "science of antiquity," encouraging Clérisseau to seek out the truth and to refute the work of others. This concern with truth can also be seen in his remarks on the problems of the arch of Orange. Further indications of the high regard Winckelmann had for Clérisseau's views are found in his expression of regret that they had never gone to Palestrina, because Winckelmann disliked earlier studies by others.[62]

Clérisseau had made numerous corrections and observations on the first edition of Winckelmann's *History of Ancient Art;* the author comments on them and states that he will incorporate them in the new edition.[63]

Clérisseau's answers to the above letters, which are lost, apparently expressed his discouragement, because on December 9 Winckelmann encouraged him by writing: "France should congratulate you for drawing from obscurity the monuments of ancient grandeur and making famous what until now was only known from rough sketches." Winckelmann wrote of his activity at Pompeii during the past few months, revealing his passionate concern with archaeological study. The last letter, dated February 3, 1768, compliments Clérisseau on his work at Nîmes[64] and once again shows Winckelmann's kindness.

On December 1, 1763, Clérisseau married Thérèse, the daughter of the sculptor Pierre L'Estache, (c. 1688 – 1774), in the Church of S. Luigi de Francesi.[65] L'Estache had been the interim director of the French Academy in Rome, following the death of Vleughels in December 1737, and served until August 17, 1738, when the new director, Jean François de Troy, took over.[66] Clérisseau was forty-two and Thérèse was presumably younger, though her father was about seventy-five at the time. She is referred to in Winckelmann's letter of December 9, 1767.[67] The added responsibility of a wife may account for the drawing instruction that Clérisseau gave to architectural students who had come to Rome as part of their education, like Robert Adam before them.[68] One pupil, Vogel, who did no work, is mentioned in Winckelmann's letter of November 26, 1763, to Caspar Füssli.[69] The best-known pupil was Friedrich von Erdmannsdorff, the future architect of Franz of Anhalt-Dessau, whose diary is invaluable. He describes their first meeting in his Roman diary on December 28, 1765:

> . . . we made the acquaintance of M. Clerisseau the excellent architectural draughtsman. He has travelled throughout Italy, Dalmatia and Istria, which he has described in a series of views he made everywhere after nature. His finished drawings are in washes of different colors. The majestic remains of Antiquity, or ideas based on these great models of the past, are decorated with landscapes and spirited figures. . . . His work is highly thought of in England.[70]

On May 3 of the following year, he wrote to a friend that he often went to Winckelmann's with the Prince of Mechlenburg, then spent the rest of the morning and day drawing or reading; in the evening he visited Clérisseau.[71]

Von Erdmannsdorff's surviving drawings of actual and imaginary Roman ruins and decorative details resemble those of his teacher. There also exists a series of twenty-four prints (published in 1797 by von Erdmannsdorff) after architectural studies made in Rome, which show the influence of Clérisseau. They bear such titles as "The Arch of Titus in the Roman Forum" and "The Ruins of the Temple of Mars Ultor in the Forum of Nerva."[72]

Even more important was Clérisseau's influence on von Erdmannsdorff's architecture, particularly the palace at Wörlitz, 1768 – 73. When August Rode published his monograph on von Erdmannsdorff in 1801, he included a brief summary of Clérisseau's career, in which he pointed out that Clérisseau had never seen

Greek buildings (except at Paestum), and therefore had worked only with Roman monuments. He stressed Clérisseau's love of ornament and richness, his lack of noble simplicity, and the stress he put on buildings of the Corinthian order, often completely at odds with what Rode called purified taste. Rode finds these same characteristics in the work of von Erdmannsdorff.[73] Rode's comments, though expressing the later prejudice of an advocate of the Greek Revival, point up the lasting influence of Clérisseau on von Erdmannsdorff, through whom the latter became acquainted with Piranesi. In fact, Piranesi dedicated one of his plates to von Erdmannsdorff.[74]

In addition to various projects and his teaching during this period, Clérisseau produced a great number of drawings of ruin scenes, because, as Robert Adam aptly said, it is "to draw his ruins by which he lives."[75] Edward Edwards wrote that once, on a wager, Clérisseau "executed fifty different drawings between morning and evening and all were allowed to have merit and variety."[76] Fortunately, there are many signed and dated drawings from these years, and our discussion will focus on these. Clérisseau continued to produce more or less exact renditions of ancient ruin scenes of major monuments known as *vedute essata*. He had first begun to do these as part of his training as a student in Rome, and he continued to do them after he left the Academy. Many of them are in the Hermitage. The drawings made for the Diocletian's Palace publication, for the abandoned Desgodetz project, and for the book on the Roman baths, would come under this heading, as would those of Pola. While some of these were executed as illustrations for archaeological studies, a great many were produced to be sold to travelers, particularly the English, who wanted views of their favorite monuments to take home. Typical of such drawings is "The Colosseum and Meta Sudans," signed and dated 1765, the earliest of the dated views of the scene, formerly in the collection of the late Ralph Edwards (Fig. 94).[77]

The most important group of *vedute essata,* dating from 1766 on is a series of twenty-one commissioned by Charles, Lord Hope, and James Hope, later the third Earl of Hopetoun, who visited Rome between 1761 and 1763.[78] Through James Adam they commissioned Clérisseau to make these at the rate of five pounds each. The drawings arrived in London in 1766, and were forwarded by James to Hopetoun House, where nine remain today; ten others are in another branch of the family; two are now lost.[79] Seven of these drawings are signed and dated 1766. They represent such Roman subjects as the Arch of Titus, the Forum of Nerva, the Arch of the Goldsmiths, the Ponto Rotto, and other Italian scenes, including Virgil's tomb and miscellaneous ancient views.

The most interesting of these is a representation of the "Ponto Rotto," dated 1766.[80] It is the only view of the subject by Clérisseau known to me. It is crudely done and the buildings in the background are flat in feeling; oddly enough, the figures in the foreground seem livelier than usual. More typical is the drawing of the "Arch of the Goldsmiths," also signed and dated 1766. This has recently flaked, revealing the surprising fact that it is painted over an engraving—undoubtedly the Cunego print after Clérisseau, which it resembles in every way. The print was one of the set of fourteen after Clérisseau depicting ruins of Rome, Pola, and Naples, published in 1766 by J. Brett.[81]

Figure 94. C.-L. Clérisseau, "The Colosseum and Meta
Sudans," 1765, London, formerly Ralph Edwards Collection

The majority of Clérisseau pictures, however, were of two other types. The
first, known as *vedute ideate,* again shows a recognizable building or ruin depicted
in a picturesque setting, usually with additional buildings or monuments. This type
is best illustrated by two drawings formerly thought to be imaginary but which I
have identified as depicting the Temple of Minerva at Assisi.

One, belonging to the Duke of Buccleuch and Queensberry, is signed and dated
1759 (Fig. 95),[82] and so actually predates the period under discussion. At first it
might seem to be a *vedute essata,* but if one examines the other signed but not
dated drawing of this scene, which is in the Wells College Collection,[83] one sees
how different the two settings are. While the temple, unusual in having stairs
between the columns instead of in front of them, is identical in both drawings, the
remainder of the scene is entirely different. The Buccleuch drawing has an ornate
fountain and more elaborate Palladian and Gothic touches, whereas the Wells
drawing has a simpler background with a giant bridge and different figures. The
two drawings differ in both size and technique. The Buccleuch drawing is executed
partly in a bright gouache of blues and reds, partly in watercolor of blue and
yellow; the smaller Wells drawing is in the usual brown ink and brown wash,
heightened with green and white accents of gouache. The Wells version is undated;
it perhaps dates from the 1760s, but it may be later. From my study of about two
thousand Clérisseau drawings, it has become apparent that the same scene appears
repeatedly over a period of at least thirty years. Although the original drawing was
undoubtedly made on the spot and no doubt preserved, or a copy made for

Figure 95. C.-L. Clérisseau, "The Temple of Minerva at Assisi," 1759,
Drumlanrig Castle, Dumfriesshire, Duke of Buccleuch and Queensberry

reference, the later versions, varying in elaboration, could have been produced at any time, as certain dated drawings prove.

The largest number of works by Clérisseau are of the third type, known as *vedute di fantasia.* Sometimes part of a scene will be recognizable, so that these pictures may seem closely related to the *vedute ideate,* but they are usually handled in a freer way, combining elements from various sites or creating imaginary ones. The earliest dated example of the type is an Italian scene in a French collection, signed and dated 1759 (Fig. 96),[84] which depicts a ruined, decorated vault with columns screening a niche, peasants on precariously arranged fragments, and the familiar fountain opposite. The combination of Corinthian pilasters and columns, Augustan entablature, tabernacle with inset relief above it, and fragments of ancient stucco works never occurred in antiquity. Clérisseau's minute depiction of every detail, made possible by the medium of gouache and his skillful arrangement, keeps this thought from occurring to the beholder.

In addition to "The Colosseum and Meta Sudans" and the pictures commissioned by the Hope family, there are numerous other dated drawings from 1762–67. The majority of these are *vedute di fantasia.* The earliest one has a motif that was repeated three times during these years and several times in later or undated drawings. This picture, simply called "Ruins," is in the Louvre (Fig. 97).[85] It was one of Clérisseau's reception pieces for admission to the Académie Royale de Peinture et de Sculpture in 1768. It depicts Clérisseau's usual corner view of a vaulted interior; the dominant feature is an elaborate doorway topped by consoles supporting a lintel, all of which, in turn, are framed by Corinthian columns carrying an entablature crowned by a triangular pediment. If this doorway has a basis in antique fact, I have yet to find it. Peasants are seen in the doorway, resting on architectural fragments. To the right, a large segmental arch, with a partially destroyed relief above, opens onto a landscape. The very next year, this basic composition was repeated in a gouache now in the Soane Museum.[86] The door is nearly identical, though the friezes have been removed. The niche to the right of the door is now empty, and more figures have been added. The arch is semicircular, the wall above is restored and pierced with windows, and the landscape has been replaced by buildings which close the distant view. The same basic elements occur in a third version, dated 1764, which was sold at Sotheby's in 1975, and in an almost identical drawing in the Marquis of Linlithgow's collection, dated 1766, that belongs to the set commissioned by the Hope family.[87] This combines elements from both the previous pictures: the arch and wall from the Soane variation and the frieze from the Louvre version. Other changes occur in the figure grouping, niche contents, and landscape.

The inner doorway alone, crowned by a pediment, appears in a drawing with the same basic composition reversed. This, signed and dated 1764 or 1765, is in the collection of Sir Brinsley Ford (Fig. 98).[88] There are numerous variations: A groin vault has replaced the barrel vault and the landscape differs, as do the decorative details and figures.

Another popular theme, a ruined Roman bath with some resemblance to the Grotto of Egeria, appears at this time, first in a gouache, signed and dated *Roma,* 1763, in the Royal Collection (Fig. 99)[89] and repeated the next year in a drawing in

Figure 96. C.-L. Clérisseau, "Italian Scene," 1759, private collection,
France (from J. Lejeaux, "Charles-Louis Clérisseau, architect et peintre
de ruines . . . ," *La Revue de l'art*, LIV, Apr. 1927, 127)

Figure 97. C.-L. Clérisseau, "Ruins,"
1762, Paris, Louvre

Figure 98. C.-L. Clérisseau, "Architectural
Capriccio," 1764 [5?], London,
Brinsley Ford Collection

Figure 99. C.-L. Clérisseau, "Bathers in a Ruined
Roman Bath," 1763, Windsor Castle Royal
Library, Her Majesty Queen Elizabeth II

the Robert Hull Fleming Museum, Burlington, Vermont, again in 1765 in an almost identical version now in the Louvre,⁹⁰ and later in several variations, both dated and undated. Once again the observer looks at an angled view into a ruined interior. The worn columns, niches with vases, and muted yet precise detail in shades of warm browns and grays accented by blue and red are identical in feeling to that of the Ruin Room. Apart from the difference in scale and the spatial arrangement of the walls, the effect of both is identical: the very plausible depiction of an ancient building, seemingly real but in fact imaginary. This is true of each of the many variations on this theme and illustrates Clérisseau's later exhortation against the servile copying of antiquity in favor of capturing its spirit.⁹¹

The other dated drawings by Clérisseau made in Italy in the 1760s represent similar interior scenes, including "The Interior of a Vaulted Hall" of 1764, now in the Soane Museum (Fig. 100).⁹² Although this is not a version of the series of baths, it has the same basic conception of an angled, interior view showing a colonnade on one side and a vista seen through an architectural frame. It is interesting to note that in this drawing the basic composition — a barrel-vaulted room terminating in a semicircular apse, which is separated from the main room by a screen of columns — appears in what is perhaps Robert Adam's most successful room, the Library at Kenwood, built in 1767–69 (Fig. 101). One cannot say that Adam was inspired by this specific drawing, because "The Reconstruction, based on the Roman Baths," made by Adam in about 1755, showed a smaller screened niche in the middle of a side wall (see Fig. 47), as did Clérisseau's drawing of an antique house (see Fig. 45). Adam had already used the motif in the hall and dining room at Syon, which was begun about 1761. However, Clérisseau's 1764 drawing once again emphasizes Adam's indebtedness to Clérisseau. It is also likely that both men were inspired by Vignola's Villa at Caprarola, which they had visited. Kent's Temple of Venus at Stowe may also have been influential.

The last dated drawing of this period to be discussed is perhaps the most important, because it is one of two drawings of antique decorative details dated February 1766. Now in the Hermitage, it represents, in beautiful soft green, red, and yellow watercolor, an antique ceiling, and bears the notation in Italian that it was "found in a sort of quarry in Feb. 1766 on Mount Celio . . ." (Fig. 102).⁹³ The colors and the delicacy of the forms, as well as the linear organization of the composition into a series of floral bands with panels between them, are very similar to Adam's ceiling designs of the 1760s.⁹⁴

If this discussion of drawings concentrates on subject more than style, it is because Clérisseau's style had already been formed by this time. Basically inspired by a combination of influences from Panini and Piranesi, his style remained constant throughout his career. There are, however, certain pictures dating from the late 1750s and 1760s that show a stronger Piranesi influence than is usual for works of this period.

The best example of this is a drawing of the Temple of Clitumnus at Spoleto, signed and dated 1759, which is in the collection of the Duke of Buccleuch and Queensberry (Fig. 103).⁹⁵ In comparison with a representation of the same temple, now in the Hermitage (see Fig. 22), which was perhaps made on the spot in the 1750s, the Hermitage picture appears to be the weaker representation, with soft

Figure 100. C.-L. Clérisseau, "Interior of a
Vaulted Hall," 1764, London, Soane Museum

Figure 101. Robert Adam, Library, 1767–69,
Kenwood House, London

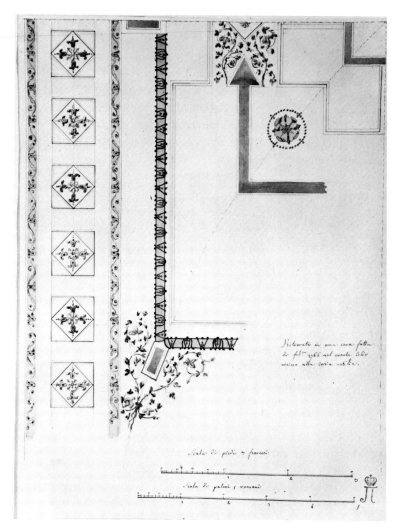

Figure 102. C.-L. Clérisseau, "Ceiling
Sketch," 1766, Hermitage

shadows and an ordinary Roman arch supporting the bridge. The Buccleuch picture is more dramatic and powerful, sharper in forms, and stronger in light and shade,[96] with a broad semicircular arch of the type later carried further and made more dramatic in the paintings of Hubert Robert (1733–1808) and the architecture of Claude-Nicolas Ledoux (1736–1806). One explanation for this dramatic change could be Piranesi's representation of this same subject, "il Tempio del Clitumno. . . ," Plate 26 from his *Antichità romane de' tempi della repubblica*, published in 1748 (Fig. 104),[97] which has not only the same dramatic power but also the arched bridge. We have noted earlier how Clérisseau was influenced by other prints in the same series, though his results were less dramatic.

Piranesi's continuing influence is also found in a series of initials, set before ancient scenes (Fig. 105), which are tamer variations of similar devices published by Piranesi, particularly in his *Della magnificenza ed architettura de' Romani*, 1761 (Fig. 106),[98] or a drawing of cupids from a frieze in the Villa Borghese (Fig. 107), which is the same subject as that depicted in a Piranesi print published in *Vasi, candelabri, cippi, sarcophagi, tripodi* of 1768–78. Of course, Clérisseau's drawing may not be based directly on that of Piranesi, but may instead stem from a common antique source.[99]

A series of six drawings of country houses in the Hermitage, such as the one illustrated here called "A Country House" (Fig. 108), consisting of houses built into ruins, is reminiscent of Piranesi's etchings from *Le Rovine del Castello dell'Acqui Giulia*, published in 1761.[100] There one sees the same combination of jagged upright ruins with lower, modern appendages. Though both share a contrast of light and dark with an emphasis on the encroachment of the overgrowth on the ruins, the Piranesi etchings are far more dramatic and masterful, while the Clérisseau drawings are clearer in the architectural forms.

The great collection of Clérisseau in the Hermitage contains three portfolios devoted to drawings of antique trophies, vases, candelabra, altars, sarcophagi, tables, and chairs, which resemble the collections etched in Piranesi's *Vasi, candelabri . . .* and in his *Trofeo di Ottaviano Augusto* of 1753.[101] Compared to Piranesi's drawings, Clérisseau's are less dramatic. They were undoubtedly made as an album of motifs and sources for future commissions and projects rather than as works of art in their own right. A study of helmets (Fig. 109) and one of candelabra (Fig. 110), compared with a single large Piranesi of candelabrum, indicates that they were intended to be part of such an album (Fig. 111).[102]

Our discussion of Clérisseau's Italian drawings of the 1760s ends on a puzzling note. Among the ones in the Fitzwilliam Museum is one of a ruined coffered dome supported by a ring of Ionic columns, which, in turn, is surrounded on the left by a curving wall pierced by pedimented windows (Fig. 112).[103] In the midst of the colonnade is the usual artful arrangement of architectural fragments, including a framed inscription. Three figures are seen at the left. A larger version of this same composition, with slight variations in the architectural fragments and different figures, is in the Russell collection in Montreal.[104] A variant, without the outside wall beyond the "ambulatory," or the remains of the dome, was formerly in the collection of C. A. Mincieux, Geneva.[105] All of these drawings show the left portion of the colonnade with the curving wall beyond at the extreme left. However, there is another drawing of this scene in the Fitzwilliam Museum, which is

Figure 103. C.-L. Clérisseau, "Temple of Clitumnos at Spoleto" (bridge and temple), 1759, Drumlanrig Castle, Dumfriesshire, Duke of Buccleuch and Queensberry

Figure 104. Giovanni Battista Piranesi, "Il Tempio del Clitumno . . . ," 1743–48, etching,
F 68, Pl. 26, *Antichità romane de' tempi della repubblica*

Figure 105. C.-L. Clérisseau, "Initials," Hermitage

Figure 106. Giovanni Battista Piranesi, "Initial Letters,"
1761, etchings, *Della magnificenza ed architettura
de' Romani* (from A.H. Mayor, *Giovanni
Battista Piranesi*, New York, 1952, Figs. 63–64)

Figure 107. C.-L. Clérisseau, "Frieze," Hermitage

Figure 108. C.-L. Clérisseau, "Country House," Hermitage

Figure 109. C.-L. Clérisseau, "Helmets," Hermitage

Figure 110. C.-L. Clérisseau, "Candelabra," Hermitage

Figure 111. Giovanni Battista Piranesi, "Candelabro antico," 1778, etching, F 700 (?), *Vasi, candelabri, cippi, sarcophagi, tripodi, lucerne ed ornamenti antichi*

Figure 112. C.-L. Clérisseau, "Ruined Coffered
Dome," Cambridge, Fitzwilliam Museum

Figure 113. Charles Natoire, "Ruines: compositions
d´architecture," Montpellier, Faculté de
Médecine de Montpellier, Atger Collection

almost a mirror image of the one mentioned above.[106] Slight variations exist in the vegetation and the stone near the figures, and one segmental pediment has been made triangular. The shadows cast by the cornice on top of the pile are also different. The arrangement of the architectural remains, placed at various angles in the center of the colonnade, is reversed in the second Fitzwilliam drawing, which precludes the possibility that the drawing represents the other half of the building. Therefore, the second Fitzwilliam drawing is a reversal of the composition of the first and of the other versions of that composition already mentioned.

These drawings present a difficult problem. Charles Natoire, the director of the French Academy in Rome from 1752–74, produced, from about 1756 to 1775, a great number of lovely drawings of scenes of Rome and the surrounding countryside, depicting not only the Renaissance villas and gardens but also the ancient ruins. Among these is a signed work entitled, "Ruines: compositions d'architecture" (Fig. 113),[107] which is related to the second Fitzwilliam drawing. It represents the same reversed composition: The architectural debris is identical in arrangement and detail, as is the composition of the figures, changed only by the addition of a mother with children at the right. The major variations are the differences in the lighting on the columns and fragments, the substitution of unfluted shafts for Clérisseau's characteristically fluted ones (which are always depicted with worn joints), and changes in the vegetation around the base of the columns.

Inasmuch as Natoire and Clérisseau did not part on the best of terms in 1754 and, as far as is known, never met again, it is hard to explain the close similarity of these two drawings. The most obvious answer is that both represent an actual ruin which both men drew, although no source has been found. There is also the problem of the reversal of the composition by Clérisseau. Natoire may have copied Clérisseau or vice versa, but it is hard to believe that either of those men would do this, common though such a practice was among students at the Academy.[108] The composition appears in other Clérisseau works and, in the arrangement of elements and in mood, resembles many other of his imaginary drawings. Despite the fact that the Natoire drawing comes from an album containing dated drawings from 1764–72, I have not been able to establish a precise date for it nor for any of the Clérisseau representations.

Thus, the years Clérisseau was on his own in Italy (1763 to 1767) were marked by a great variety of activities which, in many ways, makes this the most interesting period of his life. Now, after nearly nineteen successful years in Italy, he decided to return to France and undertake an archaeological project on his own.

V

The Return to France
Southern France and Paris:

1767–71

Clérisseau left Italy in the summer of 1767, most likely for professional reasons, as he wished to undertake a study of the Roman remains in the southern part of France.[1]

According to Clérisseau, there was a great deal to include in such a publication. In 1557 J. P. d'Albenes had published his *Discours historial de l'antique et illustre cité de Nismes,* with inaccurate illustrations, which were also published by Palladio. Desgodetz had planned to include Nîmes in his survey, but the measured drawings he had made in 1674 were lost when he was captured by pirates.[2] Other minor historical studies of the seventeenth and early eighteenth centuries added little.[3] These facts are summarized in the preface to Clérisseau's first, and as it turned out, only, volume of his study, *Antiquités de la France: Première Partie, Monumens de Nismes.*[4] He believed there was a need for a careful, accurate study correcting the mistakes of others. He added, in typical Clérisseau fashion, that he hoped the readers would not take offense at his criticism, but would realize that it was in the name of progress.[5]

The book was primarily concerned with the accurate measurement, depiction, and restoration of the monuments. Clérisseau's preface indicates, however, that he was also concerned with the buildings as works of art. He declared, for example, that Rome does not have a more perfect monument than Nîmes's Maison Carrée,[6] and he stressed the importance of harmony, order, grandeur, and variety in architecture. Most revealing of his approach was his statement that imitation is not reasonable; rather, one should study the spirit in which the original was made.[7] He ended this section by exhorting the reader: "Therefore let us learn from the ancients rules to which we should submit our practices. Let us remove this mark of servitude and cold imitation that disparage our buildings." [8]

Clérisseau's enthusiasm for his studies at Nîmes, Arles, St. Rémy, Orange, and St. Chamas was not tempered by the various archaeological problems mentioned in the previous chapter. The letters from Winckelmann are the main source of information about Clérisseau's archaeological activities in southern France, for Clérisseau sent him copies of inscriptions and precise accounts of an unusual triumphal arch, a tomb at Arles, and a sarcophagus. He also promised to send him drawings of the Pont du Gard and the arch and tomb at St. Rémy. [9]

Winckelmann commented wisely on these matters, asked questions, and offered advice. He praised Clérisseau for having the courage to work on the proscenium of the theater at Orange [10] and reminded him of the great contribution he would make to France. [11] Winckelmann also stated remarkably modern principles of archaeological research and writing: "Write as much as possible in the presence of the actual object and return to it if you have second thoughts." [12] He added, "One has no right to omit or neglect anything even if it seems unimportant to the ordinary person, because it may be important to the enlightened." [13] Winckelmann stressed giving "discoveries to the public with proper interpretations." [14]

Few of Clérisseau's drawings made in connection with his studies in southern France are known today. [15] The most important is a very large drawing of the triumphal arch at Orange, which is inscribed as being measured and drawn by Clérisseau in 1768 (Fig. 114). [16] Dating from the time the artist was still in southern France it was either done in front of the monument or is a replica of one that was. It must be the large drawing of the arch which was still in the artist's possession at the time of his death. [17] The high finish, detail, and unusual size suggest that it was to be for a plate in one of the later volumes of Clérisseau's study. Another drawing, "The Triumphal Arch and Tomb of the Julii at St. Rémy" (Fig. 115), is related to one mentioned in the Winckelmann correspondence. Although the drawing is dated 1769, [18] it must be based on a study done on the spot. When compared with a photograph of the scene (Fig. 116), it is evident that Clérisseau moved the two monuments closer together to form a better composition, or perhaps to show each in "its most picturesque position." [19] In the Royal Institute of British Architects Library in London, the series of Hardwick albums includes a drawing labeled (in a later hand, possibly that of Thomas Hardwick), "from an original by Clérisseau," and in another hand, "Dessous de l'Archivolte de L'Arc de St. Remi" (Fig. 117). [20] This drawing is very possibly by one of the Italian draftsmen, such as Giuseppi Manocchi (1731–82), who worked for the Adams in Italy and England, and so probably goes back to a Clérisseau original. The only other known Clérisseau drawing of the antiquities of southern France has been identified as the theater at Orange (Fig. 118). [21] This recalls Winckelmann's comment about Clérisseau's activity there.

Clérisseau's book came out in 1778. Lack of money prevented him from publishing the remaining volumes implied by the title *Antiquités de La France: Premier Partie, Monumens des Nismes.* [22] In 1804 a second, enlarged edition, edited by his son-in-law, J. G. Legrand, appeared. [23] This book should be accorded a place among the first archaeological studies of the Roman Revival, following Wood and Dawkins' *The Ruins of Palmyra* and *The Ruins of Baalbek* of 1753 and

Figure 114. C.-L. Clérisseau, "Triumphal Arch at Orange," 1768, Essen, de Belder Collection

Figure 115. C.-L. Clérisseau, "The Triumphal Arch and Tomb of the
Julii at St. Rémy," 1769, London, Victoria and Albert Museum

Figure 116. St. Rémy, Triumphal Arch and Tomb of the Julii

Figure 117. Giuseppi Manocchi (?)
after Clérisseau (?),
"Dessaux de l Archivolte de L'Arc
de St. Remi," London, Royal Institute
of British Architects Library

1757, respectively, and Adam's *Ruins of the Palace of the Emperor Diocletian at Spalatro in Dalmatia* of 1764. More than the others, it inspired Europeans to take an interest in the antiquities on their own soil.[24]

Soon after Clérisseau arrived in southern France, he received the commission to design a large house for a rich Marseille merchant, Louis-Nicholas Borély (1692 – 1768). Borély had begun to build a large villa on an extensive site in 1766, and it is not clear how much, if any, progress had been made by the time he hired Clérisseau to design the façade.[25] Clérisseau's drawing for this, dated in Marseille on Sep-

Figure 118. C.-L. Clérisseau, "Theater at Orange,"
Cambridge, Fitzwilliam Museum

tember 1, 1767, has been preserved (Fig. 119).[26] Basically, it is a long rectangle with a projecting central pavilion crowned by a pediment and flat attic; the ends are treated as slightly projecting pavilions. The entire design is organized horizontally and resembles a great number of eighteenth-century French buildings of the Louis XVI style in its severity and basic organization. Its most distinctive features are the great number of enrichments planned for the façade. The three pavilions were to be framed by pilasters, which were fluted on the ground floor and plain on the second, thus keeping the horizontal emphasis. Most striking were the inset panels placed above each of the windows of the pavilions, as well as above the other first-floor windows. Those above the three ground-floor windows, on each side of the central pavilion, were continuous frieze-like panels. The inset panels on the ground floor of the pavilions were to contain Classical scenes, while the long panel between them was to have acanthuslike rinceau patterns with winged figures based on Classical friezes from Clérisseau's collection of drawings, such as one from Hadrian's Villa (Fig. 120).[27] The inset panels above the first floor were to be filled with a variety of Classical decorative motifs: a rinceau with winged figures, acanthus and anthemion, sphinxes and cupids with garlands and paterae.[28] The crowning decorations were to be the Borély arms carved into the pediment. Statues were to stand on the balconies of the ground-floor windows of the end pavilions, and round niches containing busts were planned for the corresponding space above. The central door and the two window-doors were not to be framed in the severe manner of the rest of the openings, but were to be crowned by consoles and a cornice with an inset arabesque frieze over the main entrance. Beneath the windows, flanking the entrance, were to be consoles set between garlanded swags.

This handsome design, with its wealth of rich details derived from antiquity, was not built.[29] Evidently the design was too advanced for Borély. Louis-Nicholas, or possibly his son Louis-Joseph (1731–85), complained that the design was "too Italian." On January 31, 1768, Borély paid 200 livres for new plans by Marie-Joseph Peyre (1730–88).[30] The building was finally executed by the architect Esprit-Joseph Brun (1710–1804) between 1768 and 1778 (Fig. 121).[31] While the death of Louis-Nicholas Borély and the resulting financial difficulties are often cited as the reason Clérisseau's design was abandoned, there may have been another. Clérisseau left southern France for Paris later that year.[32] His design was not appreciated by a later generation, as is shown by the writing of Léon Lagrange in 1860.[33]

A comparison of the drawing (see Fig. 119) and the façade as executed (see Fig. 121) confirms Lagrange's description of the changes. The only remaining decorations are the two statues in the pediment. The pilasters of the end pavilion have been replaced by drafted stonework on the ground floor and rectangular panels on the floor above. The entrance, simply framed, has a single console as a keystone — the only remnant of Clérisseau's elaborate ornament. The end window-doors are simple, like all the others, without Clérisseau's balconies or statues.

The interior, decorated by the painter Louis Chaix (c. 1740–1811), a pupil of Vien, who returned from Rome in 1776,[34] may bear some slight relationship to Clérisseau's style, but there is no evidence that he or Peyre did any drawings for the interior. When Thomas Jefferson visited the Château in 1787, he commented only

Figure 119. C.-L. Clérisseau, "Façade Design," Château Borély, Marseille, Sept. 1767, Marseille, Musee Borély

Figure 120. C.-L. Clérisseau, "Fragment de la Ville Adriani à Tivoli," Hermitage

Figure 121. Esprit-Joseph Brun, Façade as Executed, Château Borély, Marseille (from *Monographie Château Borély*, Paris, 1908, Pl. 2)

Figure 122. C.-L. Clérisseau, "Architectural Ruins," 1771, London, Soane Museum

Figure 123. C.-L. Clérisseau, "Architectural Scene,"
1769, London, formerly Frank T. Sabin

Figure 124. C.-L. Clérisseau, "Drawing of Architectural
Interior," Cambridge, Fitzwilliam Museum

on the wind pumps.[35] Yet, at the time, Jefferson was collaborating with Clérisseau on the design of the Virginia Capitol.

Sometime in 1768 Clérisseau returned to Paris after an absence of nearly twenty years.[36] According to Abbé Barthélémy, Clérisseau found it difficult to make a living there. In a letter dated September 1, 1768, he pointed out that Clérisseau needed a patron and was not appreciated in his own country.[37] However, things improved in 1769. On September 2, Clérisseau was accepted as a member of the Académie Royale de Peinture et de Sculpture under the category of a painter of architecture. He was the first architect to be admitted to this society.[38] He presented two gouaches entitled "Bains" and "Ruines d'architecture." A month later he exhibited two works at the Paris Salon: "Vues des ruines d'Italie" and "Une Chambre sépulchrale." [39] These were described in the *Mercure de France* of October as being drawings of fantasy, beautiful in color, with excellent perspective, but with figures of a quality inferior to the architecture and handled so differently that perhaps they were by another hand.[40]

Stylistically, Clérisseau's other drawings of this period are like those from his Italian years. Sometimes old compositions reappear, as in a drawing of 1771 of a Roman wall, now in the Soane Museum (Fig. 122), which repeats a work commissioned by the Hopes in 1761–63 and delivered in 1766.[41]

Yet Clérisseau also created new ruin compositions, such as a 1769 scene of an interior (Fig. 123).[42] This has the familiar door motif of the early 1760s, now used to separate two rooms. It also has arched niches screened off by columns supporting a straight entablature, with the resulting lunette left open. This form, used in the entrance gates at Spalato, has been noted as a favorite of Robert Adam during this period. On the verso of one of the large number of Clérisseaus in the Fitzwilliam, a pen-and-ink underdrawing, or more correctly, an unfinished drawing, has been discovered (Fig. 124).[43] This represents part of another version of the picture or of a 1770 picture now in the Soane. There is also a later version dated 1782 in the Hermitage. The unfinished drawing gives a clear idea of how Clérisseau constructed his pictures. One can see the pencil lines as he first drew the scene in perspective, then the architectural details, based on his great stock of drawings, were added in pencil. Later, everything was outlined in black ink and, if completed, rendered with gouache. The very complete preliminary drawing in perspective of the basic structure and the many details help to give even the most fantastic ruin scene a sense of reality. The result is a convincing re-creation of antiquity.

One other activity of these years about which we know very little is Clérisseau's acting as a dealer or purchaser of works of art for other people. We know from his letter to the Adam brothers that he bought works of art for them during the 1760s,[44] and he evidently continued this practice. Clérisseau purchased at the sale of Ange Laurent de La Livre de Jully in Paris on May 2, 1770, two paintings for the Duke of Richmond: lot 33, La Hyre's "Conversion of St. Paul" for 140 livres, and lot 40, Patel's "Landscape with Corinthian Architecture" (with figures by Boucher) for 500 livres. At the sale of M. Le Comte de Guiche, organized by Rémy on March 4–7, 1771, Clérisseau purchased a Rubens painting, "Landscape with a Cart Crossing a Ford," for "l'Ambassadeur de l'Angleterre," [45] who must be Simon, Lord Harcourt (1714–77). The Rubens painting, which may be a copy, is still owned by the Harcourts and is now at Stanton Harcourt.[46]

VI

Clérisseau in England in the 1770s

Clérisseau went to England in 1771, according to Mariette, in his writings before 1774. He considered it best, for now Clérisseau would no longer remain idle, as he had been in Paris.[1] Things had not gone well in Paris. All Clérisseau had done since returning to Paris from southern France in 1768 was to produce excellent and inventive drawings of ruin scenes, for which the English paid him well.[2] This might have been a reason for his crossing the English Channel. A more substantial reason is that he could have followed up on the Adams' invitation to help with their various projects, as they had suggested earlier. Edward Edwards confirms this in his *Anecdotes of Painters* (1808), in which he gives Clérisseau's address in London.

> This artist was born in Paris and was brought to England by Robert Adam the architect. He resided some time in Great Marlborough Street. . . .[3]

These were busy years for the Adam architectural office. Not only was this the period of the great town houses — those for Sir Watkin Williams-Wynn, 1772–74; the Earl of Derby, 1773–74; and the Countess of Home, 1775–77 — but it was also the time of the vast but ill-fated Adelphi project of 1768–75. Clérisseau's role in these projects is difficult to assess. First of all, there is to date no direct evidence of his part in any of the Adams' projects. Lady Derby, however, was among the foreign subscribers to Clérisseau's book on Nîmes. More important is the fact that both Robert and James had been his pupils and that many of the Italian draftsmen, who had been trained in Italy by Clérisseau and the Adams to copy decorative details and ruin scenes and later to design in the Clérisseau-Adam style, had been brought to England by the Adam brothers.

Among them was Antonio Zucchi (1716–1795), the Venetian artist who often drew the figures in Clérisseau's pictures.[4] Zucchi had been greatly influenced by Clérisseau in Italy while they were both involved in the production of the book on Spalato. He toured southern Italy with Clérisseau and James Adam, and came to England about 1776. During the late 1760s and the 1770s Zucchi painted a great number of large, decorative ruin scenes, such as those in the dining room at Osterley Park (Fig. 125) and one of a triumphal arch in ruins included in the design (but not executed) for the anteroom at Lansdowne (Shelburne) House.[5] These works resemble Clérisseau's in every detail. If it were not for the fact that the Osterley Park paintings are signed by Zucchi and dated 1767,[6] we would probably attribute them to Clérisseau. There can be no doubt that Zucchi based his work on Clérisseau's pictures.

By the 1770s the Adam style had changed. The decoration had become flatter, more attenuated and elegant, with a subsequent loss of the vigor that Clérisseau had imparted to the Adams' work. Their office still employed so many of the people trained by Clérisseau himself, that it is difficult to distinguish Clérisseau's hand in the works produced by the Adams' draftsmen.

The Library of the Royal Institute of British Architects contains a series of volumes, known as the Hardwick Albums or Guard Books, of decorative drawings and tracings of rinceaux, friezes, arabesques, and floral and figural forms derived from Roman antiquity and Renaissance Rome.[7] More than half of the drawings are by Giuseppe Manocchi, whom the Adam brothers brought to England as early as 1763.[8] About twenty of the other drawings bear the inscription "Clérisseau fin[it]." A few are inscribed "Clérisseau perf[init]," suggesting that these are drawings by other artists touched up by Clérisseau. One is illustrated here (Fig. 126).[9] The assumption that this drawing is a copy is proven by the existence of a Clérisseau original in the Hermitage.[10]

The Adam material in the Soane Museum contains two drawings from a volume entitled "Drawings of Roman and Italian Decorative Work in Rome."[11] One in black ink depicts a variety of ancient motifs in a clear linear style (Fig. 127). The other is a ceiling design, touched with watercolor in the roundels and diamonds. Both are studies of decorative details from Roman or Renaissance stuccoes or wall paintings. The drawings contain many elements of the Adam decorative style: the slender curving Classical forms, garlands, tiny figures, urns, arabesques, bas-reliefs, and tendril-like decorations. It is not far-fetched to consider them part of the stock of the Adam office for use in various projects. The original Clérisseaus from which they were copied are in the Hermitage. A study of decorative details (Fig. 128) is the source for Figure 127. A drawing entitled "Bain delinié au palais des empereurs" is the original of the corresponding Soane drawing of diamonds and roundels.[12] The copies seem flat and linear in comparison with the richly plastic Clérisseau originals. Damie Stillman believes the two Soane drawings are not by Robert Adam but by one of the draftsmen; they were either done in Italy, when Clérisseau was training the draftsmen, or in England from drawings he had brought with him. They are important in that they show the use of Clérisseau's antique designs in the Adam office.

Figure 125. Robert Adam, Dining Room, c. 1766–68, Osterley Park House, Middlesex

Figure 126. Clérisseau pupil, "Acanthus," London,
Royal Institute of British Architects Library

Figure 127. Robert Adam (?), "Ceiling Design after Ancient Examples," London, Soane Museum

Figure 128. C.-L. Clérisseau, "Decorative Details," Hermitage

In 1765 the Earl of Shelburne, later to become the Marquess of Lansdowne, bought the unfinished house in Berkeley Square that Robert Adam had designed for the Earl of Bute.[13] It was more or less finished by the end of the decade, with the exception of the gallery, which was then only a shell 103 feet long and 29 feet wide. Adam's design of the mid-1760s for the library consisted of a central rectangle and two octagonal flanking chambers to be separated from the center by single-story screens of columns. This design was not followed, however. When Lansdowne went to Italy in 1771 he met Gavin Hamilton (1723–98), the archaeologist, painter, and dealer, who persuaded him to expand his antique sculpture collection and to turn the unfinished library into a gallery. Hamilton's specifications for the gallery were given to Francesco Panini, son of Giovanni Paolo Panini, who sent drawings to Lansdowne. Panini's design consisted of only one room occupying the central section and one of Adam's octagons. The other octagon presumably would have been a separate room.

Nothing was done about the project, and on February 18, 1772, Hamilton wrote to Lansdowne describing the details of the finished drawings of the Panini project. Using terms like "Real plaster," "bosso releivos," "Cameos," and a "slight ornament of bronze," he pointed out that Clérisseau's "great taste" would be of the utmost importance to the project.

> With regard to the execution of all the other ornaments, great care should be observed with regard to the harmony of colours, all of which your Lordship will find expressed as well as possible in so small a scale. Mr. Clerisseau who has an excellent eye, will be able to direct everything of this sort with great taste.[14]

Lansdowne already knew of Clérisseau, who had, perhaps at the suggestion of Hamilton, written to Lord Lansdowne on May 27, 1771, mentioning various paintings, including a Poussin and the Rubens discussed in the preceding chapter.[15]

It is unlikely that Robert Adam was involved, as relations between Lansdowne and Adam had been strained since 1771, when the nobleman opposed the act of Parliament that enabled the Adams to acquire a small bay in the Thames in order to build the Adelphi on more secure foundations.

Hamilton had lived in Rome since 1756 and was a friend of Robert Adam. He was also well acquainted with Clérisseau. Aware of Clérisseau's jealous temperament, he cautioned Lansdowne, fearing that Clérisseau might do more than simply "direct everything," and might even try to alter the Panini design. On December 26 he wrote:

> What interests me chiefly is the gallery, and if Clérisseau makes any alterations in part, or in the general plan, I should be glad to see a drawing in small, so as to enclose it in a letter. Any slight sketch will be sufficient at first so as to understand his meaning, and I assure your Lordship that I am altogether impartial, and desire nothing more than that he may think of something more grand and noble than that of Panini though I believe it will be difficult unless he changes the whole plan.[16]

This eventually happened. Lansdowne returned to the idea of a library, and wrote Hamilton that the gallery scheme had been abandoned. He then asked Clérisseau for a design, the drawing for which is dated 1774 (Fig. 129).[17]

Restricted by the established dimensions of the room, Clérisseau returned to Adam's three-part division of the library, with a large central space and two flanking ones, which he designed as domed squares in place of the octagons planned by Adam (Figs. 130, 131). The openings between the spaces were widened, and Clérisseau substituted a screen of colossal Corinthian columns in place of Adam's small Ionic order. The result was effectively a large, subdivided space quite unlike Adam's original plan of three rooms. While screens of columns had been used by Adam to separate the apsidal ends of the library at Kenwood in the late 1760s, which has been called a prototype for this design,[18] they had also frequently been used by Clérisseau in his imaginative ruin scenes. In fact, the motif of giant Corinthian columns flanked by pilasters, acting as an open wall, goes back at least as far as a drawing in France from 1759 (see Fig. 96) as well as to the side wall of the Ruin Room in S. Trinità dei Monti.

Clérisseau conceived of the central area as a large hall with colossal columns at the ends; a beautiful garland and patera frieze would encircle the room. The ceiling was to be coved and divided into panels decorated with rinceaux. Lighting came from clerestory windows above. The end rooms, smaller and square in shape, were to have six-sided domes each lighted by a lantern or, alternatively, lighted by lunettes cut into the sides as well as by a lantern (see Fig. 131). The design of the frieze for the ends repeated that of the central room. All of the details — the vertical bands of arabesques at the corners, the strips separating the bookcases, the panels and coffers of the domes, the molding on the balconies, and the lunettes — were carefully and accurately drawn with direct reference to antiquity.

In Clérisseau's project of 1767 for Château Borély in Marseille (see Fig. 119), he applied archaeologically correct panels, moldings, and sculpture to a basically Louis XVI building. In the Lansdowne project, Clérisseau attempted to capture the architectural spirit of antiquity. While the central space is a typical French hall of the eighteenth century, the Corinthian columns give it an archaeological correctness and power, as do the authority of the details. The domed spaces also are intended to be Roman.

Some critics, such as Stillman,[19] think that the project lacks the élan of Robert Adam, but I find it has a vigor that Adam's design lacks. Nevertheless, this project came to naught when it was superseded in 1779 by a design of François-Joseph Bélanger, which was itself not executed.

Clérisseau succeeded in having carried out his design for a garden alcove and screen for Lansdowne House. A drawing of it (either by Clérisseau himself or a tracing of the lost original by Sir John Soane) is inscribed in Soane's hand: "Clérisseau for Lord Shelburne in Berkeley Square. Screen in Garden. N.B. The Great Arch failed abt. 1776" (Fig. 132).[20] The drawing is the only evidence we have for the commission, which, unlike so many others by Clérisseau, was actually executed, as the mention of the collapse of the arch makes clear. The building had as its central motif a semicircular niched apse covered by a diamond-coffered half-dome set within a rectangular framework and topped by an elaborate cornice.

Flanking the center were lower wings, flat on top, whose height coincided with that of the central apse below the half-dome. The wings and central apse were pierced by semicircular niches containing statues and surmounted by roundels carved with motifs seen before in Clérisseau's Château Borély design as well as in some of his drawings done in Italy. The central niche was rectangular and contained a garden seat; the niche was surmounted by a rectangular relief. The exact date of the design is not known, but Pierre du Prey has suggested one of about 1772 when Henry Holland was involved in the building; Soane was his clerk and so could have obtained the original drawing or copied it.[21]

The alcove and screen which eventually replaced Clérisseau's (Fig. 133) is attributed to Sir Robert Smirke, who executed the gallery, but its similarity to Clérisseau's original suggests that Smirke merely modified Clérisseau's design. Smirke lowered the height of the central apse, necessitating the removal of the roundels and rectangular plaque. He emphasized the opening of the arch with moldings that may have strengthened it. The central rectangular niche was replaced by a semicircular niche. This modification of the central section necessitated changes in the wings. The roundels were removed, and additional moldings and an elaborate cornice were added to fill the space. Since the wings retained their original height, they no longer corresponded to the springing of the central half-dome. Smirke also added pitched roofs to the wings, creating triangular half-pediments reminiscent of Palladio. While these may have helped unify the whole design, they did not fit well with the flat-topped central structure, which resembled Clérisseau's original design.

There is one other connection between Lansdowne and Clérisseau. In a memorandum by Lord Shelburne (as he was then titled) of February 1777 describing the sculpture of the blue room of his house, he added the following note to item number 13, "Basso Relievo":

> The Chimney Piece mark'd in the plan sent is not that which exists but an idea of Cipriani's for Mr. H'[olland']s consideration and advice — to be afterwards executed at Rome if a good design can be had and [any] fragments [can be found] to compose it. The present is done after a design of Clérisseau's much too slight for the room as now fitted up, and particularly for the Basso Relievo above.[22]

Unfortunately, this chimney piece has not been traced. The sculpture in question, "A Relief of Homer Meditating upon the Iliad," is shown installed over a mantelpiece in the entrance, or porter's hall, in a photograph of 1922.[23] The chimney piece was engraved in Robert and James Adam's *Works in Architecture*, published between 1778 and 1822. Damie Stillman has assured me that it was designed by Adam, and, in support, cites a drawing in the Soane Museum.[24] It is highly unlikely that this hall is the one called the blue room, and there is no evidence to show which of the rooms was so named. It could have possibly been one of the flanking anterooms demolished along with the rest of the front of the house after it was sold in 1929. It was certainly neither the drawing room, now reassembled in the Philadelphia Museum of Art, nor the dining room, now in the Metropolitan Museum of Art. Careful investigation of these and the remnant still standing has

Figure 129. C.-L. Clérisseau, "Longitudinal section of
Lansdowne Gallery Project," 1774, London, Soane Museum

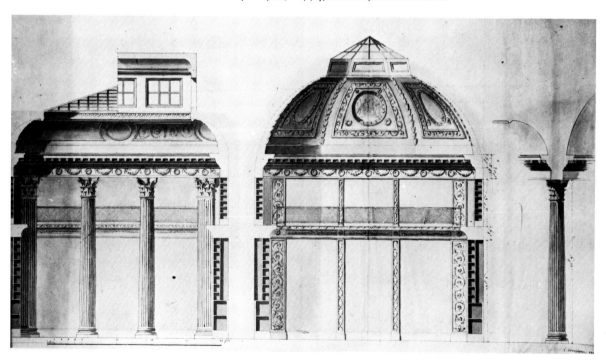

Figure 130. C.-L. Clérisseau, "Plan of Lansdowne Gallery Project,"
1774, London, Soane Museum

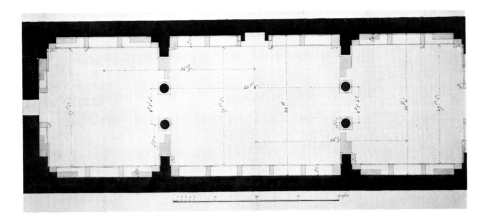

Figure 131. C.-L. Clérisseau, "Cross section of Dome,
Lansdowne Gallery Project," London, Soane Museum

Figure 132. Sir John Soane after Clérisseau (?), "Arch for
Lansdowne House," 1771, London, Victoria and Albert Museum

Figure 133. Lansdowne arch as executed

revealed nothing.[25] The date of the elusive fireplace cannot be ascertained. Does it date from the period between 1763–1767 when the house was originally designed by Adam, who used a design by Clérisseau (as Lord Shelburne wrote), or is it from the period between 1772–74, when Clérisseau was employed by Lansdowne? On a more positive note, "Milord Schelburne" was among the subscribers to Clérisseau's 1778 volume on Nîmes.[26]

During Clérisseau's years in England, he continued the production of his decorative scenes of real and imaginary antique scenes, which had always had a great appeal among the English. He exhibited these in London at the Society of Artists and the Royal Academy. Horace Walpole annotated his catalogue of the Academy's 1772 exhibition: "A Frenchman lately arrived, famous for the beauty and neatness of his drawings from the Antique. He was the master of Mr. Adam when at Rome." He also commented on two of the four Clérisseau drawings exhibited. Concerning no. 49, "A Bath Composed After the Manner of the Ancients," he wrote: "too much like a scene in an opera" and his comment on no. 50, "A Sepulchral Chamber Composed after the Ancients," was "charming taste."[27]

On February 2, 1779, Baron Grimm wrote to Catherine the Great that when Lord Harcourt (the second Earl, 1714–77) left his position as Ambassador to France he returned to England with Clérisseau, who had three fat portfolios of drawings that he hoped George III would purchase. Clérisseau claimed that the King was eager to see the portfolios, but Lord Bute opposed the idea. Clérisseau's volumes were seized by customs, who maintained that it was impossible for a single man to have done all of them and that he was merely the merchant of the work. This enraged Clérisseau, who cried, "It's my blood, the purest of my blood. I value my portfolios three millions sterling."[28] This visit probably occurred between May 25, 1772, when Lord Harcourt was listed as a general in the Army and returned to England, and before October 9 of that year, when he was named lord lieutenant of Ireland.[29]

It is possible that, at this time, Clérisseau was asked to replace six mirrors in the central section of a mid-seventeenth-century French cabinet, now at Windsor Castle. This he did with gouache scenes of Roman ruins (Fig. 134).[30] Three of the drawings cover the two slanting sides and back wall of a recess in the center of the desk. They are separated by carved wooden corkscrew columns, which support the ceiling of the recess executed in trompe l'oeil (probably not by Clérisseau). The other two drawings flank the recess. At first glance the drawings seem continuous in depicting an antique interior, the two outside drawings being the side walls and the center one a niched end—a sort of miniature ruin room. A closer look at the side drawings shows that the antique scenes are shown from a different viewpoint.

During this period, Clérisseau's work was adapted as part of the decoration on another piece of furniture, the elaborate George III satinwood-and-marquetry cabinet-on-stand made for the Craven family, probably for William, sixth Baron Craven (1738–81), who inherited the Craven properties from his uncle in 1769. The drawers and central cupboard front are inlaid with views of medieval castles and abbeys. Most of these are based on prints from *Bucks' Antiquities,* published in 1774, though the view of Combe Abbey is taken from an earlier publication.

Figure 134. Cabinet with inset scenes by Clérisseau, Windsor Castle
Royal Library, Her Majesty Queen Elizabeth II

The inside of the cabinet doors have inlaid scenes of Classical ruins in engraved, stained, and shaded woods. At least one of these is based on the Clérisseau print "The Temple of Augustus at Pola," from the series published in 1766.[31]

Clérisseau was not the first artist to introduce gouache into England, but he was one of the early exponents of this new medium, and his work, together with that of Marco Ricci (1676–1730), who came to England in 1708, inspired other artists such as Paul Sandby (1725–1809) to use it. Sandby's interest in Clérisseau went beyond his use of gouache. For one thing, he had provided some of the figures for the large plates of Spalato.[32] In 1777–78 Sandby produced a series of architectural scenes of Italy in brown aquatint, after Clérisseau and others. Sandby published some himself, and others in conjunction with Archibald Robertson.[33] He also owned pictures by Clérisseau, including one now in a private collection.[34]

Clérisseau, then living on Great Marlborough Street, exhibited four pictures at the Royal Academy in 1772:

49. "A Bath composed after the Manner of the Ancients."

50. "A Sepulchral Chamber, composed after the Manner of the Ancients."

51. "A View of the forum of Nerva."

52. "A Ruin of a Triumphal Arch."[35]

The *London Chronicle*, May 2–5, 1772, no. 2402, noted that "These drawings have uncommon merit being remarkable for taste, correctness and a variety of teints—a circumstance seldom met with in compositions of architecture."[36]

The vagueness of Clérisseau's titles and the repetition of many of his compositions make it difficult to identify any of these specific pictures, though it seems very possible that number 50 is the "Interior of a Sepulchral Chamber," signed and dated 1772, that is now in the Soane Museum (Fig. 135). The Soane picture is a repetition, with only slight variations in detail, of another made in the previous year, now in a French collection.[37] Stylistically the two are no different from Clérisseau's earlier works; once again, this plausible created scene was obviously assembled from a variety of antique sources. The Ariadnelike figure at the left, the sarcophagus at the right, the usual urn in a niche, and the rinceaux fragments are all carefully arranged in barrel-and-groin vaulted rooms framed with round and segmental arched openings.

Clérisseau also exhibited at the Society of Artists in 1775, 1776, and even as late as 1790.[38] His address is given in a biographical sketch preceding the exhibition listings as "at Mr. Torres' the Golden Head, behind the Opera House, Market Lane, Haymarket." The entry for 1775 also states that he was then "at Paris."

The four drawings exhibited in 1775, after Clérisseau's departure, are of particular interest because they have remained together in England. They were:

61. "The Temple of Vesta at Tivola, a stained drawing."

62. "Nymphaeum at Castel Gandolfo, a stained drawing."

63. "Nymphaeum with a view of Palazolo, a stained drawing."

64. "The Temple of the Sun and the Moon at Rome."[39]

Figure 135. C.-L. Clérisseau, "Interior of a Sepulchral
Chamber," 1772, London, Soane Museum

Figure 136. C.-L. Clérisseau, "Nymphaeum at Castel
Gandolfo," Cambridge, Fitzwilliam Museum

These four works were bequeathed to the Fitzwilliam Museum in 1816 by the seventh Viscount Fitzwilliam. Not only are the titles identical, but three of the four drawings are signed and dated 1774.[40] Again, one notices Clérisseau's method of production. The view of the Nymphaeum at Castel Gondolfo looking inward, exhibited as number 62 (Fig. 136),[41] was based on Clérisseau's original drawing done on the spot and probably the one now in the Hermitage.[42] The Hermitage drawing is a study of the architecture per se, an archaeologically exact study of it as an *aide-mémoire*; whereas the later one, with its picturesquely disposed figures, has a greater emphasis on the variety of texture and the details — it has, in short, been conceived as a decorative view of antiquity.

There are numerous other drawings dating from Clérisseau's years in England. One of the most interesting is the "View of the House of the Crescenzi," signed and dated 1774, now at Burton Constable in the collection of Mr. and Mrs. John Chichester-Constable. A note in the 1791 inventory in the Constable archives states that it was a gift of "Brown," presumably Lancelot "Capability" Brown, the landscape gardener.[43] It is obviously based on Clérisseau's drawing of the same subject in the Hermitage.[44] Another is a large, handsome drawing of the Arch of Constantine, done in 1771, which shows the monument as it looked before 1732, when the heads of the Attic figures were restored by Pietro Bracci.[45] Was Clérisseau following the tradition of not showing ancient monuments in their actual condition? Or was he being a purist by eliminating a recent restoration?

Clérisseau's work inspired many imitators. The Irish architect James Gandon (1742 – 1823), who had worked for Sir William Chambers, produced numerous pastiches in the 1770s and 1780s, and even enlarged a Clérisseau drawing for Sir Watkin Williams-Wynn, the Adam patron who owned several works by Clérisseau.[46] Joseph Bonomi, among others, also produced drawings in this style.

Clérisseau had long enjoyed the patronage of the English. During his many years of residence in Italy, his pictures had a great appeal to those making the grand tour. But he was equally successful when he came to England, and this success continued even after his departure.

VII

Clérisseau in Paris:

1773-80

The exact time of Clérisseau's return to France is not known. He was there in 1775, when the catalogue of his works included in the Society of Artists exhibition in London noted that he was "at Paris."[1] He was almost certainly in Paris when his pictures were included in the Paris Salon in the autumn of 1773.[2] It would seem likely that he was in London in order to submit his design for the library to Lord Shelburne in 1774, but he may have sent it from France. One of the main reasons for believing that he was back in France by the fall of 1773 is that during these months he was engaged in making the designs for a Roman house for Catherine the Great. Charles Cochin, Secretary of the Académie Royale de Peinture et de Sculpture, had recommended Clérisseau for this work.

In France Clérisseau resumed his production of decorative scenes of ruins. At the Salon of 1775 he exhibited several of these. Diderot commented rather unfavorably on one of them:

> As for those architectural compositions in the Ancient style [91] they are gouache and of an earthy color, the touch is heavy and without spirit. The man exaggerates his merit and has never done anything after nature. In his place I should draw and copy excellent pictures. He could learn for this is what LePrince and others have done.[3]

Bachaumont, on the other hand, praised these drawings for their sound taste, bold execution, and profound knowledge of ancient architecture.[4] Typical of this period is a signed and dated "Ruin Scene" of 1775, formerly in the Musée Fourché at Orléans (Fig. 137.)[5] It shows no decline in Clérisseau's style. One might assume

Figure 137. C.-L. Clérisseau, "Ruin Scene," 1775,
formerly at Orléans, Musée Fourché, destroyed

either that Diderot was prejudiced against this type of picture or that he saw one of
Clérisseau's duller works.

On November 25, 1775, Clérisseau received a *logement* at the Louvre on the
first floor of the Pavillon du Gouvernement.[6]

Clérisseau's work for Laurent Grimod de la Reynière (1737–90), which is important for our understanding of the beginnings of the Louis XVI style, has been the
subject of considerable discussion. Confusion has been caused by the fact that
Clérisseau designed two salons for him. Clérisseau's decoration of the grand salon
of Grimod de la Reynière's new house on the rue Boissy d'Anglas, facing the
Champs-Elysées and the Place Louis XV (now the Place de la Concorde), has been
variously dated from as early as 1769 by Louis Réau to as late as 1782 by Bauchal.
Various dates in between have also been suggested by others.[7] Not one of these
scholars, nor many others, with the exception of Mlle. Jeanne Lejeaux, was aware
that Clérisseau decorated the salons of *two* different houses for Grimod de la
Reynière.[8] The most extensive description of the decorations, usually identified
with the Boissy d'Anglas house, does not refer to it at all but rather to the earlier
salon in a house on the rue Grange-Batelière.

The first mention of Clérisseau's association with these two residences for Grimod de la Reynière is in Janson's edition of Winckelmann's *Lettres Familières,* published in 1781. The following is a note to the extracts of the Winckelmann-Clérisseau correspondence.

> . . . we have by him (Clérisseau) two salons which he decorated properly in arabesques for M. de la Reynière, director general of the post office. The first of these is in his old mansion, rue Grange-Batelière, the history painting is by M. Peiron, pensionnaire of the King. The second is in the new mansion on the Champs-Elysées with the history painting by M. Le Chevalier Poussin.[9]

The first residence is also mentioned in Thiéry's *Guide des amateurs et des étrangers voyageurs à Paris,* published in 1787.

> . . . one finds on the left of the rue Grange-Batelière occupied by beautiful hotels. . . . the one that was built by Carpentier, architect to the King for M. Bouret which later belonged to M. de la Bord, then to M. de la Reynière, and lastly to M. Le Duc de Choiseul. One should notice especially a square salon *(salon carré)* which forms a salon for company, decorated with a Corinthian order in wood, the doors and vaults are decorated in the antique style. The historical part of the decoration, consisting of bas-reliefs and the ceiling was done by Perron, Painter to the King. All of the decoration of this room was designed and executed after the drawings of M. Clérisseau, Painter to the King. This artist was limited by the arcades and pilasters already built.[10]

Thiéry's statement clearly refers to an existing house. This statement is confirmed by notary deeds and by Gustave Desnoiresterre's biography of Laurent Grimod de la Reynière, which states that after the death of his father he lived in the rue Neuve des Petit-Champs, and then went to live at the Hôtel Laborde at 3 Grange-Batelière.[11] Laborde sold the house to him for 450,000 livres on September 11, 1770.[12] Grimod purchased the building in order to give himself time to construct his magnificent town house on the rue de la Bonne-Morue (later rue Boissy d'Anglas), which he had purchased on September 12, 1769.[13]

The documents give a fair idea of the decoration of the room. Thiéry's description makes it clear that Clérisseau had to work within an existing room; he also mentions the Corinthian order (columns and pilasters) in wood, and doors and vaults in the antique style. Janson adds that there were painted arabesques. Both writers mention the history paintings, which, according to Thiéry, consisted of imitations of bas-reliefs and the ceiling painting. The spelling of the artist's name is given variously as "Peiron" by Janson and "Perron" by Thiéry, and can be identified as that of Jean-Francois-Pierre Peyron (1744–1814), a history painter who arrived in Paris in 1767. He worked in the studio of Lagrénee the elder and later helped Dandré Bardon on his publication *Collection sur costume des anciennes.* In August 1773 Peyron won the Prix de Rome with a painting of the "The Death of Seneca," and in September 1774 he entered the Ecole royale des élèves protégés and received his *Brevet* on August 31, 1775. He left for Rome in October of that year. In 1781 he returned to France and was admitted to the Academy in 1787. He would have been young at the time that Grimod de la Reynière's house was being decorated, and in the midst of his training before departing for Rome.[14] This identification is strengthened by the fact that in the sale of Clérisseau's possessions after his death, number 15 was a Peyron ink drawing, heightened in white in the style of an antique bas-relief representing a sacrifice.[15] This was perhaps a sketch for one of the overdoor paintings in the salon. Furthermore, Janson refers to Peiron as being a pensioner of the King, and Thiéry called him painter to the King, both posts which Peyron held. Further strengthening the identification with Peyron, it should be noted that Thiéry makes the same spelling error when discussing Peyron as inspector of the Gobelins.[16]

Although Grimod de la Reynière acquired the house in 1770, the decoration must have been done later. The most likely date is between September 1773 and September 1774. By this time Clérisseau would have returned from England, but Peyron would not yet have entered the Ecole des élèves protégés, where he would not have been allowed to undertake commissions.

Documents and later descriptions of the building before its destruction in 1886 provide details about the salon. The deed of April 2, 1778, when Grimod sold the house to Pierre Poncet and Jean Theverin, mentions the "boiserie of the Salon composed of six pilasters painted gray and four overdoor paintings done on linen."[17] During the Revolution many of the rooms of the building were used as stables,[18] but the salon was still intact in 1805 when it was described as having two major doors with carved ornaments and paired arabesques in the panels, with a carved cornice and panel painted on linen above each door; two other doors with the same composition and six Corinthian pilasters are also mentioned.[19]

The building changed hands several times before it was purchased by the government in 1812 and in 1821 it became, as part of the Opéra, a famous *foyer de la danse*[20] where "one could touch the capitals with a hand."[21] Eugène Lami's print of 1841 shows only Clérisseau's wooden pilasters and an elaborate cornice above (Fig. 138). All the rest of the original decoration by Clérisseau and Peyron must have disappeared by this time. The building caught fire on October 28, 1873,[22] but the salon was not damaged. Shortly thereafter A. de Champeaux, curator of the Library of the Union Central des Arts Décoratifs, wrote that the room was decorated with carved wood Corinthian columns and that the overdoors, frieze of the cornice, and ceiling had been painted earlier in the new Pompeian style by Peyron after Clérisseau (he wrote "Perron" which suggests his information had derived from Thiéry). Most important of all, he says that the boiseries survived, were sold, and sent to England.[23] They have yet to be located.

As already mentioned, Laurent Grimod de la Reynière bought the land for his new town house late in 1769. Construction of the building was delayed and the building permit was not issued until November 25, 1775.[24] When Grimod de la Reynière sold his Grange-Batelière house to Pierre Poncet and Jean Theverin on April 2, 1778, the deed specified that, for the price of purchase, the owners were to build a new house for him, using Barré as architect, on the land he owned on the rue de la Bonne Morue. The deed further specified that the new building was to be ready for decoration by June 30, 1779.[25]

The Janson statement, probably written in 1781, has already been quoted in part because it also refers to the first salon. We recall his statement that "the new

Figure 138. "The Green Room of the Opera" (first Grimod
de la Reynière Salon), print by Staines after Lami

mansion on the Champs-Elysées was properly decorated with arabesques by Clérisseau with history painting by M. Le Chevalier Poussin."[26]

Thiéry, who described the first house, also described the second.

> At the beginning of the Champs-Elysées you see the house of M. Grimod de
> la Reynière, Administrator general of the Post Office, built by M. Barré,
> Architect, in which you will notice a square salon decorated from the
> drawings of M. Clérisseau, Painter to the King and first Architect of the
> Empress of Russia. This salon, in the arabesque style, is decorated with
> much sculpture and gilt. The history paintings were executed by M. de la
> Vallée, surnamed Le Chevalier Poussin.[27]

The most important source of information about this room, however, is the
description and drawings of the hotel made in 1782 by the Polish architect Jana
Christyana Kamsetzer (1753–93) while he was in Paris studying the latest styles.
Kamsetzer made seven drawings, including plans, sections, and exterior and interior elevations.[28]

The plan of the house, as depicted by Kamsetzer, shows the location of the
salon at left center (Fig. 139).[29] He describes it thus:

> *The Great Room,* or salon, which is the principal ornament of the house, is
> between the rooms of Monsieur and Madame. One can see the elevation of
> it in plates 3 and 4. It is decorated with arabesques painted in colors on a
> white ground on canvas mounted on a stretcher. These arabesques are

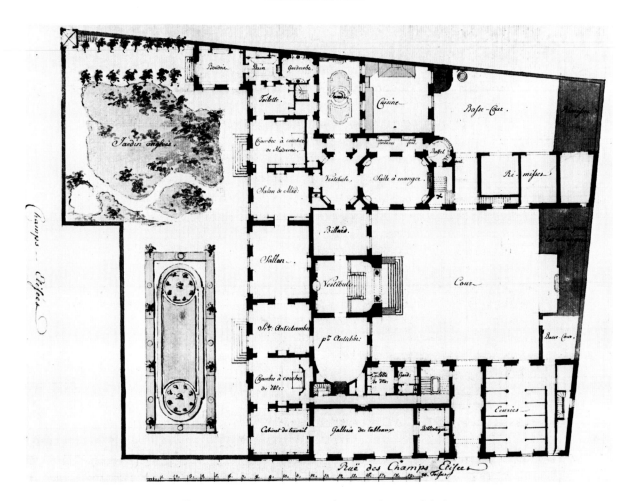

Figure 139. J. C. Kamsetzer, "Plan, Hôtel Grimod de la
Reynière, Paris," Warsaw, University Library

arranged in compartments surrounded by rich gold borders like those surrounding the large mirrors opposite the windows.

The leaves of the doors are of rosewood, and have panels of gray wood decorated with applied trophies in relief. The frieze, crowned by a cyma moulding, forms the cornice, and is ornamented with festoons of flowers and leaves in relief.

The ceiling, plate 5, is in the shape of a large oval with a festoon border of fruits in relief, the picture which is found there represents the three times of the day. Surrounding this is an ornament of figures and vases in half-color.[30]

Kamsetzer went on to describe the carpet and, very briefly, the furniture; he finishes his description of the room by saying that the drawings give an idea of the mirrors, bronzes, and marbles.[31]

Another description of the Grimod de la Reynière salon, contained in the *Almanach des Artistes* of 1777, will not be discussed until later. It has been interpreted by Croft-Murray as describing the room Kamsetzer drew.[32]

Until recently the assumption has always been that this salon was destroyed before the house was torn down in 1928 to make way for the new United States Embassy.[33] Réau believed that the decoration did not survive the French Revolution,[34] during which time it was owned by Grimod de la Reynière's son, Alexandre Balthazar Grimod de la Reynière (1758–1838), the famous gastronome. After his death the building was used by various embassies and clubs until it was acquired by the United States Government.[35] Edward Croft-Murray has convincingly suggested that the Neo-Classic decorations on canvas panels, formerly at Ashburnham Place, near Battle, Sussex, attributed to James "Athenian" Stuart (1713–88), are in all probability the original panels from the salon of the Hôtel Grimod de la Reynière.[36] These are now in the Victoria and Albert Museum. Croft-Murray further suggests that the panels may have been acquired in the 1850's by Bertram, fourth Earl of Ashburnham (1797–1878), who then had them installed at Ashburnham Place. However, he admits the possibility that the panels may be replicas of the original set.[37]

The Kamsetzer drawings of the room (Figs. 140, 141)[38] and its plan (see Fig. 139) indicate that there were eight large panels of arabesques: two of them flanking the fireplace, two at each end of the framing doors, and two presumably between the three windows which repeat the arrangement of the fireplace wall. The drawing of the fireplace wall shows two rinceau strips (see Fig. 140), while the end wall has four (see Fig. 141); thus it appears that the room would have had twelve panels. These totals are the same for the paintings now in the Victoria and Albert Museum (Fig. 142).[39]

The composition of the arabesque panels is the same in the Kamsetzer drawing and the Ashburnham Place panels. Both have large oval scenes in the center, and small roundels above the rectangular plaques framed by arabesque patterns with urns and scrolls. The delicacy of the colors of the original is not apparent in the photographs. The arabesque ornament of the elaborately foliated scrollwork, festoons, flowers, drapery, birds, vases, and tiny medallions is carried out in shades

Figure 140. J. C. Kamsetzer, "Décoration du Salon du côté de la Cheminée,
Hôtel Grimod de la Reynière, Paris," Warsaw, University Library

Figure 141. J. C. Kamsetzer, "Décoration du Salon du côté de la Porte,
Hôtel Grimod de la Reynière, Paris," Warsaw, University Library

Figure 142. C.-L. Clérisseau, Panels from Ashburnham
Place, Sussex, now in London,
Victoria and Albert Museum

of pink, gray, blue-gray, and gray-green heightened with gold, all against a white background. The large ovals, representing the early life of Ulysses, are in full color, while the roundels and rectangular "reliefs" are painted in warm buff on green, Pompeian red, blue, or blue-gray backgrounds. The rinceau strips are in shades of gray against gold-flecked backgrounds. The individual scenes are different, except for one or two of the large paintings;[40] this may be the result of artistic license on Kamsetzer's part. The rinceau strips are exactly as drawn. Therefore, the Ashburnham Place panels are from the salon of Grimod de la Reynière's new house. Croft-Murray's reservations about their being the originals because they are on canvas instead of wood are unfounded, as Kamsetzer clearly states that the paintings were on canvas.

The role of Etienne de la Vallée, later Lavallée-Poussin (c. 1733–93), in the design is not clear. Thiéry writes of him as carrying out the history paintings, and adds that the room was decorated from the drawings of Clérisseau, a statement suggesting that La Vallée may have done the actual painting after Clérisseau's design. This seems likely because La Vallée was primarily a painter, not a designer. He would have been sympathetic to the ideas of Clérisseau because both men had similar antiquarian backgrounds in Italy and were friends of Piranesi. About 1778

La Vallée-Poussin published a book of arabesque designs, *Nouvelles Collection d'arabesques propres à la décoration des appartements,* better known from its 1810 publication by Alexandre LeNoir.

A. de Champeaux was the first to recognize that four paintings representing architecture, painting, sculpture, and music, attributed by M. Feral to Vincent, were part of the decoration carried out by La Vallée for the Hôtel Grimod de la Reynière (Figs. 143, 144). They were in the 1893 sale of Nissim de Comondo, who had been President of the Cercle de l'Union Artistique ou de l'Epatant, an organization which occupied the building beginning in 1887.[41] Each of the four figures in the paintings is placed in the midst of lyrical arabesque decoration. They are undoubtedly part of the original decoration of the building, for the figure representing architecture holds a plan of the house (see Fig. 143), which is identical with the plan drawn by Kamsetzer (see Fig. 139). Champeaux and later M. J. Ballot mistakenly believed these paintings to be part of the salon decoration.[42] This is clearly impossible. From the plan of the town house (see Fig. 139) and Kamsetzer's description, it is not possible to tell where the pictures might have been installed, though perhaps they were in Madame Grimod's salon just beyond the main salon. All four of the panels are the same height, 85 7/8 inches (218 cm.). Two of them, painting and music, are narrower, being 18 15/16 inches (48 cm.) wide. They would therefore fit on either side of the fireplace, while the wider ones, architecture and sculpture, approximately 27 7/8 inches (58 cm.) wide, could have gone in the space between the window and the opposite wall.[43] Kamsetzer mentions that in 1782 Madame Grimod's salon had not yet been finished, and we know that by 1788 La Vallée had not been paid for his work.[44] The case for locating these panels in the smaller salon is strengthened by the possible identification of the woman in the music panel (see Fig. 144) as Madame de Genlis (Félicité du Crest de Saint Aubin) 1746–1831.[45] This gifted musician was often a guest at the house.[46] The identification of the man shown in architecture as Clérisseau has been suggested,[47] but he is more likely to be Barré, the architect of the building, as he is shown holding its plan.

A description of the "Salon de M. de la Reynière newly decorated by M. Clérisseau" appeared in the *Almanach des Artistes* in 1777.[48] This description has been interpreted as applying to the salon in the new, or second, town house,[49] despite the fact that, as reprinted in Duvaux's *Livre-Journal,* it directly follows another *Almanach* item of the same year which refers to M. de la Reynière as living at the rue Grange-Batelière.[50] The *Almanach* description of the room is as follows:

The Salon of Mr. de la Reynière, recently decorated by M. Clérisseau. The pleasant new genre which this artist has used in the arrangement of this salon makes it one of the most beautiful and distinguished. The noble style in which it is treated corresponds to the grandeur of the room which is thirty-eight feet long by twenty-eight wide and high. Consequently the spectator experiences increasing satisfaction as he examines the different parts. The accord and connection between the various elements produce an harmonious whole which one is obliged to admire, and one's astonishment heightens when one notices that the artist was restricted by an existing order and several other defects that he was obliged to keep. He has been able to change them in such a way as to remove ornaments in bad taste and replace them with others of a better choice, so that it is impossible to tell without foreknowledge that this work is a restoration.

The fireplace you see is of precious marble expertly adorned with bronze. It fits perfectly with the four gilt candelabra which grace the four corners of the salon and which are on pedestals of the same marble as the fireplace. These candelabra, the craftsmanship of which is carefully worked, were made by M. Deplessis, the famous Parisian bronze chaser.

The ceiling is eight feet high above the cornice and forty-two feet long. It is entirely the composition of this architect and a perfect match for the rest of the decoration. The four doors are treated in a very interesting way. The painting which ornaments the panels and the over-door harmonizes with that of the ceiling and the adornments which encircle this room are very pleasing and a valuable accomplishment.

Mirrors, the effect of which is so attractive, when they reflect and multiply interesting objects as in the salon of M. de la Reynière. . . . Finally, the beautiful salon that we cite as a model, honors equally the good taste of its owner and the talents of the artist. . . .[51]

This very general description could apply to either house, yet certain items and details indicate that it refers to the earlier room. The problem of the address has already been mentioned, but the strongest reason for believing that the earlier room is being discussed is the reference to its skillful remodeling and the removal of those parts in poor taste. This cannot be a description of a newly built house, and it will be remembered that Thiéry, in describing the first Grimod de la Reynière salon, stated that Clérisseau had to adapt his design to the old forms.[52] The mention of four doors corresponds to the 1805 document describing the first salon, whereas Kamsetzer's drawing and plan show only two doors in the second salon. It is true that the candelabra mentioned in the *Almanach* description of Le Brun are shown in the Kamsetzer drawings (see Figs. 139, 140), but one can assume that Grimod took with him to his new house such elegant pieces. The similarity of the fireplace in the Kamsetzer drawing with the description of the one mentioned in the *Almanach* can be explained. The deed of April 2, 1778, when Grimod sold the Grange-Batelière house, specified that the marble fireplace in the grand salon would have to be replaced, as he was taking the original with him. He also took the four overdoor panels by Peyron.[53] One of these may have been drawn by Kamsetzer, as the painting shown in his drawing (see Fig. 141) is far different in style from the La Vallée-Poussin panels in the Victoria and Albert Museum. The *Almanach*'s statement that the salon was recently decorated by 1777 has led scholars to interpret this as referring to the second salon, yet it can apply equally well to the first salon.

The problem of dating the second house is now clear. First of all, it must have been built after 1777, the year when La Vallée-Poussin, who is mentioned by both Janson and Thiéry as having executed the historical paintings, arrived back from Rome after a stay of nearly fourteen years.[54] Grimod de la Reynière sold his house on the rue Grange-Batelière on April 2, 1778, with the understanding that the

Figure 143. La Vallée-Poussin,
"Architecture" and "Sculpture,"
panels for Hôtel Grimod de la
Reynière, present whereabouts unknown

Figure 144. La Vallée-Poussin,
"Music" and "Painting," panels
for Hôtel Grimod de la Reynière,
present whereabouts unknown

purchasers, Pierre Poncet, entrepreneur of the Kings's buildings, and Jean-Jacques Theverin, would build his new house and have it ready for decorating no later than June 30, 1779. The completion of the sale was on February 11, 1781.[55] Therefore the decoration of the new salon took place between July 1779 and, at the latest, early 1781, when Janson first mentioned the decoration in his note to the French translation of Winckelmann.[56] This salon was completed by 1782, not only because Kamsetzer drew it then, but also because Prince Paul, son of Catherine the Great, and his wife, Marie Feodorovna, while traveling as the Comte and Comtesse du Nord, admired it when they visited Paris that year. After asking who had designed the room, they were introduced to Clérisseau by their host, Grimod de la Reynière.[57]

While we know a great deal less about the first salon of 1773–74, the descriptions of it do mention arabesques, pilasters, and decorations in the Pompeian style. These two rooms, designed by Clérisseau with different collaborators, were executed within approximately six years of each other for the same client. As part of the decoration (Peyron's overdoor paintings, the marble fireplace, and the four candelabra) of the first salon was taken to the second one, we can assume that the two rooms were similar in character even though one was a remodeling and the other a new creation. This is confirmed by the fact that Le Brun's *Almanach* description of the first salon has been thought to apply to the second one, which was drawn in detail by Kamsetzer.

Characteristic of both salons were arabesque decoration, painted doors with Classical details, overdoor paintings of Classical scenes, and probably *grotteschi* panels set into rectangular wall frames. We know from the Kamsetzer drawings that such panels were in the second salon. Thus, the major elements of the new Neo-classic style of decoration are to be seen in both rooms.

Clérisseau may have introduced the style into France,[58] but Piranesi, in *Diverse maniere d'adornare i cammini ed ogni altra parte degli edifizi* of 1769, was the first to show the new, archaeologically correct *grotteschi*, or arabesques, as wall decoration.[59] The black-and-white designs in the book are thinner and more spidery than the elegant and assured work by Clérisseau seen in the panels in the Victoria and Albert and represented in the Kamsetzer drawings.

The earliest arabesque panels (the main characteristic of the new style according to Kimball and others) in France date to 1777 and have been thought to be those by François-Josèphe Bélanger (1744–1818) at Bagatelle. Bélanger's panels have the same delicate quality of Clérisseau's work. This is not surprising for several reasons. In 1769 Bélanger had sought Clérisseau's advice in designing a pavilion in the garden of the Hôtel de Brancas for the Comte de Lauraguais. It even has been suggested that Clérisseau designed *grotteschi* panels for this interior.[60] Furthermore, in 1769 Clérisseau had persuaded Bélanger to send to Rome for Clérisseau's pupil, Nicolas-François-David Lhuiller (d. 1793), who brought with him to France a copy of Piranesi's *Diverse maniere*. This book was a revelation to Bélanger[61] and undoubtedly played a role in his work.

The Grimod de la Reynière arabesque panels have much in common with those of the Adam houses of the late 1760s, such as those at Osterley Park (see Fig. 125). Both have inset plaques of various shapes, vases, fantastic creatures, and arabesque

Figure 145. C.-L. Clérisseau, "Arabesque," Hermitage

foliage. However, Adam's heavier, more robust, white stucco decorations are set on a colored ground, while Clérisseau's are painted in colors against an off-white background (see Fig. 142). The similarity is to be expected, considering Clérisseau's influence on Adam and their use of the same ancient Roman and Renaissance sources. Although Damie Stillman admits that Adam's early arabesques of 1759 for Castle Ashby and Hatchlands are strongly influenced by Clérisseau, he believes that those at Osterley go beyond Clérisseau. He also thinks that Clérisseau's panels for Grimod suggest a knowledge of rooms such as later Adam ones at Osterley and at Kenwood (see Fig. 101), which Clérisseau must have seen when he was in England in the early 1770s.[62] That he was influenced by these seems unlikely, as Clérisseau, with a far greater knowledge of Roman and Renaissance arabesques than Adam, had no need to copy his pupil.

An examination of Clérisseau's drawings makes his independence even more obvious. For example, "Arabesques," one of numerous similar drawings after ancient Roman and Renaissance works now in the Hermitage is part of a group entitled "Arabesques and Ornaments after Antique Monuments" (Fig. 145).[63] It shows all the elements of the Grimod design: the rinceau strips, the round and rectangular plaques, the scrolls, and every detail of the decoration. Such drawings as this, done in Italy by Clérisseau, are surely the inspiration for the Grimod salon.

Clérisseau's originality and his creative ability in the use of ancient Roman and Renaissance decorative forms in wall decoration become even more apparent in his work for Catherine the Great. In 1773 Clérisseau designed a Roman house for the Empress, and his design, which may antedate the first Grimod de la Reynière salon, has all the elements — panels, strips of arabesques, overdoor scenes, and elaborately carved doors — seen in that room.

Clérisseau, Piranesi, Adam, and others working in the middle of the eighteenth century were inspired by the ancient wall paintings, stuccoes, and carvings as well as by the Renaissance works that had been freely adapted from antiquity. The result in each case is somewhat different, yet all of these prove Clérisseau's statement that the arabesques are an "inexhaustible source for decorating in a beautiful way the interiors and exteriors of modern buildings."[64]

During the 1770s Clérisseau was involved, as were many others, with the redecoration and reinstallation of the Grand Gallery of the Louvre under the supervision of Hubert Robert. In October 1777 he suggested that the sculpture be put in the window embrasures, and the following year he was one of a group of architects who fought to preserve the vault at the east end that had been designed by Nicolas Poussin.[65] The same year he advocated the use of natural light, either from skylights or from the vaults. Further, he spoke of the need for remodeling the gallery in order to give it better proportions.[66] Also in 1778, Clérisseau's first and only volume on the Roman antiquities of France appeared.[67] Clérisseau also continued his modest activity as an art dealer, no doubt supplementing his income and being of service to his friends.[68]

VIII

Clérisseau and Catherine the Great:

1773–87

On September 2, 1773, Catherine the Great of Russia, inspired by Michel François Dandré Bardon's volume, *Collection sur costume des anciens* (Paris, 1772), a gift of the sculptor Etienne-Maurice Falconet (1716–91), asked Falconet to write Charles Cochin, Secretary of the Académie Royale de Peinture et de Sculpture, for the name of an architect who could design a house in "Antique" style to be erected in the gardens at Tsarskoe-Selo. This was to be " . . . arranged on the inside *à l'antique* with all of the rooms decorated in the same manner according to their different uses and all the furniture designed accordingly, the house not too large or too small . . . "[1] In November Cochin proposed Clérisseau.[2] On December 6, Catherine agreed that he had all the qualifications to design the house, and asked when the drawings would be ready and how much they would cost.[3] By December 24 the designs—whether they were sketches or finished drawings is not clear— had been submitted.

Catherine was furious because of the immensity of the projected building and its impracticality for northern Russia.[4] Instead of the small house set in a garden that she had expected, Clérisseau had designed a grandiose Roman palace. To date we have not discovered exactly when the final drawings were formally submitted.[5] There are nineteen drawings, including an enormous plan, eight interior elevations, five pairs of arabesque panels, and five drawings of other decorative details. These were accompanied by a five-page explanation, including a copy of the program. All this material is now in the Hermitage.[6]

The plan (Fig. 146) resembles part of Hadrian's Villa at Tivoli.[7] It consists of an elaborate palace containing all the usual rooms, with the addition of a full comple-

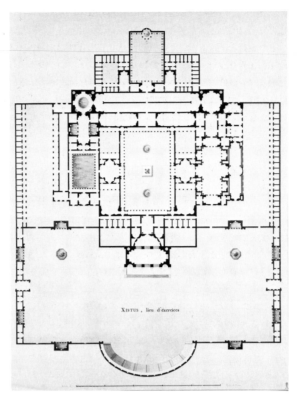

Figure 146. C.-L. Clérisseau, "Plan of The
Roman House Project," Hermitage

ment of Roman baths, plus a series of rooms for religious rites. Situated around the
building itself are exercise areas, an amphitheater, and servants' quarters. The
ceremonial disposition of the rooms, as well as the complexity of their shapes, is in
many ways reminiscent of Diocletian's Palace at Spalato (see Fig. 61). The comparison with Spalato is not exact, however, because Clérisseau's design is that of a huge
villa, not a fortified palace. Perhaps the design for Catherine the Great can best be
described as the Baths of Caracalla set into Hadrian's Villa.

The most striking features of the plan are the various shapes of the rooms
inspired by Clérisseau's study of antiquity. The rectangular grand vestibule (A on
plan) terminates in semicircular apses which have niches carved in them; beyond is
a semicircular room leading to a small vestibule (a). The main focus of the plan is
the open court (T), which Clérisseau called the "Cavedium displuviatum," an area
serving as the center of circulation. The residential quarters are off to the right, the
bath complex to the left. Beyond the court is an assortment of rooms, including the
cryptoporticus, library, tennis court, and temple complex. The plan exaggerates
the formality of Roman architecture, with its sequences of large and small spaces,
its inclusion of vestibules before major rooms, and its axial organization.

Clérisseau's complete description of each room of the house emphasizes his inclusion of all the features of a typical Roman palace. These include (I use Clérisseau's spelling and capitalization): an elaborate Triclinium (B on plan), Pynacotaeca (C), Cubiculum noctes (D), Lararium (F), and Oecus (Q). Also included are the great variety of rooms that make up a Roman bath: Callidarium (H), Piscina (K), Laconicum (L), Apodilerium for undressing (i), Unctarium (g), and Hypocostum (h). The house contained such necessary features as rooms for slaves (P) and service quarters (t).[8] Not only were the names and functions of the rooms influenced by Clérisseau's desire to emulate ancient Rome, but the forms of the rooms were suggested by his study of Roman baths and palaces. The two circular rooms with alternating square and semicircular niches, the Callidarium (H), and the Oecus (Q), were inspired by such buildings as the one Robert Adam referred to as the Temple of Jupiter (now identified as Diocletian's Mausoleum) at Spalato (see Fig. 61). The use of screens of columns to separate niches from the main part of a room, as in the Triclinium (B), can be seen in Clérisseau's imaginative drawings of the 1750s and 1760s (see Figs. 46, 100), which Robert Adam used in his architecture of the 1760s.

Unfortunately, the elevations of the interior are not identified, and seem to have been designed for rectangular or square rooms rather than for the varieties of forms shown in the plan (see Fig. 146). The first impression given by the elevations is of the overwhelming amount of decoration: ruin scenes, rinceau strips, historical scenes, friezes, bas-reliefs, arabesques, and other decorative panels. This array had been carefully organized by Clérisseau, who often conceived of a wall in terms of four horizontal bands. In a typical elevation (Fig. 147),[9] the topmost decoration consists of alternating rectangular and circular historical scenes, painted in imitation of bas-reliefs and framed by plain, flat bands. Beneath these, separated by a simple molding, is the major decorative area of the wall, in this case three large ruin scenes, each set directly under one of the long scenes of the top level. Vertically separating the large scenes are strips of arabesques which extend down through the third area to the fourth band, or wainscoting. Their pilaster-like effect is increased by the projection of the wainscoting to receive them at the bottom, and by their placement under the round paintings at the top of the wall. Roman busts project from the middle of the arabesques. The large ruin scenes are further set off, above and below, by decorative scrolls and Classical scenes. The third band, immediately above the wainscoting, consists of smaller scenes of ruins flanked by roundels and framed with rinceaux. These small pictures are separately framed with the same flat moldings of the large ruin scenes above them. The wainscoting, divided into panels, is decorated with a variety of Roman scrolls and other motifs from antiquity.

The other drawings represent variations within this basic organization. If the doors are shown, they extend up through the two lower bands, and the space above them may have a somewhat different arrangement consisting of a large ruin scene set in the third panel between the doors and of octagonally framed historical scenes placed above doorways (Fig. 148).[10] In such cases there is an elaborate rinceau frieze below the cornice, and this is repeated at the corner in the form of wider vertical strips framing the two doors and the space between them. The use of

Figure 147. C.-L. Clérisseau, "The Roman House Project, Interior Elevation," Hermitage

Figure 148. C.-L. Clérisseau, "The Roman House Project, Interior Elevation," Hermitage

rinceaux has already been seen in the design for the Lansdowne library, contemporary with these designs.[11] The elevations of the larger rooms display the same form, but with variations in the Classical details, the size of scenes, and the organization of motifs, as can be seen in the large drawing of a room with long windows, perhaps the Pynacotaeca (C on plan) (see Fig. 85).[12] The curved ceiling was treated in a similar way. In all these drawings the dominant feature is a scene of ruins, except in two elevation drawings, one of which is a statue in a niche (perhaps trompe l'oeil) occupying the central area (Fig. 149).[13] The basic organization of the rich decoration in these two drawings is similar to that of the others. Clérisseau, unlike Adam, breaks the wall into small panels and, when large paintings of ruin scenes are included, in a manner similar to Adam's design for Osterley (see Fig. 125), Clérisseau surrounds them with stucco decorations presumably to have been painted in bright colors. His decoration is delicate and feathery, as has been seen in the second Grimod de la Reynière salon, yet, in the design for Catherine, this delicacy is less apparent as the multiplicity and closeness of the units gives the project an overdecorated feeling. Even so, Clérisseau's Russian house shows in individual parts some of the delicacy of Adam's work of 1759 at Castle Ashby and Hatchlands, yet also seems to adumbrate his later work of 1780, as in the third drawing room at Cumberland House, Pall Mall (Fig. 150).

Besides the overall drawings for the walls, the designs for the house include elaborate arabesque panels (Fig. 151), and details of various other panel decorations (Fig. 152).[14] This second set is especially interesting because it shows that, inventive as Clérisseau was in composing in the antique style, he sometimes copied the antique exactly. The upper panel shown here is based on a relief from the forum of Trajan, now in the Lateran Museum, Rome.[15] The lower panel is probably based on a frieze from Frascati, now also in the Lateran Museum.[16]

Catherine rejected these designs because of their grandiosity. Falconet tried to mediate by attempting to placate Clérisseau and Cochin on the one hand and the Empress on the other.[17] Catherine and Falconet were reluctant to consent to Clérisseau's demands for payment; though Cochin and Prince Galitzin advised them that Clérisseau should be paid, there is no evidence that he was remunerated.[18]

Evidently all was forgotten by 1778 when Catherine was advised to buy drawings by Clérisseau; she asked Baron Grimm to handle the matter for her.[19] At the same time, Catherine's son, the future Emperor Paul, visited Clérisseau in Paris, where he asked to see the complete set of drawings for the Roman house.[20] Grimm reported his difficulties in dealing with Clérisseau, but was able to buy about 1,170 of the latter's drawings in 1779.[21] Clérisseau's description of the collection is included in Appendix B. It is not clear whether the purchase was made to appease Clérisseau for the loss of the earlier commission, as there may also have been other reasons. Catherine admired French culture in general and, in spite of her difficult dealings with Clérisseau, admired his drawing in particular. Two other opinions reinforced her; Hofret Reiffenstein (1719–93), one of her agents, praised Clérisseau's work,[22] and Catherine also knew that her son thought highly of Clérisseau's drawings. Catherine also made him an honorary member of the Imperial Academy of Arts.[23]

Figure 149. C.-L. Clérisseau, "The Roman House
Project, Interior Elevation," Hermitage

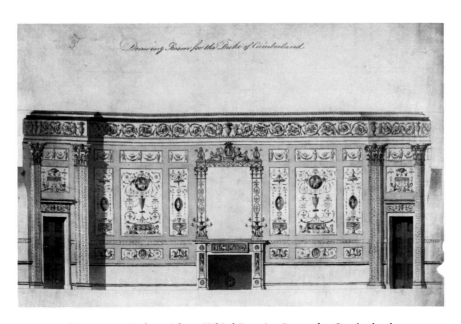

Figure 150. Robert Adam, "Third Drawing Room for Cumberland
House," c. 1780, London, Soane Museum

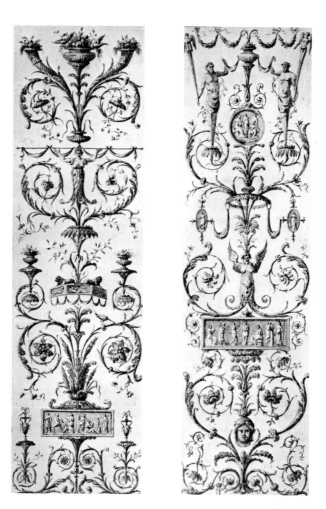

Figure 151. C.-L. Clérisseau, "The Roman House Project, Arabesque Panels," ink and gouache, Hermitage

Figure 152. C.-L. Clérisseau, "The Roman House Project,
Decorative Panels," Hermitage

On November 7, 1780, Catherine wrote Baron Grimm that she wanted Clérisseau
to design a triumphal arch to be built in Russia by Charles Cameron (c. 1740–
1812), the Scottish architect and author of *The Baths of the Romans* (London,
1772), who was then working for her.[24] She requested a complete set of drawings
and a model. In 1781 the model and the drawings (Figs. 153, 154) were sent to
Russia; Catherine found the arch too large and too expensive to build and the
project was abandoned.[25] The drawings are in the Hermitage and the model in the
Academy of Fine Arts at Leningrad.[26] It was to be gigantic in size, with three large
portals. Of these, the center one is depicted with a large, elaborately decorated
semicircular arch; the other two are rectangular openings with Doric columns
supporting flat entablatures and sculpture groups on top. Each portal was to be
flanked by groups of statues executed by the sculptor François Gillet, who also
designed the decorated bases and roundels above. The shorter sides of the arch
were likewise to have portals. Around the top was to be a rinceau frieze surmounted by a cornice, above which was a low attic with additional moldings. The
geometrical severity of the composition resembles Clérisseau's Palais at Metz (see
Fig. 165), which was being built at this time (see Chapter X). The section drawings
give some idea of the complexity of the arch design. The side and end portals were
to have elaborate coffered vaults supported inside by Doric columns, so that the
whole interior of the arch would be open. A stairway led to the vaulted attic and to
the top of the arch. The interior walls were also to be decorated with roundels and
reliefs. If the arch had been executed, it might well have been one of the great
triumphal arches of all time.

Even though the arch was never built, Clérisseau's design was not without
influence. Giacomo Quarenghi (1744–1817), the Italian architect working for
Catherine, unpacked the model and later used it as the inspiration for his own
much smaller arch, built in St. Petersburg in 1814. And, in final recognition of

Figure 153. C.-L. Clérisseau, Triumphal Arch Project,
"Façade Principale," Hermitage

Figure 154. C.-L. Clérisseau, Model of Triumphal Arch, detail,
Leningrad, Academy of Fine Arts (from L. Réau and G. Loukomski,
Catherine La Grande . . . , Paris, 1930, 19)

Figure 155. C.-L. Clérisseau, "Architectural Fantasy," 1784, Hermitage

Clérisseau's ambitious designs, Catherine bestowed on Clérisseau the title of "Premier Architecte de Sa Majesté Impériale."[27]

Catherine not only decided that Cameron was to execute Clérisseau's arch, but also later wrote Clérisseau that Cameron was using Clérisseau's drawings in the decoration of her new apartments.[28] In effect, the Cameron Gallery and other rooms at Tsarskoe-Selo, carried out in agate and crystal, were decorated by Clérisseau himself. After the devastation of World War II, when so many of these rooms were destroyed, Clérisseau's drawings and those of Cameron were used in the reconstruction.

When Catherine's son, Prince Paul, and his wife were traveling incognito as the Comte and Comtesse du Nord, they visited Paris in 1782. Clérisseau wanted to pay his respects, but at first he was not received. As mentioned earlier, the royal couple met Clérisseau several days later in the salon of the Hôtel Grimod de la Reynière. There are three accounts of this meeting: one in a letter to Catherine from Baron Grimm on November 4, 1782; a second recorded by Baroness Oberkirch in her *Mémoires;* and a third by de Bachaumont in his *Mémoires secretes.*

According to Baron Grimm's account, several days after Clérisseau's failure to meet them the Russian Prince and Princess went to see the residence of Grimod de la Reynière, where Clérisseau had decorated the main salon. There were more than forty people present and Clérisseau was among the guests. The beauty of the room so struck the Prince that he asked who had designed it, whereupon M. de la Reynière presented Clérisseau. Though received with royal politeness, Clérisseau was rude to the Prince. The Princess tactfully came to the rescue, telling Clérisseau how much she liked the salon, and asked him to send her the drawings and the model. Clérisseau replied that he had already sent the model and the drawings to the Empress. When the Princess explained that she wanted them herself, Clérisseau refused.[29]

Baroness Oberkirch gives a different version. According to her, Clérisseau asked the Prince why he had not spoken to him before. When the Prince replied that he had nothing to say to Clérisseau, the Frenchman answered that he would report this to the Empress. The Prince told him to do so, and everyone was embarrassed.[30] De Bachaumont's briefer account agrees with that of Baroness Oberkirch.[31]

Despite this contretemps, Clérisseau sent Catherine drawings during the 1780s,[32] among them "An Architectural Fantasy" (Fig. 155).[33] Clérisseau maintained this custom for several years, and made it obvious that he expected to be paid, even though Catherine had not ordered them. Finally, in 1787, she instructed Baron Grimm to tell Clérisseau to stop sending them,[34] thus ending her connection with the French artist.

In many ways Clérisseau's relations with Catherine the Great epitomized his career. Although a pioneer and talented designer in the Neo-Classic style, his originality and craftsmanship were never fully recognized. His projects were either not executed or were used by others, and his inability to get along with people added to his difficulties.

IX

Clérisseau, Thomas Jefferson, and the Virginia Capitol:

1785 – 90

In July 1784, Thomas Jefferson left America for France to take up his duties as minister there. For several years he had been concerned with the design for a state capitol building for Richmond, Virginia. On March 29, 1785, James Buchanan and William Hay, two directors of the public buildings, wrote to Jefferson asking him to "consult an able Architect on a plan fit for a Capitol, and assist him with the information of which you are possessed. . . . we wish to unite economy with elegance and dignity."[1] In his reply five months later, Jefferson explained:

> It was a considerable time before I could find an architect whose taste had been formed on a study of ancient models of this art; the styles of architecture in this capital being far from chaste. I at length heard of one, to whom I immediately addressed myself, and who perfectly fulfills my wishes. He has studied 20 years in Rome, and has given proofs of his skill and taste by a publication of some antiquities of this country.[2]

Jefferson did not mention the name of the architect in this letter, nor did he in his letter of September 20, 1785, to James Madison:

> I engaged an Architect of capital abilities in this business. Much time was requisite, after the external form was agreed on, to make the internal distribution convenient to the three branches of government. . . . The plan however was settled. We took for our model what is called the Maison quarrée of Nismes, one of the most beautiful, if not the most beautiful and precious morsel of architecture left us by antiquity. . . . It is very simple but it is noble beyond expression, and would have done honour to our

country as presenting to travellers a morsel of taste in our infancy promising much for our maturer age.[3]

In a later letter to Buchanan and Hay, Jefferson told them of the selection of the Maison Carrée (see Fig. 156) as the model and the reasons for this choice. He wrote that, in considering the problem, two possible procedures presented themselves: one was to have an architect make an original design according to his fancy, the other was to take a model already devised and approved by "the suffrage of the world." Jefferson did not hesitate to decide that the latter method was the best and that the model should be the Maison Carrée at Nîmes, which he called, "the most perfect and precious remain of antiquity in existence." He added that he had not yet seen the building, and knew it only from drawings and others' accounts (presumably Clérisseau's, though he is not specifically named).

When Clérisseau is mentioned as the architect, Jefferson gives a clear indication of impending difficulties in altering the original design.

> As it was impossible for a foreign artist to know what number and sizes of apartments would suit the different corps of our government, nor how they should be connected with one another, I undertook to form that arrangement, and this being done, I committed them to an Architect (Monsieur Clérisseau) who had studied this art 20 years in Rome, who had particularly studied and measured the Maison quarrée of Nismes, and had published a book containing 4 most excellent plans, descriptions, and observations on it. He was too well acquainted with the merit of that building to find himself restrained by my injunctions not to depart from his model. In one instance only he persuaded me to admit of this. That was to make the Portico two columns deep only, instead of three as the original is. His reason was that this latter depth would too much darken the apartments. Economy might be added as a second reason. I consented to it to satisfy him, and the plans are so drawn. I knew that it would still be easy to execute the building with a depth of three columns, and it is what I would certainly recommend. We know that the Maison quarrée has pleased universally for near 2000 years. By leaving out a column, the proportions will be changed and perhaps the effect may be injured more than is expected. What is good is often spoiled by trying to make it better.[4]

Besides the modifications of the portico depth, Clérisseau suggested, at least in part, another change mentioned many years later in Jefferson's *Autobiography*.

> I applied to M. Clerissault, who had published drawings of the Antiquities of Nismes, . . . to have me a model of the building made in stucco, only changing the order from Corinthian to Ionic, on account of the difficulty of the Corinthian capitals. I yielded, with reluctance, to the taste of Clerissault, in his preference of the modern capital of Scamozzi to the more noble capital of antiquity.[5]

The drawings were sent with Jefferson's letter of January 26, 1786, to Buchanan and Hay. They included "the ground plan, the elevation of the front, and the elevation of the side. The architect having been much busied, and knowing that this was all which would be necessary in the beginning, has not yet finished the Sections of the building."[6] Jefferson added that the models of the front and side in plaster would follow later. Although the completed model was ready in June 1786, it did not leave Le Havre until the following December.[7] The model (Fig. 157) had been made by Jean-Pierre Fouquet (1752–1829), "the artist whom Choiseul Gouffier had carried with him to Constantinople, and employed, while ambassador there, in making those beautiful models of the remains of Grecian architecture which, are to be seen in Paris."[8]

The cornerstone of the Capitol had been laid as early as August 17, 1785,[9] and the foundations begun long before the drawings or the model arrived. The builder, Samuel Dobie, therefore had to adapt the plan to the existing foundations, whose dimensions had been determined by those in charge in Richmond.[10] Three years and two months later, on October 20, 1788, the General Assembly held its first meeting in the building, which was not yet completed. In 1792 the building was still under construction: The cornices were unfinished and much plastering remained to be done. As late as 1797 the hollow brick columns still lacked bases and capitals, and the red brick exterior was not covered with stucco until 1798.[11]

For the sake of economy, the main entablature was made of wood and the enframements of openings were of stucco,[12] although from the beginning Jefferson had envisioned them in stone.[13] The monumental flight of stairs planned for the front of the portico was omitted and windows were inserted in the base of the building instead, presumably to save still more money and to get additional light into the basement offices. Entrance to the building was by means of doors at the sides.

An engraving of about 1830 (Fig. 158) shows the building as it looked when first completed. In 1906 wings were added, the columns enlarged, and their capitals and bases replaced. At the same time, the wooden architrave and frieze were replaced by stone and terra-cotta substitutions.[14] Finally, steps were placed across the front, and the windows in the pediment were removed.[15]

The interior has been so elaborately remodeled over the years that nothing of the original detail remains. The building today is not only very different from the one envisaged by Clérisseau and Jefferson but also greatly changed from the one erected in the 1780s. The adaptations and modifications necessitated by financial and other reasons, as well as the later alterations, make it very difficult to appraise the design, not to mention determine its authorship.

Clérisseau's role in designing the Capitol has been much debated. Fiske Kimball argues persuasively that the building is essentially Jefferson's and that Clérisseau was merely a consultant.[16] Kimball points out that Jefferson's first plans for the Capitol were probably made about 1780, some five years before he met Clérisseau. These plans already showed the Capitol in the form of a temple with a portico at each end (Fig. 159).[17] We may suppose it was at the same time that Jefferson made elaborate calculations about the size and decorations of the proposed rooms. These were later translated into French, and Marie Kimball has suggested that they were given to Clérisseau by Jefferson as a guide.[18]

Figure 156. Maison Carrée, Nîmes, first century A.D.

Figure 157. Fouquet after C.-L. Clérisseau design, model
of Virginia State Capitol, Virginia Capitol

Figure 158. Virginia State Capitol, c. 1830, print, McCormick Collection

Figure 159. Thomas Jefferson, "First Floor
of Capitol," c. 1780, San Marino, CA,
Henry E. Huntington Library

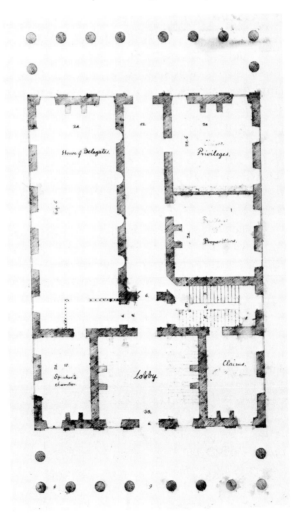

All this does not necessarily mean that the design was solely Jefferson's. We shall never be sure because the documents do not make clear Clérisseau's part in designing the building. All we have is Clérisseau's account of charges and expenditures for architectural work of June 2, 1786.

Debourse pour Monsieur Jeferson.

Les plans de prisons, Coupe et elevation	2 louis
Les plans due model, premier et Rez de chaussé	2 louis
L'elevation de la facade	2 louis
Elevation Laterale	2 louis
Les antiquités de nismes	3 louis
Toutes les mesures et profil lexecution du model	1 louis
	12 louis

Il faut observer que tous ces dessins ont eté obligé destre
fait deux fois avant de les dessiner proprement.[19]

Jefferson entered the following in his account book on the same day: "pd. Clerissault for a book 72 f. pd. do. for plans for state of Virginia 288 f." When he submitted his accounts to the State of Virginia on December 9, 1789, he included the following item: "1786 June 2 pd. Clerissault for his assistance in drawing the plans of the Capitol and Prison 288. 0."[20]

In a letter of June 1786 accompanying his account, Clérisseau wrote that Jefferson was satisfied with the way he had seconded his client's intention.[21] Three years later, Jefferson bought from the Paris silversmith Jean-Baptist-Claude Odiot "a coffee pot as a present to Clerissault for his trouble with the drawings etc. of public buildings, 423 livres."[22]

The drawings for the Capitol offer no more conclusive evidence of the extent of Clérisseau's assistance. None of the surviving drawings can be among those prepared by Clérisseau and sent to Richmond, because they differ from the design. Everyone agrees that the model represents the form of the design as it was intended to be executed. It is assumed that the final drawings, referred to in Jefferson's letter of January 26, 1786, were those lent to Pierre L'Enfant in 1791, now lost.[23] Two drawings, now in the Massachusetts Historical Society (Figs. 160, 161), have been interpreted as being by Jefferson on the basis of style and mediums, with corrections in soft pencil by Clérisseau. They are studies for the building, but differ in many ways from the final design seen in the model. These drawings attributed to Jefferson are certainly inspired by the Maison Carrée, but with the engaged columns replaced by two banks of windows. The portico was made shallower, and the capitals changed to Ionic. Kimball suggests that the soft-pencil alterations of the pitch of the pediment, the addition of consoles, the enframements of openings, and the panels were made by Clérisseau.[24] Most of these changes can be seen in the model. In addition, the moldings, cornice, panels, and capitals of the model have been even further modified, and the columns have been fluted. The result is less a literal copy of the Maison Carrée, as envisioned by Jefferson in his writing and drawings, than a design in the eighteenth-century Roman style of Clérisseau. This is indicated by the sophisticated quality of the model and the garland panels reminiscent of those Clérisseau had designed for Château Borély (see Fig. 119). Similar

Figure 160. Thomas Jefferson and C.-L. Clérisseau,
"Study Front Elevation Virginia State Capitol,"
c. 1785, Boston, Massachusetts Historical Society

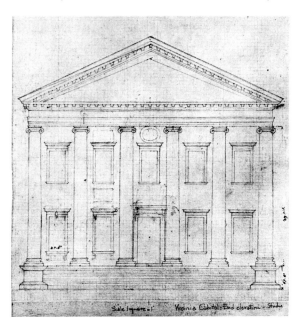

Figure 161. Thomas Jefferson and C.-L. Clérisseau,
"Study Side Elevation Virginia State Capitol,"
c. 1785, Boston, Massachusetts Historical Society

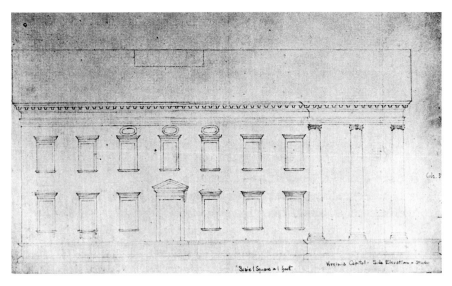

inset panels can be seen in the Palais du Gouverneur at Metz (see Fig. 164). In fact, the composition of the entire side elevation of the model is similar to the building at Metz, which was actually designed, though not completed, before the Virginia Capitol. The Scamozzi type of Ionic capitals on the model were also, as Jefferson wrote in his *Autobiography,* Clérisseau's idea.[25] Jefferson had wanted the purer Ionic of the ancients as shown in his drawing (see Fig. 161), but had been overruled by Clérisseau.

In execution, many other modifications of the design for the Capitol were made. The garlands in the panels were omitted, as were the inset panels above the second story. The columns were not fluted as indicated in the model, and pilasters, not part of the original design, were added to the sides of the building in place of the half-columns of the Maison Carrée. The pilasters do not appear in any of the known drawings of the Capitol, and may have been Samuel Dobie's idea. Although these modifications, including the omission of the portico stairs and the change in materials referred to earlier, probably resulted from a need for economy, Kimball suggests that the omission of the garlands in the panels may represent the new "Greek" taste for simple forms that was developing in the late 1790s, at the time when this part of the building was completed. Kimball suggests that this is a consequence of the presence of Benjamin Latrobe in Richmond at this time.[26]

It is purposeless to discuss the interior of the building in depth because it was greatly modified in execution and has been remodeled over the years. One of Jefferson's early plans[27] shows the three-column-deep portico desired by him and rejected by Clérisseau. That plan also has a large central room with columns which bears little relation to the rotunda of today. However, the existing room preserves more of Jefferson's original building than any other part, even though later doors and moldings give it a strong Edwardian flavor. As far as we can tell, the legislature rooms were almost purely the work of Dobie. The evidence for this is the drawing made at the time of the collapse of the building in the 1870s, which shows a provincial Adam interior, not at all in the Jeffersonian Classical manner.[28] In the design of the interior, as with the exterior, economy evidently played a major role.

Any architectural collaboration raises the question of how much was contributed by each party. While the basic idea for the temple form and the copying of a specific model clearly came from Jefferson, Clérisseau's greater architectural expertise entered into both the design as a whole as well as the specific details. The reduction of the portico depth, the treatment of the windows, the inset plaques, and the change of the capitals from the Corinthian originals to the easier-to-carve Ionic, are features entirely due to Clérisseau. He took Jefferson's idea and adapted the ancient form to a modern building; the result was one of the first large-scale buildings directly based on a specific Roman temple.

Jefferson wrote to William Short in 1789,

"Our new Capitol when the corrections are made of which it is susceptible will be an edifice of first rate dignity. Whenever it shall be finished with its proper ornaments belonging to it (which will not be in this age) it will be worthy of being exhibited alongside the most celebrated remains of antiquity. It's *(sic)* extreme convenience has acquired it universal approbation."[29]

X

The Later Years: Metz, the Weimar Project, and the Second Edition of the Book on Nîmes

Between 1776 and 1778[1] Clérisseau had been asked by the Maréchal de Broglie, Governor of Evêches, to design the Palais du Gouverneur at Metz, now the Palais de Justice. Why he was awarded this commission for the building is not known. The drawings for the ground and first floors, preserved in the local archives, are dated 1778 (Figs. 162–168).[2] Construction started soon after they were finished, but the work dragged on and the building was not completed until about 1785. The plans, which were closely followed, depict it as a U-shaped structure with a large court closed off by a low screen wall containing the entrance gate. At the far right are attached low service buildings, which create a second small court; as executed, this was greatly reduced in size. It appears that Clérisseau merely submitted the plans and returned to Paris, leaving the execution of the design to others.

On approaching the Palais, which is set by itself in a park, one is struck by its tremendous size and mass. Until the twentieth century, it remained the largest structure in Metz. The severity and simplicity of the building are readily apparent, but are relieved by much sculptural decoration, including the piled-up proto-Empire trophies raised on pedestals flanking the entrance gate, the bas-relief in the lunette above, and the allegorical group crowning the geometrically conceived entrance. Human figures in some illustrations give some idea of the great size of the entrance and its flanking windows, as well as of the building as a whole. The façades at the ends of the screen wall containing the entrance express the basic organization of the building. The high ground floor, with its tall windows and smaller ones above, repeats the motifs of the gateway screen; then comes a heavy

Figure 162. C.-L. Clérisseau, "Palais du Gouverneur at Metz,
ground floor plan," 1778, Metz, Archives

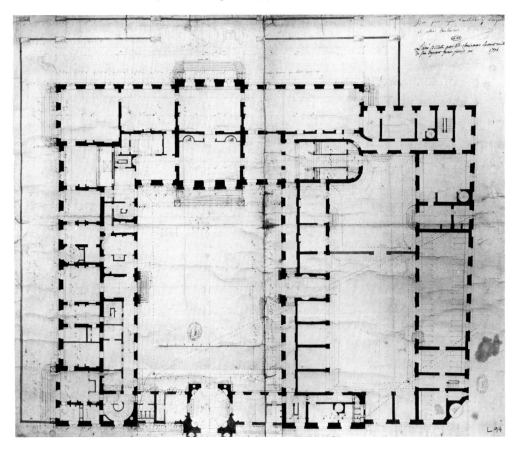

Figure 163. C.-L. Clérisseau, "Palais du Gouverneur at Metz, first floor plan," 1778, Metz, Archives

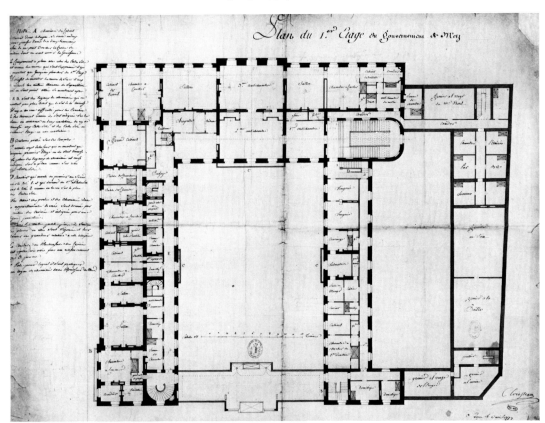

Figure 164. C.-L. Clérisseau, Palais du Gouverneur, Metz
elevations, 1778, Metz, Archives

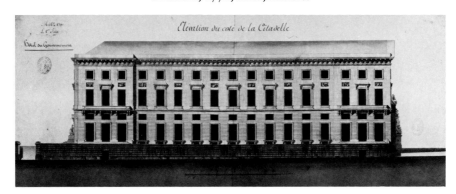

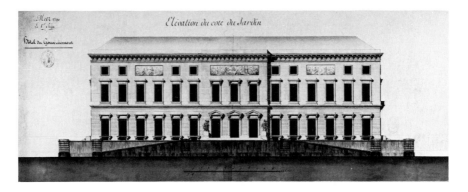

Figure 165. C.-L. Clérisseau, Palais du Gouverneur, Metz, general view

Figure 166. C.-L. Clérisseau, Palais du Gouverneur, Metz, entrance

stringcourse, which is also the top element of the screen. Above this are tall, richly framed, main-floor windows with entablatures supported by consoles, and finally a top floor of squarer, simpler windows. All of the openings are small in terms of the great expanse of flat, undecorated wall. The two sides of the U are crowned by elaborately carved pediments containing allegorical subjects. Below the pediments is the elaborate entablature, with a frieze of triglyphs and metopes, which encircles the whole building.

After passing through the domed gateway, one reaches the huge U-shaped court, about 150 by 110 feet (Figs. 167, 168). Here the three surrounding façades of the court repeat the basic organization seen on the outside of the building; only the treatment of the elaborate entrances to the building from the court is different. Those on the sides of the court are single openings set in severe masonry frames, with open lunettes resembling relieving arches above the lintels. Straight ahead is a set of three pedimented doors forming the main entrance to the building. The richest decoration in the court is on the first floor above these two side entrances: Here the central windows, flanked by statues representing figures of local heroes, are crowned with large historical friezes carved by the sculptor François Masson.[3] Some of the flanking windows of this main floor have simple frames with small reliefs of classical trophies inset above; others, however, have elaborate frames with console-supported entablatures. The top of the wall is crowned by the main entablature, with its simple parapet above, already mentioned as running around the entire building, repeating the form of the top of the entrance gate screen.

The outside façades of the building repeat the same organization. Pavilions are suggested at the ends of the long side in order to break the monotony of the expanse of wall, to which inset reliefs give additional variety. The rear façade, facing the Moselle River, has on the ground floor a central pavilion with sculptural decoration.

While the use of inset panels, carved pediments, and statues recalls Clérisseau's design for Château Borély (see Fig. 119), many of the details here are not so Classical. The entrance trophies and some of the small reliefs were undoubtedly inspired by those on the base of the column of Trajan, which had been drawn by Clérisseau and Piranesi. Most of the reliefs are of relatively recent historical scenes: One depicts the Duke de Guise at the siege of Metz in 1552, another the Treaty of Versailles of 1783. The statues do not represent ancient figures but rather such modern heroes as Guise, Montmorency, Vielleville, and Gannor.

The basic form of the building is typical of the Louis XVI style, and may have been inspired by J. F. Blondel's Hôtel de Ville in Metz of a few years earlier.[4] However, its tremendous size and its profuse wall decoration, contrasting with vast flat areas of wall, are unusual. Janson realized this as early as 1781, when he wrote that "this very large building has the character of grandeur and simplicity which recall antiquity."[5] The geometrical austerity of the massive, often unadorned, forms show Clérisseau's characteristic ability to capture something of the underlying formal quality of Roman architecture. Even the reliefs of modern subjects seem to emulate the spirit of antiquity. In one of the portfolios of drawings that Clérisseau sold to Catherine the Great in 1779, while the Palais at Metz was being built, he wrote that he sought "to conserve the antique character and the

Figure 167. C.-L. Clérisseau, Palais du Gouverneur, Metz, view of courtyard

Figure 168. C.-L. Clérisseau, Palais du Gouverneur, Metz,
sections showing court, 1778, Metz, Archives

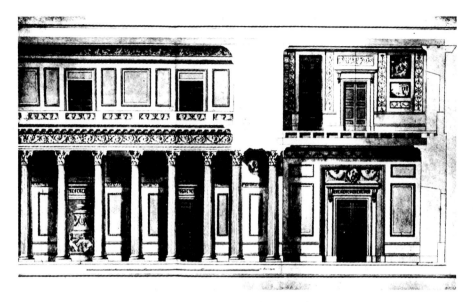

Figure 169. C.-L. Clérisseau, "Great Hall Project for Palace in Weimar,"
1792, present whereabouts unknown (from A Doebber, "Das Schloss
in Weimar," *Zeitschrift des Vereins für Thüringische
Geschichte* . . . , n. f., 3rd supp., 1911, Pl. 7)

air of grandeur which was part of all the antique monuments."[6] This reinforces the
degree to which he was conscious of ancient Roman sources in his designs.

Between 1792 and 1794 Clérisseau, then in his seventies, was involved in the
decoration of the great hall and adjoining room of the Palace at Weimar. His
former pupil, Friedrich von Erdmannsdorff, may have suggested that he be employed, but it was Goethe who wrote Clérisseau, on July 1, 1792, asking for a
design.[7] Letters were exchanged, and eventually the drawings, at least one of which
is dated 1794, were sent to Weimar.[8] Clérisseau was paid for the drawings, but his
project was not executed.[9] His design for the great hall (Fig. 169) had a balcony on
four sides supported by his favorite giant Corinthian columns surmounted by a
rinceau frieze, a combination seen earlier in his Lansdowne library project (see Fig.
129). The walls themselves are divided into panels with friezes and decorative areas
above, and are crowned by a cornice of swags. The elaborate doors recall Clérisseau's similar treatment at Metz (see Fig. 164). The balcony is also reminiscent of
the Metz building. Above it, the transition from wall to ceiling is made with an
elaborate, decorated cove molding similar to that in Clérisseau's second salon for
Grimod de la Reynière (see Fig. 140). The adjoining room was to be decorated with
arabesque panels alternating with ruin scenes, recalling his Roman house design
(see Fig. 147). It is unclear why the project was not carried out as designed, but
probably by that time Clérisseau's Roman style was found to be no longer in
fashion. The hall, as executed in 1802–1803 by Nicolaus Friedrich von Thouret
(1767–1845) and succeeded by Heinrich Gentz (1766–1811), is much simpler
and starker, in keeping with the incoming Greek mode. The columns have become

Ionic and the doors and walls are simple; the only decoration consists of the deep frieze encircling the room and the statues in the niches. Apart from the basic conception of a hall with a balcony supported by columns, the only trace of Clérisseau's design in the room, as finally executed, is the use of a cornice of swags for the balcony frieze.

The Weimar design is the last known architectural project by Clérisseau. However, during these last years of activity, in the 1780s and early 1790s, and in spite of the French Revolution, he had continued to produce characteristic scenes of ruins without any decline in artistic power. Works in various museums show no diminution of his ability to repeat old compositions and invent new ones. Some of the works of this period were exhibited at the Salon of 1783, when Diderot, in analyzing Clérisseau's drawings of "The Arch of Constantine" and "The Interior of a Sepulchral Chamber," congratulated him on his fine taste in arrangement and invention.[10] Diderot complained, as he had earlier, of Clérisseau's limited range of color. As late as 1790 Clérisseau sent six drawings to the exhibition of the Society of Artists in London.[11]

Undoubtedly at the suggestion of von Erdmannsdorff, Clérisseau sold thirteen drawings, one dated 1778 and six of them dated 1790, to Duke Leopold Friedrich Franz von Anhalt-Dessau. These were for the decoration of one of the rooms of the Villa Hamilton, a pavilion designed by von Erdmannsdorff for the gardens of the Palace at Wörlitz between 1791 and 1794.[12] The building was inspired by Sir William Hamilton's villa near Naples, which the architect had visited in 1766. Here Clérisseau repeated many of his earlier subjects, including temples in Rome, Tivoli, and Pola, and introduced some new themes. Earlier, between 1768 and 1773, von Erdmannsdorff had designed the palace at Wörlitz where the wall and ceiling decorations were executed by Johann Fischer (active c. 1760 to after 1800). These included in the Pompeian-style library a fresco portrait of Clérisseau based on a drawing possibly by Fischer or possibly by a French artist (see frontispiece).[13] The drawing may have been sent to Wörlitz or brought by von Erdmannsdorff, as Clérisseau is not known to have visited there either in the 1760s and 1770s or in the 1790s.

The drawings produced by Clérisseau during the last decade of the century declined in number and sometimes in quality. A beautiful one from 1793, in a French private collection, is most accomplished,[14] but later ones dated 1800 and 1801 show a falling off in the depiction of detail and a lack of assurance.[15]

A recently discovered sketchbook, inside of which is written "Clérisseau commence à Montpellier en 1793," contains fourteen drawings in pencil, pen, and wash, three of which are inscribed "Dans le temple de Diane à Nismes en 1793," "Restes d'un temple antique que l'on voit à Vienne," and "Tombeau de la fille d'Youy au jardin des plantes." The others are landscapes, sketches of figures, and studies of ancient remains. While many of the subjects, and in one or two cases the compositions, resemble Clérisseau's work in a general way, these quick and free sketches are stylistically unlike any of the drawings known to me.[16] It is tempting to think that Clérisseau, in his seventies, resumed his study of the Roman remains in southern France, but these charming, slight sketches are not archaeological studies. Were it not for the inscription on the inside of the carnet, Clérisseau's name would not have been suggested.

As in earlier years, Clérisseau's work was widely collected by a variety of people. The architect Etienne-Louis Boullée had three in his collection at his death in 1799, and Clérisseau's neighbor in Auteuil, François Baudelaire (the poet's father), had the same number.[17] Although Clérisseau had not been in England since the early 1770s, he did not sever his ties there. In April 1788 he wrote Charles Greville (1749–1809) about a commission for either M. Darnault or Greville for the design of some bookcases with pictures above them.[18]

Clérisseau does not seem to have been active as an artist during the last twenty-five years of his life, yet these were years of glory for him. In December 1793 J. B. P. Lebrun of the Commission des Arts visited the art collections in Auteuil of Clérisseau, on which his neighbor Hubert Robert and one other unnamed collector reported in detail.[19] In 1801 Napoleon asked for a list of the ten best architects (as well as other artists) who might be considered for membership in the Classe des Beaux-Arts of the Institut, and Clérisseau was named third in a nonalphabetical list.[20] The second edition of his book on the antiquities of Nîmes appeared in 1804. It was prepared by him in collaboration with his son-in-law J. G. Legrand.[21] The same year Napoleon granted him a yearly pension of 600 francs.[22] He exhibited at the Salon of 1808;[23] a portrait of him drawn in the following year shows him as well preserved.[24] In 1810 he was made a member of the Academy of Rouen, and in 1815 Louis XVIII made him a member of the Légion d'Honneur,[25] three years before Percier was decorated.

Clérisseau died at Auteuil on January 19, 1820, aged ninety-nine. His wife and daughter inherited his house at 14 rue Molière, valued at 30,000 francs, and his furniture, worth 4.250 francs.[26] His valuable library, the finest of any architect of his time, and the works of art he owned were sold at auction in December of the same year.[27] By then, he had completely outlived his time, though he had been honored by both Napoleon and the Bourbon Restoration within the previous decade — his death and the sale of his possessions seemed to have created little stir.

Appendix A

Observations sur le Palais projetté pour Sa Majesté Impériale
par le Sr Clerisseau d'après le programe qui lui a été remis par
M. Cochin secretaire de L'accademie Royale de Peinture et Sculpture de Paris,
auquel M. Falconet l'avoir Envoié, par ordre de l'Impératrice et dont il Joint
icy la Copie. [Hermitage, Portfolio N 19, 1773-74]

Copie du Programe

On demande qu'un ou plusieurs de nos Artistes Français veuille-bien
fouiller dans l'antiquité Grecque et Romane pour y trouver une Maison
toute meublée; c'est a dire qu'on demande les desseins d'une Maison
antique, dont l'Exterieur soit décoré precisement comme l'etoient celles
des Romains tant pour le Plan que pour l'Elevation, et dont l'Intérieur
savoir Sales, Chambres, Cabinets etc. soit construit décoré et meublé sur le
costume antique le plus Exactement qu'il sera possible de l'observer.

   On désire que cette Maison ne soit ni fort Grande ni fort petite, elle doit
être bâtie dans un Jardin. On demande que pour la Salle à manger la forme
des Triclinaires soit Exactement observée, et On désireroit qu'il en fut
dessiné, et en Renfoncement quarré et en demie cercle, afin que l'on puisse
choisir ce qui plaira davantage. On demande aussi que chaque meuble soit
dessiné àpart afin qu'en Pais Etranger cela puisse être Executé avec Exactitude.

   Enfin il s'agit de faire une Résumé du siècle et du Pais des Cesars, des
Augustes, des Cicerons, des Mécénas et de faire une Maison pour loger tous
ces Gens là dans une seule Personne.

Après la lecture de ce Programe le Sr Clérisseau crut pouvoir donner carriere à son imagination et rassembler toutes les connoissances qu'il avoit de l'antiquité pour composer le Plan qu'il a l'honneur d'envoier à Sa Majesté; il a taché d'entrer dans l'Esprit du programe qui prescrit la Rigidité du Costume antique: et a composé ce Palais comme s'il eut dû le présenter à Auguste pour être Exécuté à Frascati.* Quand à l'observation du programe qui ordonne que cette Maison ne soit ni fort grande ni fort petite, le Sr Clérisseau n'a jamais pensé que Sa Majesté Impériale voulut faire Exécuter en entier dans son Climat, un projet fait pour l'Italie. Mais il a cru devoir composer ce plan avec tous ses accessoires et dans la Grandeur convenable à la Majesté du Souverain auquel il est destiné, afin que L'Impératrice pui se former une Idée parfaite dela demeure des Cesars, qu'elle put connoitre le Genre de leur décoration intérieure et Extérieure par les Elevations, Coupes et différents détails que le Sr Clériseau Esperoir y Joindre, Si Sa Majesté avoir été contente du plan. Enfin si quelques une de ses pièces avoir assés flatté L'Impératrice pour qu'elle en désirat voir l'Execution, le Sr Clériseau les auroie alors réunies avec ordre dans un même Pavillon et auroit fourni tous les moyens de l'Exécuter dans un Jardin comme le programe le dénote.

Noms et Usage des différentes pièces du Plan désignées par les lettres de Renvoi Suivante.

A. *atrium*, Grand Vestibule principale entrée du Palais.

a. *Vestibulum*, Vestibules moins considérables qui précedirent les pièces principales.

B. *Triclinium*, Grande salle de festins. b. Emplacements pour les musiciens et pantomimes qui jouvient pendant le repas. x. Grands Buffets ou étoient arrangés Cimétriquement des vases d'or et d'argent. z. passages pour le service de la Cuisine àlaquelle on descendoit par de petits Escaliers pratiqués à coté. b. *modica caenatio*. Salle à manger plus petite pour les Repas ordinaires.

C. *pynacotaeca*, Grande Gallerie ou l'Empereur conservoit ses portraits de famille et autres éffets très prétieux. Cette Gallerie étoit échauffée ainsi que la Grande salle de festins par de Grand fours pratiques dans l'Epaisseur des murs lesquels se nommoient *hipocostum*.

D. *Cubiculum noctes*, Chambre à Coucher de l'Empereur.

E. *Cella frigidaria*, Sallon frais.

F. *Lararium*, Chapelle ou l'Empereur conservoit ses Dieux Eutélaire

G. *Cripto porticus*, trés Grande Gallerie couverte et rémplie de tableaux, Sculpture et autres objets Curieux, pour se promener pendant la chaleur et le mauvais tems.

H. *Callidarium*, Bains chauds échauffés par dessous. c. sont des Baignoires particulieres.

I. *pronigeum*, Bains tièdes.

K. *piscina*, Bains froids découverts Environnés de Colonnes contenant un grand Bassin assés profond pour y nager.

* Campagne délicieuse et Environs de Rome

L. *Laconicum,* Chambres pour transpirer.

i. *apodilerium,* Chambres pour se deshabiller.

g. *unctuarium,* Chambre pour se parfumer.

h. *hypocostum,* Lieu qui servoit à contenir le feu.

M. *Spheristerium,* Jeu de Paulme.

N. *Bibliotecha,* Bibliotèque.

O. *Porticus servorum,* portique intérieur et Extérieur où se promenoient les Esclaves pendant la Chaleur où la pluie. devant ces portiques est une Grande Cour à leur usage le Long delaquelle sont distribuer leur habitations. La Cour et les habitations apposéer à celle-cy à la droite du plan, étoient destinées aux Soldats de la Garde de l'Empereur, les petites cours et les Logements Situer aux deux Cotés du Grand Vestibule d'entrée, étoient pour les officiers du Palais.

P. *Cubiculum amplum,* Salle des Esclaves.

p. *Cubiculum minus,* petites chambres dont l'usage différoit suivant celui des Grandes pièces qu'elles avoisinoient, celles qui environnent la chambre à Coucher par Exemple servoient à retirer les officiers et les Esclaves utiles au Service de l'Empereur, comme ces pièces ont peu d'Elevation il y en avoit d'autres au'dessus pour le même usage, on y arrivoit par un petit Escalier qui les avoisinoit.

Q. *Oecus,* Grande Sallon où l'Empereur donnoit ses audiences.

R. temple consacré à la Divinité adoptée par l'Empereur.

S. *purificatorium,* purificatoires ou les prêtres se lavoient avant d'entrer au temple. les Cours et les Logements qui accompagnent ces pièces étoient destinés aux Prêtres et contenoient aussi des Etables pour les Victimes.

J. *Area Sacra,* Cour Sacrée environnée de colonnes devant des Pilastres, entre chaque Colonne étoit placée la Statue de l'Empereur où Impératrice qui avoient acquis le titre de *Divin* et audessus entre chaque Pilastre étoit un bas relief qui représentoit l'action mémorable qui liu avoit acquis ce titre Glorieux.

T. *Caveduim displuviatum,* Cours découverte environnée de Logements et d'une Gallerie couverte formée par des Colonnes afin de communiquer à couvert d'un Coté du Palais à l'autre au milieu de cette Cour est une piramide et deux fontaines Jaillissantes.

t. *areola,* petite cour de dégagement pour le Service, au fond desquelles sont des portiques et des Serres marquées s nominée *apotheca. r transitus,* passages de dégagement.

U. *propiteum,* porche qui donnoit entrée à l' enceinte du Palais par *le xistus. xistus,* lieu d'Exercice où se donnoient des jeux, des fêtes, des Courses, et des Combats d'hommes et d'animaux, ce lieu étoit embelli par des fontaines Jaillissantes où les Athletes alloient se désalterer, il étoit aussi environné de bains nominés *Lavacrum* ou les Athletes alloient laver la Sueur et la poussière dont ils étoient couverts pendant les Exercices. Ces Bains étoient décorés de Colonnes, à Coté étoient les Logements des Gladiateurs et les Retraites des bêtes feroces qui combattoient. au milieu du xiste en face de l'entrée du Palais étoit place l'amphiteatre marqué y. *amphitheatrum,* Lieu où l'Empereur et toute sa Cour se plaçoit pour vour les Jeux et Couronner les Vainqueurs, l'ensemble de ce lieu étoit décoré avec Simétrie et une noble simplicité qui n'en Excluoit point la magnificence.

Derrière l'Amphitheatre est l'Echelle du Plan

Il faut observer que la pluspart des pièces sont Eclairées par en haut et que le Sr Cleriseau a tous les détails néçéssaires pour achever les Coupes et Elevations de ce Palais comme est la Coupe du Museum.

Appendix B

Observations sur les différentes
Boîtes qui Composent la Collection
au nombre de 18.

[Hermitage, Portfolio n 19, 1778. Presumably by Clérisseau but the rather haphazard use of accents suggests that this text may have been written or transcribed by someone whose native language was not French.]

La Boîte A contient Près de Cent Chapiteaux variés, tous d'après l'antique; cette Recherche est d'autant plus prétieuse que la pluspart de ces Chapiteaux n'existent plus. Les uns ont été transportés dans différents Pais, d'autres sont entierement mutilés, et d'autres enfin ont servi à faire différents ouvrages de Sculpture comme Bustes, Vases, Etc. l'intention de l'auteur étoit de dessiner les plus intéressants de pareille Grandeur à celui qui est marqué A aussi dans le Grand portefeuille L'avantage qui seroit résulté de ses desseins terminés, eut été de conserver aux arts la forme de ces fragments prétieux et de tendre par là à leur perfection.

La Suite de plafonds qui achevent cette Boéte est aussi puisée dans différents monuments antiques, qui sont chacun désignés au bas du dessein.

La Boîte B contient différentes recherches sur les armes, le costume et les différents instruments des anciens; ces différentes pièces sont puisés d'après des bas reliefs des statues et des peintures antiques où d'après des desseins fort anciens et fort rares qui avoient été puisér dans la même Source.

La Boîte C contient des vases et des candelabres antiques où composés dans le meme Stile. Come on Remarque dans tous ces Vases des formes très nobles, très simples et très variées, qu'ils sont revetus d'ornements Riches et de fort bon Gout, la pluspart pouroient s'exécuter en différentes matieres dans diverses manufactures et en remplacer plusieurs d'une forme triviale et d'un mauvais stile dont en fait communement usage, pour ce l'intention de l'auteur étoit de les Epurer et dessiner plus en grand, en appliquant chacun suivant sa convenance et le dessinant à etre Exécuté en Terre, en Bronse, en argent etc. suivant la nature de sa forme et de ses ornements.

La Boîte D contient des autels antiques des Cercophages où tombeaux qui renfermoient des Corps embaumés, des urnes Cinéraires, des Lampes sepulchrales, des meubles, des pieds de tables etc. ces différentes pièces peuvent encore Servir à la décoration soit intérieur, Soit Extérieure des appartements modernes en les appliquant chacun convenablement. L'auteur avoit aussi projetté d'enformer différents meubles comme poéles, tables, Buffets, Cuvettes, Tombeaux, Exécutables en terre, en marbre, Bois, Bronse Etc.

Les trois Boîtes marquées E contiennent des ornements et arabesques dessinés d'après les monuments antiques soit en peintures, soit en Sculptures. Ces Ornements sont une Source inépuisable pour décorer dans un beau Stile l'intérieur où l'Extérieur des batiments modernes, des meubles et même des habits. Les uns étant propre à être sculptés en marbre, en parie, en Bois, en platre et en Bronses, d'autre en peinture sur le platre; le Bois, la toile, et d'autres enfin en Broderie de soie, d'or et d'argent sur les Etoffes. C'est pour réunir ces différents matériaux que l'auteur a composé le Museum qui en dans le Grand portefeuille.

Les trois Boîtes marquées F contiennent des vues représentant les différent monuments qui subsistent encore à Rome, aux Environs et à différents endroits de l'Italie; ces desseins sont des intentions que l'auteur apris durant son Séjour en Italie, pour enformer des desseins plus terminer où des tableaux. La forme de ces différents monuments peut Encore être utile aux peintres d'histoire et de Paisage qui les emploient souvent comme accessoires dans leurs tableaux.

Les deux Boîtes marquées G contiennent des compositions dans le stile antique, le But que l'auteur s'est proposé dans ces desseins a été de composer des tableaux pittoresques, qui conservassent le Caractére antique et l'air de Grandeur imprimé à tous les monuments des anciens. Les uns sont Supposés être la Ruine d'un seul monument considérable, quelques uns la réunion de plusieurs monuments ensemble, d'autres représentent seulement des fragments qui par leur Grandeur et leur Richesse semblent avoir appartenu à des monuments remarquables.

Les lettres majuscules qui se trouvent dans une des Boîtes, Etoient composées pour orner la diction d'un ouvrage.

Les deux Grandes Boîtes marquées H contiennent des vües des différents monuments de l'Italie dans un format plus grand que celles contenuér dans les Boîtes marquées F elles sont prises dans le même principe et destinées aux mêmes fins.

La Grande Boîte marquée I contient des compositions dans le Stile antique, dans un format plus grand que celles contenues dans les Boîtes marquées G mais absolument dans le même Stile.

L'autre Grande Boîte marquée I. H. Est un mélange des vües d'Italie et de Compositions dans le Stile antique du même format et dans le même Caractere que les desseins des deux Grandes Boîtes marquées l'une d'un I et l'autre d'un H.

Le deux plus Grandes Boîtes contiennent des vües d'Italie qu'il auroit fallu un temps très considérable pour terminer comme l'auteur le désiroit. Son projet étant de les faire Graver dans la même Grandeur qu'elles sont dessinées, afin que tous les amateurs et les artistes puissent avoir devant les yeux des monuments qu'ils se proposent devoir où qu'ils ont déja vus, Il y en à même déja 14 de Gravées dont les planches sont à Londres, mais comme l'auteur a craint de retarder la Jouissance de l'Impératrice il les Joint à sa Collection dans l'Etat où elles se trouvent (*) pour remplir le vuide que l'auteur Eprouvera lorsquil sera dénué. detoutes ses Etudes, il se propose de donner au public plusieurs des objets qui composent la Collection de l'Impératrice et dont il a Extrait des pensées d'après la permission qu'elle a bien voulù lui en accorder et il demande comme un Grace particuliere À Sa Majesté Impériale, de Souffrir quil lui en dédie les Gravures en mettant au bas qu'elles sont tirées du Museum de L'Impératrice de Russie.

(*) pour mieux jouir de l'effect de ces dessins il faut
les regarder un peu de loin et aux lumieres

Appendix C
List of Signed and Dated Drawings by Clérisseau

Date	Title	Location
1753(?)	Arch of Pola, Istria	Christie's, London, Mar. 7, 1984
1754(?)	Arch and Tomb at St. Rémy	Christie's, Mar. 7, 1984
1755	Roman Ruins with Artist	Sotheby's, Feb. 5, 1937
1755	Interior of a Classical Building	Richard Philip
1759	Temple of Minerva, Assisi	Duke of Buccleuch, Drumlanrig Castle, no. 78
1759	Temple of Clitumnus, Spoleto	Duke of Buccleuch, no. 80
1759	Italian Scene	Private coll., France
1759	Italian Scene	Sestieri, Rome in 1965
1760	Temple of Augustus, Pola	Duke of Buccleuch, no. 79
1760	Arch of Augustus, Pola	Bernardi, Praetoria
1760	Temple of Augustus, Pola	Bernardi, Praetoria
1761	Ruined Basilica	ex-Thomas Worsley, Christie's, July 4, 1978, no. 111
1761	Therme at Baia	Didier Aaron, Paris, 1978
1762	Ruins (Door)	Louvre, no. 25242
1762(5)	Ruins	Gore, Ringwood, England
1763	Ruins	Cailleux, Paris in 1988
1763	Ruins with Fountain and Arch	Soane, no. 137
1763	Interior of Ancient Chamber	Soane, no. 129
1763	Ruin of a Roman Bath	Windsor Royal Collection, 13027
1763	Ruin Scene	S. Davidson, Santa Barbara, CA

1764	Vaulted Hall	Soane, no. 64
1764	Capriccio (Door)	Angier, Paris in 1975
1764(5)	Ruins (Door)	B. Ford, London
1764	Roman Bath	Fleming Museum, Burlington, VT
1764	Triumphal Arch and other Monuments	Breteuil sale
1765	Roman Bath	Louvre, no. 25243
1765	Architectural Ruins	Soane, no. 110
1765	Roman Bath	Soane, no. 122
1765	Colosseum	ex-Ralph Edwards, London
1766	Interior with Ruined Vault	Soane, no. F 160(447)
1766	Ponto Rotto	Marquess of Linlithgow, no. L1
1766	Arch of the Goldsmiths	Marquess of Linlithgow, no. L5
.1766	Temple of Antoninus	Marquess of Linlithgow, no. L2
1766	Forum of Nerva	Marquess of Linlithgow, no. L3
1766	Arch of Titus	Soane, no. F 161(448)
1766	Tomb of Vergil	Marquess of Linlithgow, no. L7
1766	Ruins of an Arch	Marquess of Linlithgow, no. L9
1766	Ceiling Sketch	Hermitage, no. 1859
1766	Ceiling Sketch	Hermitage, no. 1860
1767	Château Borély design	Borély, Marseille
1768	Arch at Orange	de Belder, Essen
1769	Falls at Tivoli	Victoria and Albert, no. 14-1872
1769	Classical Scene	ex-Mathews, Poole, England
1769	Ruin Interior	ex-F.T. Sabin, London
1769	Ruin Interior	ex-F.T. Sabin
1769	Ruin Interior	Temple Newsam, Leeds
1769	Ruin Interior	Peretti, Rome
1769	Arch and Tomb at St. Rémy	Victoria and Albert, no. E5151-1910
1770	Ruins	Huntington Library and Art Gallery, San Marino, CA
1770	Baths of Caracalla	Hermitage, no. 2476
1770	Ruins	Musée Cantini, Marseille
1770	Ruined Colonnade	Peretti, Rome
1770	Roman Bath	Marseille
1770	Vaulted Hall	Soane, no. 67
1770	Colosseum	ex-L.G. Duke, Count de Salis in 1971

1770	Ruins, Interior	ex-Christie Miller
1770	Bath	Versailles auction in 1973
1770	Temple of Concord	Versailles auction in 1975
1771	Ruins Side Wall	Soane, no. 68
1771	Architectural Interior	Soane, no. 65
1771	Ruins, Interior	Soane, no. 209
1771	Ruins Interior Sepulchre	Private coll., France
1771	Arch of Constantine	Pröchel, Munich
1772	Ruins Interior Sepulchre	Soane, no. 119
1772	Temple of Concord	Versailles in 1973
1772	Ruins Through Arch	Christie's, Apr. 12, 1983
1772	Capriccio	Sotheby's, Britwell Coll., Mar. 20, 1979 (no. 323)
1773	Ruins	ex-Walker, Galleries, London
1773	Ruins Interior Sepulchre	Soane, no. 97
1774	Castel Gandolfo Nymphaeum	Fitzwilliam, Cambridge, no. 3669
1774	View of Pozzuoli	Fitzwilliam, no. 3670
1774	Temple of the Sibyl, Tivoli	Fitzwilliam, no. 3671
1774	House of Crescentius	Chichester Constable
1774	Ruins	ex-Walker
1774	Ruins	Christie's, 1967 (same as above or copy ?)
1774	Three Designs for Lansdowne Library	Soane, no. LXVIII, 5
1775	Ruins	ex-Gould, New York
1775	Ruins	ex-Mitchell, London
1775	Ruins	ex-Mitchell, London
1775	Ruins	Orleans (destroyed)
1775	Ruins	Knole
1776	Ruins	Knole
1776	Ruins	Knole
1778	Roman Ruins	Wörlitz, no. 1–43
1780	Arch for St. Petersburg and drawings	Hermitage
1781	Ruins, Statue	Hermitage, 16927
1781	Ruins, Bath	Hermitage, 16923
1781	Arch of Titus	Hermitage, 16925
1781	Ruins	Hermitage, 16924
1781	Arch of Constantine	Hermitage, 16916
1781	Ruins with a Niche	ex-Hermitage
1782	Ruins, Triumphal Arch	ex-Hermitage
1782	Interior	Albertina
1782	Ruins	Uffizi
1782	Ruins	Hermitage, 16915
1782	Ruins	Hermitage, 16919

1782	Ruins	Hermitage, 16922
1782	Ruins	Hermitage, 16926
1782	Ruins	Hermitage, 43672
1783	Ruins	Hermitage, 11485
1784	Ruins	Hermitage, 11551
1784	Ruins	Sotheby's, 1976
1788	Ruins, Door	Besançon
1788	Ruins	Besançon
1788	Ruins	Polakovits, Paris
1790	Ruins, Temple of Vesta, Tivoli	Wörlitz, no. 1-47
1790	Rear, Temple of Augustus Pola	Wörlitz, no. 1-42
1790	Ruins, Fountain	Wörlitz, no. 1-37
1790	Ruins, Interior	Wörlitz, no. 1-38
1790	Ruins	Wörlitz, no. 1-40
1792	Palace Salon Design	Weimar
1793 (?)	Sketchbook	ex-Prouté, Paris
1793	Ruins	ex-Cailleux, Paris
1798	Ruins	ex-Parsons, New York
1800	Pantheon	Pupil, Paris
1800	Hadrian's Villa	ex-Prouté
1801	Hadrian's Villa	ex-Prouté

Notes

Chapter 1

1. P. J. Mariette, who wrote what is generally considered to be the first biographical account in his *Abécédario* (before 1774), pub. Paris, 1853, I, 378, gave the year as 1718. The *Biographie universelle* of Paris, 1836, LXI, 125, gives 1720, and the *Nouvelle biographie générale* of 1863, Paris, X, 835, gives 1721. *Lance's Dictionnaire des architectes français,* Paris, 1872, I, 147, gives 1722, citing the registry of the Académie Royale d'Architecture as its source. This last date was followed by the majority of modern scholars and biographers until Mlle. Jeanne Lejeaux solved the problem in 1928 when she found an extract from Clérisseau's baptismal record in his dossier at the Grande Chancellerie de la Légion d'Honneur. This document states that Charles-Louis Clérisseau, the son of Jean Clérisseau, a leading merchant dealing in perfumed gloves, and Jeanne Rosselet, was baptized at the church of St. Germain l'Auxerrois in Paris on August 28, 1721.

J. Lejeaux, "Charles-Louis Clérisseau, architect et peintre des ruines, 1721–1820," *La Revue de l'Art,* LIII, Apr. 1926, 226. I am indebted to M. Ch. Du-courbal, archivist of the Musée Nationale de la Légion d'Honneur, for confirming this information. However, the father was called Rousselau Clérisseau in the memoir by Abbé Bouret during Clérisseau's illness of 1754 (A. de Montaiglon and J. Guiffrey, *Correspondence des Directeurs de l'Académie de France à Rome avec les Surintendants des Bâtiments,* Paris, 1900, XI, 17, no. 4692).

J. Lejeaux, "Charles-Louis Clérisseau, Architecte (28 août 1721–janvier 1820)," *L'Architecture,* 1928, XLI, no. 4, 115.

2. Mariette, *Abécédario,* I, 378; E. Bénézit, *Dictionnaire critique et documentaire des peintres, sculpteurs, dessinateurs et graveurs,* Paris, 1949, I, 540.

3. "Le sieur Charles-Louis Clérisseau, rue Tirechappe. Elève de M. *de Boffrand,*" Lemonnier, *Procès-verbaux,* VI, 40.

4. Mlle. Lejeaux suggests that his commercially minded father may have disapproved of an artistic vocation or that his interest may have revealed itself late. J. Lejeaux, "Clérisseau, peintre," 226.

5. Lemonnier, *Procès-verbaux,* VI, 49.

6. Lemonnier, *Procès-verbaux,* VI, 57, where the medal is also described. Seventeen forty-six is usually given by most authorities as the date of Clérisseau's award. While this is technically correct, he actually won the award for 1745 with the result that this date is sometime given (H. LePauze, *Histoire de l'Académie de France à Rome,* Paris, 1924, I. 295). This unusual procedure was followed because the 1744 awards were withheld (Lemonnier, *Procès-verbaux,* VI, 16) and were then given in 1745 with the understanding that another set of awards would be given in 1746 for 1745 (Lemonnier, *Procès-verbaux,* VI, 37). Clérisseau won this award, and François Brébion won the actual 1746 award (Lemonnier, *Procès-verbaux,* VI, 57). M. A. Duvivier, "Liste des élèves de l'ancienne Ecole Académique et de l'Ecole des Beaux-arts qui ont remporté les grand prix 1663 – 1857," *Archives de l'art francais,* Paris, 1857 – 58, V. 294. Certain biographers such as Bénézit (*Dictionnaire,* 540) and du Peloux (*Répertoire biographique et bibliographique des artistes du XVIIIe siècle français . . . ,* Paris, 1930, 28) give the date as 1751.

7. The program for the competition, as given in Lemonnier, *Procès-verbaux,* VI, 48, was as follows: "Un hôtel pour les bâtimens seulement, sans jardin. Le terrain sera de 40 toises de large sur la rue, sur la profondeur nécessaire jusqu'au mur de face sur le jardin.

"La maison aura 18 à 20 toises de face, le restant pour les basses cours, des écuries, des cuisines.

"Les élèves feront deux plans, l'un pour le rés de chaussée, l'autre pour le premier étage; ils feront aussi la façade de la maison sur la cour et une seconde façade sur le jardin; ces façades seront ornées d'architecture à volonté.

"Enfin les élèves feront une coupe par le milieu du corps de logis sur l'epaisseur du bâtiment seulement.

"L'échelle sera d'un pouce pour toise pour les plans seulement et de 2 pouces pour les élévations et la coupe." M. A.

Duvivier, "Liste des élèves de l'ancienne Ecole Académique et de l'Ecole des Beaux-arts qui ont remporté les grand prix 1663 – 1857," *Archives de l'art français,* Paris, 1857 – 58, V, 294.

8. Lemonnier, *Procès-verbaux* VI, 120 and n. 1.

9. Mlle. Lejeaux speaks of him as waiting around for months ("Clérisseau peintre," 226). Focillon places him in Rome in 1746 (*Giovanni Battista Piranesi,* new ed., Paris, 1928, 56). Hautecoeur (*Histoire,* IV, 10) correctly has him in Rome in 1749, but lists this as the date of his winning the Grand Prix; Mariette (*Abécédario,* I, 378) does not have him go to Rome until 1751.

10. De Montaiglon and Guiffrey, *Correspondance,* X, 176, no. 4678, M. d'Isle à Tournehem; Brevet d'Elève Architecte . . . pour Le Sieur Clérisseau, 184, no. 4692; Extraits des Comptes des Bâtiments du Roi, 177, no. 4681; Lemonnier, *Procès-verbaux,* VI, 120.

11. De Montaiglon and Guiffrey, *Correspondance,* X, 188, no. 4699, De Troy à Tournehem, 2 juillet 1749. A letter from de Troy on the state of the Academy on Sept. 25, 1751 (De Montaiglon and Guiffrey, *Correspondance,* X, 307) lists Clérisseau as arriving in Feb. 1749, but this is a mistake (see De Montaiglon and Guiffrey, *Correspondance,* XVIII, Errata, v). De Troy's letter further states that Clérisseau's term was to end in 1751, which is also a mistake because the normal term was then three years and Clérisseau would have been there only two years by 1751.

12. R. Wunder, "Charles Michel-Ange Challe, A Study of his Life and Work," *Apollo* LXXXVII, Jan. 1968, 24 – 25.

13. J. Harris, "Le Geay, Piranesi and International Neo-Classicism in Rome 1740 – 1750," *Essays in the History of Architecture Presented to Rudolf Wittkower,* D. Fraser, H. Hibbard, and M. Lewine, eds., New York, 1967, 188 – 96. The best discussion of Legeay is by Gilbert Erouart, *L'architecture du Pinceau. Jean-Laurent Legeay, Un Piranesien français dans l'Europe des Lumières,* Paris, 1983.

14. Gouache on paper, $5^7/8 \times 7^3/4$ in. (14.9 × 19.7 cm.) signed *"Clérisseau fecit Roma."* Formerly in the collection of the Walker Gallery, London, which published it in *Walker's Monthly*, no. 78, June, 1934 (unpaginated). Present whereabouts unknown. I am indebted to J. L. Naimaster, formerly of the Walker Gallery, for providing this information and a photograph.

15. The first mention of this is an announcement on Dec. 12, 1766, in the *Public Advertiser* of a set of six prints after drawings by Clérisseau, the figures by Zucchi. Mariette (*Abécédario*, I, 380) wrote sometime before 1774 that Clérisseau employed other artists to draw figures for him. Diderot later suggested that Clérisseau's figures were inferior to the architecture and perhaps were by another hand (D. Diderot, *Salons, 1769, 1771, 1775, 1781,* J. Seznec, ed., Oxford, 1967, 4). Goethe wrote in 1781 that Zucchi drew the figures for the buildings and the ruins of Clérisseau's pictures (J. W. Goethe, *Italian Journey,* trans. by W. H. Auden and Elizabeth Mayer, London, 1962, 157). A Roman *capriccio* with a pyramid and other buildings signed by both Clérisseau and Zucchi appeared at Christie's on July 10, 1973, no. 171. Its present whereabouts are not known.

16. See Marjorie B. Cohn, *Wash and Gouache: A Study of the Development of the Materials of Watercolor,* Cambridge, 1977, 10–11.

17. Amsterdam, Ryksmuseum, R 1963, 286, "Pulchinello," brown pen and gray wash, $11^{13}/16 \times 7^{13}/16$ in. (30 × 20 cm.), signed.

18. The best discussion of these figures is in the exhibition catalogue *Jean Barbault* by Nathalie Volle and Pierre Rosenberg, Rouen, 1974, 53–54, Pl. LXVII–LXX.

19. The cult of ruins in art is discussed in a great number of books including *The Pleasures of Ruins,* by Rose Macaulay, London, 1953, and *Fascination of Decay, Ruins: Relic–Symbol–Ornament,* by Paul Zucker, Ridgewood, N.J., 1968.

20. "Le sr. Clérisseau, architect, et bientot à la fin de ces trois année; il c'et adonné à faires des études dans la gout de *Jean Paul.* Il ya a du talent et cachant bien la perspective et l'architecture, il pouroit bien réussir dans ce genre; il a copié differend tableau d'après le *Paniny.* Il travaille actuelement a un dessin coloré que j'auray l'honneur de vous voyez," De Montaiglon and Guiffrey, *Correspondance,* X, 399, no. 4919, Natoire à Vandières, 19 juillet 1752. Vandières repeated this information in his letter to Natoire of Aug. 21 (De Montaiglon and Guiffrey, *Correspondance,* X, 406, Vandières à Natoire, 21 aoust 1752).

21. Edinburgh National Gallery of Scotland (on loan from the Society of Antiquaries), D3772. "Interior of the aqueduct of the fontana di Trevi, Rome," watercolor, $6^3/8 \times 12^3/8$ in. (16.3 × 31.4 cm.). Inscribed on the verso in Ramsay's hand: "The aqueduct of the Fontana di Trevi with the inscription of Claudius after a drawing of Clérisseau by A. R. 1755." Matthew Brettingham bought a design of a ruin from Clérisseau on Aug. 2, 1753 (Holkham mss. 744). Two drawings of Roman ruins by Clérisseau were purchased by Stephen Breckingham in Rome 1752–53. Sir Brinsley Ford kindly provided me with this information. I have been unable to trace a drawing sold at Sotheby's on Feb. 5, 1937, which is listed as being dated 1755. Two drawings with the impossible dates of 1753 and 1754 will be discussed in Chapters III and V. See also note 91.

22. "A Prospect of the Ruins of the Temple of Jupiter Capitolinus in the Campo Vacino at Rome," engraving, $10^1/2 \times 13^3/4$ in. (26.7 × 35 cm.). "Published as the Act directs April 19th 1756 by T. Major at the Golden Hind in Chandeis Street London. Clerrisseau (sic) fecit, M. Morin sculp." See Chapter II.

23. L. Hautecoeur, *L'Architecture classique à Saint Petersbourg,* Paris, 1912, 40–48.

24. Leningrad, State Hermitage Museum, no. 2323, "The Colosseum," pen and wash, $5^5/_{16} \times 14^1/_8$ in. (15 × 36 cm.). In citing the Hermitage drawings I have given English titles for those drawings whose subjects I identified and have retained French titles for those so inscribed. The few Russian titles inscribed on drawings have been translated into English. Drawings in the Hermitage are hereafter cited as just Hermitage with their number.

25. Detroit, Detroit Institute of Arts, 47.94, "The Colosseum," oil on canvas, $29^1/_8 \times 53$ in. (74 × 134.7 cm.), signed and dated 1735.

26. Hermitage, statement at the beginning of Clérisseau Portfolio N 10 (107).

27. F. Arisi, *Gian Paolo Panini*, Piacenza, 1961, 76, 294. This discussion is omitted from the second edition, Rome, 1986.

28. Numerous oil paintings have been attributed to Clérisseau, including some scenes originally given to Panini or Hubert Robert, but I question all of them because there is no evidence that Clérisseau ever painted in oils. While one of these (no. 1 below) is rather convincingly inscribed on the verso, it too lacks any stylistic relation to Clérisseau's drawings. The best known of these paintings are:

I. Manchester, Whitworth Art Gallery, University of Manchester, no. 0/6/1962, "Capriccio with Classical Ruins," oil on canvas, $25^5/_8 \times 35^5/_8$ in. (65 × 95 cm.), inscribed on verso: "C. Clerisseau *del.*" I am indebted to the late Francis Hawcroft of the Whitworth Art Gallery for arranging for me to study the painting and for providing photographs. Stylistically the picture seems related to *capricci* by Marco Ricci, such as those in the Royal Collection at Windsor Castle.

II. England, Private Collection, "The Colosseum Seen Through a Ruined Arch," oil on canvas, 40 × 50 in. (115 × 127 cm.). According to the present owner, the painting originally bore Clérisseau's signature and was dated 1759; these markings are no longer visible and infrared photographs have not revealed them. The painting resembles the work of Panini but with greater contrasts of light and dark. Servandoni has also been suggested and, on the basis of a photograph, Marianne Roland-Michel has published the picture as such in *Piranèse et Les Français* (Georges Brunel, ed.), Académie de France à Rome II, Rome, 1978, 492, Fig. 6. However, the awkward depiction of a tomb shown in perspective raises doubts about the painting being either by Clérisseau or Servandoni, although the latter's painting in the Ecole des Beaux-Arts is the closest in feeling.

III. Paris, Private Collection, "Capriccio of Classical Monuments," oil on canvas, 38 × 54 in. (96.6 × 149.99 cm.). Formerly attributed to Hubert Robert. The attribution to Clérisseau is by J. Byam Shaw, formerly of P. and D. Colnaghi and Co., on the basis of its similarity to the Whitworth painting, which had also been owned by Colnaghi. Mr. Byam Shaw also suggested that the figures resemble those of Hogarth.

IV. Rome, private collection, "Scene near Arch of Constantine," oil on canvas, 21 × $16^1/_2$ in. (53.4 × 41.3 cm.). Reproduced in *The Connoisseur*, Antique Dealer's number, June, 1959, 32. Exhibited *Il Settecento a Roma*, Rome, 1959, no. 152.

V. Rome, Gallerie Nazionale, no. 941, "Landscape with Laundresses," oil on canvas, dimensions unavailable.

VI. Rome, Gallerie Nazionale, no. 946, "Landscape with Waterfall," oil on canvas, dimensions unavailable. I am indebted to John Fleming for bringing the above two pictures to my attention.

VII. Princeton, The Art Museum, Princeton University, "Classical Landscape," oil on canvas, $14^3/_4 \times 18$ in. (37.5 × 45.7 cm.). This picture is a copy by an unknown artist of Hubert Robert's painting "Le Port de Ripetta à Rome," now in the Ecole National des Beaux-Arts, which is signed and dated 1766. Pierre Rosenberg has informed me that the Princeton painting dates from the nineteenth century. Another version of the subject by Robert, signed and dated 1761, is in the Liechtenstein Collection.

VIII. Dublin, National Gallery of Ireland, "Roman Ruins," oil on canvas, 28³/₄ × 24 in. (73 × 61 cm.). Adolfo Venturi attributed the painting to Piranesi, and Lionello Venturi to Ghisolfi. The National Gallery of Ireland kindly provided me with this information, but I have been unable to find out who suggested the attribution to Clérisseau. Attributions to Jean Barbaut and Jean Jérôme Servandoni have recently been suggested. Fiannuala Croke kindly allowed me to study the painting which bears no resemblance to Clérisseau. I am indebted to the late Curtis Baer for first bringing this painting to my attention.

IX. London, Frost and Reid, formerly, "Classical landscape with Figures," oil on canvas, 17 × 28 in. (43.3 × 71.2 cm.), and "Figures among Classical Ruins," oil on canvas 17 × 28 in. (43.3 × 71.2 cm.). Sold at Sotheby's, March 26, 1969, no. 17, a pair.

X. London, formerly Frank T. Sabin, formerly, "The Colosseum," oil on canvas, "Arch of Constantine and Colosseum," oil on canvas.

29. An unsigned drawing attributed to Clérisseau in the Royal Institute of British Architects Library, London, B3/10, was first pointed out to me as a copy of a Panini by the late Professor A. M. Friend, Jr. While there is no doubt that the drawing is a copy of the drawing in the Albertina, Inv. 2940, and that the two drawings are approximately the same size (Albertina, 14¹/₈ × 10 in.; RIBA, 13³/₄ × 9³/₄ in.), there is no evidence that the RIBA drawing is by Clérisseau. Richard Wunder assures me it is not by Panini.

30. I have already discussed Clérisseau's relations with Piranesi in somewhat more detail in a paper presented at the Colloque Piranèse et les français held at the French Academy in Rome, May 12–15, 1976. It was published as "Piranesi and Clérisseau's Vision of Classical Antiquity" in *Piranèse et les Français 1740–1790* (Académie de France à Rome II), George Brunel, ed., Rome, 1978, 303–14.

31. J. G. Legrand, "Notice historique sur la vie at sur les Ouvrages de J. B. Piranesi, Architecte, Peintre, et Graveur . . . Rédigée sur les pièces communiquées par ses fils les Compagnons et les Continuateurs de ses nombreux travaux" [Paris, 1799], Paris, Bibliothèque Nationale, Mss. nouv. acq. fr. 5968, 129 verso. This biography is published, somewhat inaccurately, in G. Morazzone, *Giovanni Battista Piranesi*, Milan, 1921, 47–77, and more accurately by Andrew Robinson in *Nouvelles de l'estampes*, 5, 1969, 191–226, in *Grapica* 2, 1976, 132–62; and in Gilbert Erouart and Monique Mosser, "A propos de La Notice Historique sur la vie et Les ouvrages de J-B Piranese: origine et fortune d'une biographie," *Piranèse et Les Français*, 213–52. This last is fully annotated.

32. "Ouvrait on une nouvelle fouille, ils y couraient, on s'y trouvaient réunis, souvent sans être avertis et mus par la même curiosité, leur domaine en devenait d'autant plus étendu, cependant ils se fussent réciproquement taxés d'une ambition démsesururée . . . et lorsque les marbriers venaient à la recherche pour trouver dans ces débris de quoi façonner un socle, un buste, un vase de marbre, et qu'ils dérangeaient Le désordre pittoresque de leurs fragmens, c'est ce que nos deux antiquaires appelaient les *incursions des Barbares dans leur états*. Cette réunion donna naissance au bel ouvrage de *Piranesi*, intitulé, *Magnificence de l'architecture des Romains*. Legrand, "Notice historique," 134 recto and verso.

33. Legrand, "Notice historique," 138 verso.

34. Henri Focillon believed that the Panini influence was dominant in the early style of Clérisseau and that only later did Piranesi become important. Focillon, *Piranesi*, 164.

35. "Parte di ampio magnifico Porto all'uso degli antichi Roman," F. 122, Plate 23, *Opere varie d'architettura prospettive, groteschi, antichità*, Rome, 1750.

36. Harris, "Le Geay," 189–96; Wunder, "Challe," 22–33. It is not clear whether Piranesi was influenced by the progressive French or vice versa. Harris argues for the French, and Wunder for Piranesi.

37. Montreal, Canadian Centre for Architecture, "Roman Temple," pen, ink, and watercolor, 15³/₄ × 26¹/₄ in. (40 × 61.7 cm.). Signed and dated 1746.

38. Harris, "Le Geay," 195.

39. Hermitage, no. 2444, Portfolio N11 (108), "Antique Fantasy," pen, ink, and gouache, 8¹/₄ × 12³/₄ in. (21 × 31 cm.).

40. Paris, Louvre, 24241, "Dessin d'Architecture," pen, brown ink, pencil, and dark wash, 14¹/₂ × 9 in. (36.9 × 22.9 cm.). This drawing came to the Louvre during the Revolution as by Clérisseau (Inventaire Morel d'Arleux, no. 11454). I am indebted to Mlle. Roseline Bacou, Conservateur, Cabinet des Dessins, for this information.

41. Werner Oechslin, following the suggestion of Jens Ericksen, has reached the same conclusion independently. See W. Oechslin "Pyramide et sphère, notes sur l'architecture révolutionaire du XVIIIᵉ siècle et ses sources italiennes," *Gazette des Beaux-Arts* 6ᵉ per. LXVII, April 1971, 219–20, Fig. 39. It was exhibited as Challe in the exhibition "Piranèse et les français 1740–1790" (Académie de France à Rome), 1976, 73–74, no. 22, illus. p. 75.

42. "Campidoglio antico" F. 9, Plate VII of first issue, Plate 10 of later one; Hermitage, no. N 2552, "Fantasy," ink and gouache, 10 × 14¹/₈ in. (25.2 × 36 cm.).

43. Hermitage, no. 2477, "Forum of Nerva," ink, gouache, and black chalk, 11⁷/₁₆ × 9³/₈ in. (29 × 23.9 cm.).

44. "Parte di Foro di Nerva," F. 46, Plate 11, *Antichità romane de' tempi della repubblica*, Rome, 1748.

45. Hermitage, no. 11468, "Forum of Augusto," ink, gouache, and pencil, 7⁵/₈ × 11³/₄ in. (19.3 × 29.8 cm.). "Il Foro di Augusto," F. 56, Plate 5, *Antichità romane de' tempi della repubblica*, Rome, 1748. I am indebted to the Department of Special Collections of the Princeton University Library for allowing me to study and have photographed their copy of the collection of Piranesi etchings. This made possible the identification of many of the Clérisseau drawings, including those of the Forum of Augustus and the Temple of Clitumnus mentioned in Chapter IV.

46. "ce sont les études de Clérisseau constamment dirigées sur l'antique, qui le firent changer de manière et lui firent abandonner ces mauvais cartouches dans le goût Napolitain, dont il composait des premiers frontispices pour y substituer ces beaux fragmens antiques d'un travail admirable qui les enrichirent depuis," Legrand, "Notice historique," 136 recto and verso.

47. Hautecoeur, *Rome et la Renaissance de L'Antiquité a La Fin du XVIIIᵉ Siecle*, Paris, 1912, 48. Natoire produced many skillful drawings of Roman ruins during these years. See Chapter II.

48. De Montaiglon and Guiffrey, *Correspondance*, X, 399, no. 4919. See note 20 for complete text. De Montaiglon and Guiffrey, *Correspondance*, X, 406, no. 4924, Vandières à Natoire, 21 aoust 1752.

49. De Montaiglon and Guiffrey, *Correspondance*, X, 411, no. 4926, Natoire à Vandières, 12 septembre 1752; 418, no. 4929, Vandières à Natoire, 16 octobre 1752; 423, no. 4931, Natoire à Vandières, 15 novembre 1752; 431, no. 4940, Vandières à Natoire, 14 janvier 1753.

50. De Montaiglon and Guiffrey, *Correspondance*, X, 307, no. 4843, Etat Présenté à M. Le Directeur Général des Elèves. . . .

51. De Montaiglon and Guiffrey, *Correspondance*, XI, 16, no. 5008, Vandières à Natoire, 28 février 1754.

52. Gusman's statement that Clérisseau, together with de Wailly, Moreau, and Peyre, explored and studied Hadrian's Villa in 1750 must be erroneous, because Peyre did not arrive until 1753 and the other two only in 1754 (P. Gusman, *La Villa Impériale de Tiber, Villa Hadriana*, Paris, 1904, 28).

53. Rome, Gabinetto della Stampe, Farnesina, Vol. 2602, n. 286, "Caricature of Clérisseau," pen and ink, 4⁵/₈ × 3¹/₈ in. (11.6 × 7.9 cm.), inscribed: "Mons. Clériso dilectante di Architettura francese, huomo benestant assai fatto da me Cav. Ghezzi 26 Xbre 1751." This is from an album of 128 pages containing 306 drawings. See F. Hermanin, "Un volume di disegni di Pier Leon Ghezzi, "*Bolletino d'Arte*, I, no. 2, Feb. 1907, 17–24; and M. Benesovich, "Ghezzi and the French Artists in Rome, "*Apollo*, LXXXV, May 1967, 340–47.

54. The original text is given in the preceding note.

55. At least five later noncaricatured portraits of Clérisseau are known to the present writer.

I. Paris, Musée Carnavalet, Album Destailleur, "Half Length Side View Wearing a Cap," black crayon, 6⁹/₁₆ × 5¹/₄ in. (16.6 × 13.3 cm.), inscribed below: "Du Genie des anciens Serère observateur, Ils sut les reproduire en ses savants ouvráges Et se heureux talents d'accord avec son coeur Font revivre la Grèce et la vertu des sages: Nota: Ces vers, comme l'original de ce dessin sont de l'architect Légrand son gendre."

II. Paris, Musée Carnavalet, Album Destailleur, "Side View of Head," black crayon, 4³/₈ × 3³/₁₆ in. (11 × 8 cm.), inscribed below: "Ce portrait de M. Clérisseau architecte a été dessiné d'apres nature en 1809: Il est parfaitement ressemblant quoique fait par surprise, c'est à dire pendant que cet artiste regardoit dess desseins dons son cabinet. C'est a M. Matary, architecte, alors mon dessinateur que je le dois.

Le Masson

Ingenieur"

III. Paris, Lucien Dorbon, "Clérisseau Seated at a Table Drawing, Seen from the Back," engraving, inscribed below in ink: "Clérisseau (Louis) peintre et architecte" and "Clérisseau architect."

IV. Norton, MA, T. J. and M. D. McCormick, "Side View Bust length facing right," black crayon, 8¹/₄ in. (21 cm.), inscribed below: "Charles Louis Clérisseau Premier Architecte de sa Maj. Imp. de Toutes les Russie." The attribution to Anton Graf was rejected by E. Berkenhagen (*Anton Graf*, Berlin, 1867, 419, no. X13). The drawing may be by Johann Fischer (active 1760 - after 1800) who executed a slightly less refined fresco after it for the library of the Schloss at Wörlitz, D. D. R., 16¹¹/₁₆ × 12⁹/₁₆ in. (42.5 × 32 cm.), inscribed "Clerisseau" [see Staatliche Schlosser and Gärten. Wörlitz, Oranienbaum, Luisium, *Charles-Louis Clérisseau 1722–1820 Ruinen Malerei* (Wörlitz, 1984), text by Burkhard Gäbler, pl. 16 where it is dated about 1772]. The drawing and fresco probably date later than this as Clérisseau looks older than fifty-one. The inscription on the drawing must be a later addition as Catherine did not give Clérisseau the title until the 1780s. See Chapter X. Reproduced as frontispiece.

Angelica Kauffmann may also have drawn him. In the sketchbook from Italy (1761–66) in the Victoria and Albert Museum, published by P. Walch ("An Early Neoclassical Sketchbook by Angelica Kauffman," *Burlington*, CXIX, no. 887, Feb. 1977, 98–111), is a portrait of an unidentified man I believe may be Clérisseau. No. 47, (illus. Walch, Fig. 21) black chalk, 7⁹/₁₆ × 5¹/₄ in. (19.2 × 13.2 cm.), depicts a man with a large nose, protruding lips, and sharp eyes, resembling other portraits of Clérisseau. That he is shown holding a book coupled with the fact that the drawing is mounted on the same sheet as a portrait of Winckelmann (and presumably followed it in the original sketchbook) reinforces this idea. I am indebted to Peter Walch for his opinion.

56. London, British Museum, 1859-8-6-269, pen and brown ink, probably over black lead, $19^{13}/_{16} \times 7^3/_4$ in. (53×19.6 cm.). I am indebted to the late Mr. Edward Croft-Murray, Keeper of Prints and Drawings, for allowing me to study this drawing.

57. "Monsieur Clérisseau Francese uno dei Monsionary nell'Acad, di Francia e sendo directores nella Med. Monsieur di Truè il Med.º Mensionario e bravissimo achitetto, il quale allo Camandolsi..l'Eremo a Frascati dell'Em^{in}. il Card^{al}. Domenico Passionei, il quale gli ordino un Disegnio..fare una specie di Arcadia, ad uso di Ticchio Nello Spiarro che a nella Suo Macchia in d.º. Romitorio, il quale lo fece a Meraviglia bene, in presenza d. d.º Em^{in}. fatto da Me Cav.^{1} Ghezzi il di 26 [16?] Agosto 1751 [2] Nella Mia eta di Anni -78-." The two dots occur in the original text and are not ellipses. Professor Robert Marshall of Sweet Briar College and the late Anthony Clark generously helped in this translation.

58. Hautecoeur, *Rome et la Renaissance,* 19.

59. J. J. Lalande, *Voyage d'un français en Italie fait dans les années 1765–66,* Paris, 1769, V, 415; L. Von Pastor, *The History of the Popes,* London, 1935, XXXV, 383.

60. J. Winckelmann, *Briefe,* H. Diepolder and W. Rehn, eds., Berlin, 1952–56, II, III, *passim.*

61. Robert Adam, "Journal of a Tour in Italy," *Library of the Fine Arts,* II, Oct. 1831, 177. This is actually the diary of James Adam. Two candelabra belonging to Cardinal Passionei were in the first Adam sale of 1773, fourth day, March 1, nos. 20 and 21 (A. Bolton, *The Architecture of Robert and James Adam,* London, 1922, I, 327). Perhaps these had been purchased by James during his visit.

62. "Le sr. *Clérisseau* travaille aussy avec beaucoup d'ardeur; il compose avec une grande facilité les morceaux de ruines," De Montaiglon and Guiffrey, *Correspondance,* X, 451, no. 4953, Natoire à Vandières, 15 mai 1753.

63. De Montaiglon and Guiffrey, *Correspondance,* X, 457, no. 4963, Vandières à Natoire, 29 juillet 1753. Charles O'Brien has convincingly argued that Clérisseau was a Jansenist sympathizer and cites a letter from him to the Jansenist magistrate, Lefebvre de Saint-Hillaire, on August 28, 1753, describing the events leading to his expulsion. Further, O'Brien believes Clérisseau later played a major role when Natoire expelled Adrian Mouton from the Academy in 1768. See Charles H. O'Brien, "New Light on the Mouton-Natoire Case (1768): Freedom of Conscience and the Role of the Jansenist," *Journal of Church and State,* 27, no. 1, 1985, 65–82.

64. De Montaiglon and Guiffrey, *Correspondance,* X, 462, no. 4968, Natoire à Vandières, 23 aoust 1753.

65. De Montaiglon and Guiffrey, *Correspondance,* X, 463–64, no. 4969, Clérisseau à Vandières, 28 aoust 1753.

66. De Montaiglon and Guiffrey, *Correspondance,* X, 465–66, no. 4971, Vandières à Natoire, 17 septembre 1753; 471, no. 4978, Vandières à Natoire, 22 septembre 1753; 472, no. 4980, Vandières à Clérisseau, 22 septembre 1753; 474, no. 4985, Natoire à Vandières, 18 octobre 1753; 478, no. 4988, Vandières à Natoire, 30 novembre 1753.

67. L. Bollea, *Lorenzo Pécheux, Maestro di Pittura nella R. Academia delle Belle Arti di Torino,* Turin, 1942, 18.

68. Bollea, *Pécheux,* 365–66.

69. Bollea, *Pécheux* 82.

70. De Montaiglon and Guiffrey, *Correspondance,* X, 482, no. 4993, Natoire à Vandières, 26 decembre 1753; XI, 6, no. 5000, Vandières, à Natoire, 24 janvier 1754; 14, no. 5006, Natoire à Vandières, 20 février 1754.

71. Mariette, *Abecedario*, 379.

72. Mariette, *Abecedario*, 379.

73. De Montaiglon and Guiffrey, *Correspondance*, XI, 17, no. 5009, "Mémoire de l'Abbé Bouret pour Clérisseau"; 18, no. 5010, Vandières à l'Abbé Bouret, 4 mars 1754.

74. De Montaiglon and Guiffrey, *Correspondance*, XI, 17, no. 5009.

75. De Montaiglon and Guiffrey, *Correspondance*, XI, 20, no. 5014, Vandières à Natoire, 13 mars 1754; 21, no. 5016, Natoire à Vandières, 26 mars 1754; 24 no. 5020, "Mémoire présenté à M. de Vandières."

76. "il et sorty de l'Académie sans me rien dire et remply de movaise humeur, comme sy on luy avoit fait encore du tort. C'est une teste attaquée; il faut le laisser pour ce qu'il est; nous en voilà enfin débarrassé," De Montaiglon and Guiffrey, *Correspondance*, XI, 30–31, no. 5026, Natoire à Vandières, 29 mai 1754.

77. ". . . non content d'avoir dessiné dans Rome les antiquités que renferme cette grande ville, il se détermina à faire les mêmes recherches dans toutes les parties d l'Itali. Il alla à Naples, et n'y eut pas un coin des environs qu'il fouillât," Mariette, *Abécédario*, 379.

78. The Hermitage drawings were originally divided into groups, each designated as a portfolio. They now have been reorganized. Piranesi's further influence will be discussed in Chapter IV.

79. See Appendix B. Hautecoeur, *St. Pétersbourg*, 40–48, gives a very general description.

80. Hermitage, no. 1860, Portfolio N I (98). See Chapter IV for a discussion of this drawing.

81. C.-L. Clérisseau letter, September 27, 1754, to a friend in France, 4 pages, sold at Sotheby's, May 9, 1972, no. 544, and now in the Fondation Custodia (coll. F. Lugt), Institut Neerlandais, Paris, no. 1972-A. 754. I am greatly indebted to Mr. Carlos van Hasselt for providing me with a photocopy of the letter and allowing me to study the original.

82. There is no mention of Clérisseau in the vast correspondence of Horace Walpole and Horace Mann.

83. C.-L. Clérisseau letter.

84. Edinburgh, Register House, Clerk of Penicuik Papers, no. 4762, Robert Adam to William, Jan. 31, 1755.

85. W. Chambers, *A Treatise on the Decorative Part of Civil Architecture with illustrations, notes and an examination of Grecian Architecture by Joseph Gwilt*, London, 1825, xxxix.

86. J. Harris, *Sir William Chambers, Knight of the Polar Star*, London, 1970, 5.

87. London, British Museum, Add. 41133 Letter Book, 2-3, Letter from William Chambers evidently to J. D. LeRoy, undated but about Nov. 17, 1769. I wish to thank Mrs. Heather Martienssen of the University of the Witwatersrand for this reference.

88. Harris, *Chambers*, 6.

89. E. Edwards, *Anecdotes of painters who have resided or been born in England with critical remarks on their production . . .*, London, 1808, 72.

90. M. Whinney, *Sculpture in Britain*, 138. Rupert Gunnis is wrong in stating that Wilton arrived in Rome in 1752 (R. Gunnis, *Dictionary of British Sculptors 1660–1851*, rev. ed., London, 1968, 434).

91. I am indebted to John Harris for his opinion on the possible times of the encounter. See also Harris, *Chambers*, 23.

92. Harris, "Le Geay," 195–96, and Figs. 33 and 35: Harris, *Chambers*, 24.

93. London, Victoria and Albert Museum, no. 3339, illustrated in Harris, "Le Geay," Fig. 34. Harris, *Chambers*, Pl. 7.

94. Harris, *Chambers*, 24.

95. W. Chambers, *Plans, Elevations, Sections and Perspective Views of the Gardens and Buildings at Kew in Surrey, the Seat of Her Royal Highness the Princess Dowager of Wales*, London, 1763, Pl. 42.

96. While this may not be clear from the Clérisseau drawings already discussed, those treated in Chapter II are very similar to those of Chambers.

97. Chambers, *Plans, Elevations,* 7. Harris, *Chambers,* 24, also mentions Chambers's 1759 design for York House with a crumbling, flower-strewn cornice.

98. London, Victoria and Albert Museum, no. 5712, location 93 B 21. Its cover is inscribed: *Recueil de Divers Dessein and Architecture and other Ornaments.* This volume contains 520 drawings. I am indebted to John Harris for assistance in finding this volume. See also J. Harris, "Sir William Chambers and His Parisian Album," *Architectural History,* VI, 1963, 54–56.

99. "Valuation and Inventory of Effects at Whitton Place, December 30, 1790.

Library

1 S. W. Chambers Finit Cleriss: 10. 10."

Mrs. Heather Martienssen first provided me with this information but read Finit as lmitn. See Harris, *Chambers,* 24.

100. *A Catalogue of a Valuable Library of Books of History, Antiquities, Architecture, etc. Late the Property of Sir William Chambers, deceased, Architect to His Majesty.* London, Christie's. Saturday July the 16th 1796, 9, no. 79. Inscribed: "bought by Gandon."

101. I have intentionally left out any discussion of the theoretical aspects of Neo-Classicism. There is no evidence that Clérisseau was familiar with the books of Marc-Antoine Laugier (1731–69). They were not included in his extensive library, which was sold after his death (*Catalogue des livres . . . du cabinet . . . Clérisseau . . . 11 . . . 16 Décembre 1820 . . . l'hôtel de Bullion*).

Chapter II

1. Edinburgh, Register House, Clerk of Penicuik Papers, Diary of Robert Adam, Jan. 1755. Ignazio Enrico Hugford (1703–78) was a well-known painter. He owned two Clérisseau pictures which later entered the Uffizi, but they cannot be traced. (J. Fleming, "The Hugfords of Florence," *The Connoisseur,* CXXVI, Dec. 1955, 204–205).

2. Until the discovery of these documents in 1955 it was thought that Adam and Clérisseau had met in France in 1754, when Adam was at the beginning of his grand tour to Italy. Drawings made on the spot show that Adam visited Nîmes on December 13, 1754, and it was assumed that he had been there in the company of Clérisseau, who later published a book on the antiquities of that city. J. Swarbrick, *Robert Adam and His Brothers, Their Lives, Work and Influence on English Architecture, Furniture and Decoration,* London, 1915, 50; J. Lees-Milne, *The Age of Adam,* London, 1947, 18. A drawing by Adam labeled "Sketch of the Tour Magne at Nîmes from the Windmill taken on the spot 13th December, 1754," is in the Soane Museum, Vol. 55, no. 60; Swarbrick, *Adam,* 52; Lees-Milne, *Adam,* 18.

3. J. Fleming, *Robert Adam and His Circle in Edinburgh and Rome,* London, 1962, 134.

4. Edinburgh, Register House, Clerk of Penicuik Papers, Diary of Robert Adam, Jan. 1755.

5. Edinburgh, Register House, Clerk of Penicuik Papers, no. 4762, Robert Adam to William, Jan. 31, 1755; Adam's original spelling and punctuation in the letters has been retained throughout.

6. Lees-Milne, *Adam,* 18; F. Kimball, *The Creation of the Rococo,* Philadelphia, 1943, 213; See Chapter I for Chambers.

7. This is apparent throughout the letters.

8. Edinburgh, Register House, Clerk of Penicuik Papers, no. 4764, Robert Adam to James, Feb. 19, 1755. Meltiths are meals.

9. On Feb. 20, 1755, Clérisseau delivered to Cardinal Alessando Albani (1692–1779) a letter of recommendation and a set of engravings of Alexander Gordon's Egyptian antiquities that the Cardinal had ordered. Vienna, Osterreichisches Staatsarchive, Haus-Hof und Staatsarchiv: Mann-Albani Correspondence, fazc. 161, Mann to Albani, Feb. 21, 1755; Fleming, *Adam*, 144.

10. The problematic relationship with Mengs will be discussed in Chapter IV.

11. Edinburgh, Register House, Clerk of Penicuik Papers, no. 4777, Robert Adam to James, July 4, 1755. For Pécheux, see Chapter I.

12. Edinburgh, Register House, Clerk of Penicuik Papers, no. 4777, Robert Adam to James, July 4, 1755.

13. Edinburgh, Register House, Clerk of Penicuik Papers, no. 4777, Robert Adam to James, July 4, 1755.

14. Hermitage, no. 2257, "Arabesque After the Antique," pen and gouache, 9³/₈ × 9¹/₂ in. (24.4 × 24 cm.); Hermitage, no. 2179, "Garland and Bucraine," pen and wash, 4³/₈ × 9¹/₂ in. (16.2 × 24.1 cm.), inscribed: "a villa Medicis a Rome." The relief depicted was originally part of the Ara Pacis. Hermitage, no. 2223. "Architectural moulding," pen and gouache, 9⁷/₁₆ × 9 in. (24 × 22.5 cm.).

15. Letter from Clérisseau to Huquier, Naples, May 1, 1755, sold Charavay, Paris, *Vente autographs 7-8 novembre 1887*, 14, no. 81, J. Locquin, *La Peinture d'histoire en France 1747 à 1785*, Paris, 1912, 104. The present whereabouts of this letter are not known. I am indebted to the British Museum and the Bibliothèque National, Paris, for making it possible for me to obtain a copy of the Charavay catalogue. Huquier is either Gabriel Huquier (1695–1772) or, more likely, his son Jacques-Gabriel Huquier (1725–1805).

16. Edinburgh, Register House, Clerk of Penicuik Papers, no. 4777, Robert Adam to James, July 4, 1755. "Mr. Wood" is Robert Wood (1716–71) of Palmyra and Baalbek fame.

17. Edinburgh, Register House, Clerk of Penicuik Papers, no. 4778, Robert Adam to Jenny, July 5, 1755. For the relationship between Adam and Piranesi, see Damie Stillman, "Robert Adam and Piranesi," *Essays in the History of Architecture Presented to Rudolf Wittkower*, D. Fraser, H. Hibbard, and M. Lewine, eds., New York 1967, 197–206 and A. A. Tait, "Reading the Ruins: Robert Adam and Piranesi in Rome," *Architectural History*, 27, 1984, 524–28.

18. Edinburgh, Register House, Clerk of Penicuik Papers, no. 4778, Robert Adam to Jenny, July 5, 1755.

19. Edinburgh, Register House, Clerk of Penicuik Papers, no. 4779, Robert Adam to Nelly, July 12, 1755. There is no mention of any of this in Legrand's biography of Piranesi.

20. Edinburgh, Register House, Clerk of Penicuik Papers, no. 4788, Robert Adam to Jenny, Oct. 14, 1755.

21. Edinburgh, Register House, Clerk of Penicuik Papers, no. 4778, Robert Adam to Jenny, July 5, 1755. "And before he [the Duke of Bridgewater] went away he engaged to take some of Clérisseau's Drawings for near to £50 Sterl."

22. J. Fleming, "Robert Adam, the Grand Tourist," *The Cornhill Magazine*, no. 1994, summer 1955, 127.

23. Edinburgh, Register House, Clerk of Penicuik Papers, no. 4764, Robert Adam to James, July 4, 1755. "Degodets" is Antoine Babuty-Desgodetz (1653–1728); Ramsay is Allan Ramsay (1713–84), the Scottish painter.

24. Edinburgh, Register House, Clerk of Penicuik Papers, no. 4811, Robert Adam to James, Sept. 11, 1756. Much later in 1758 James Adam suggested having some of the drawings engraved as part of a proposed publication, Edinburgh, Register House, Clerk of Penicuik Papers, no. 4848, Robert Adam to James, June 17, 1758; Hermitage, Portfolios N 9 (106), N 13 (110), and N 17 (114), for example.

25. C.-L. Clérisseau, *Antiquités de la France: Première Partie, Monumens de Nismes,* Paris, 1778, xiii.

26. Edinburgh, Register House, Clerk of Penicuik Papers, no. 4786, Robert Adam to James, Sept. 6, 1755. Donald was Robert Adam's valet. The letters describing the actual journey are missing.

27. The dating of Clérisseau's drawings is very difficult. While he made original drawings, usually without figures, on the spot; throughout his life he made replicas or variations of these originals. This is borne out by a study of the dated drawings. The round temple at Tivoli, for example, was represented at least seven times, and several of these replicas bear dates ranging from as early as 1774 (long after Clérisseau had left Italy) to as late as 1790. Presumably the original drawing is an undated one without figures.

28. Hermitage, no. 11624, "Temple of Clitumnus," pen, brown ink, and gouache, 11 × 15 in. (27.9 × 38.1 cm.). There is another version of this drawing in the British Museum, LB 4-1877-10-13-942, which was later given the title "Temple, possibly in Dalmatia" (L. Binyon, *Catalogue of Drawings by British Artists and Artists of Foreign Origin Working in Great Britain Preserved in the Department of Prints and Drawings in the British Museum,* London, 1898, 217, no. 4). The correct title of this scene was recognized by the present writer. The most dramatic version of this scene, signed and dated 1759, in the Collection of the Duke of Buccleuch and Queensberry, will be discussed in

Chapter IV. Hermitage, no. 1504, "Waterfall at Terni," pen, brown ink, and gouache, 11¹⁵/₁₆ × 8³/₈ in. (30.3 × 21.3 cm.); Hermitage, no. 11506, "The Arch of Augustus at Fano," pen, brown ink, and gouache, 16³/₄ × 23¹/₄ in. (42.5 × 59.1 cm.). Inscribed on verso: "Arc de Triomphe de Fano"; Norton, MA, McCormick Collection, "Arch of Augustus at Rimini," pen, brown ink, and gouache, 13 × 11 in. (33 × 27.9 cm.). Illustrated in "French Watercolors 1760–1860," University of Michigan Museum of Art, Ann Arbor, Sept. 29–Oct. 24, 1965, Pl. 5.

29. Penicuik House, Midlothian, Sir John Clerk Collection, "n 1–192 View of Antiquity in and about Rome and other Parts of Italy," 188 sketches remaining of an original 192, nearly all in pen, brown ink, and gray wash. A few heightened with watercolor, and a few are in black lead and gray wash or pen and ink only. This volume was on deposit in Edinburgh but is now back at Penicuik House. I am greatly indebted to Sir John Clerk of Penicuik for lending the volume to the Department of Prints and Drawings of the National Gallery of Scotland in order that I might study it. My work was greatly facilitated by the Keeper of Drawings, the late Keith Andrews.

30. J. Fleming, "An Italian Sketchbook by Robert Adam, Clérisseau and Others," *The Connoisseur,* CXLVII, Dec. 1960, 186–94.

31. No. 183, pen, brown ink, and gray with brown wash, 10⁵/₈ × 14⁷/₈ in. (27 × 37.7 cm.), Fleming, "Sketchbook," 187, 192. Fleming suggests that the Adam drawing may be a copy of a Clérisseau, but I think that the slight differences between the two drawings suggest that they were made independently, perhaps side by side.

32. See Chapter I.

33. This was first pointed out by A. A. Tait, "Reading the Ruins: Robert Adam and Piranesi in Rome," *Architectural History,* 27, 1984, 527. I do not agree with his attribution to Clérisseau of any of the Penicuik drawings.

34. Edinburgh, Register House, Clerk of Penicuik Papers, no. 4789, Robert Adam to James, Oct. 19, 1755.

35. Edinburgh, Register House, Clerk of Penicuik Papers, no. 4789, Robert Adam to James, Oct. 19, 1755.

36. Edinburgh, Register House, Clerk of Penicuik Papers, no. 4798, Robert Adam to Jenny, Jan. 31, 1756.

37. Allan Ramsay studied in Italy under Imperiali and Solimena from 1736 to 1738. After achieving success as a portrait painter in London, he returned on several occasions to Italy. His style combines a Scottish forthrightness with a very French feeling. The connection between Ramsay and Clérisseau was first discovered by John Fleming, "Allan Ramsay and Robert Adam in Italy," *The Connoisseur*, CXXXVII, April 1956, 78–84.

38. For example, Edinburgh, Register House, Clerk of Penicuik Papers, no. 4808, Robert Adam to William, May 29, 1756.

39. The six drawings belong to the Society of Antiquaries and are now in the National Gallery of Scotland. I am indebted to the late Keith Andrews for providing this information and for allowing me to study the drawings.
  I. D. 1023, "Inside the Colosseum, Rome," watercolor, 21 × 15 1/8 in. (53.3 × 38.2 cm.).
  II. D. 1027, "The Temple of Venus and Rome, in the Forum," pen and watercolor, 12 × 18 in. (30.4 × 45.6 cm.).
  III. D. 3772, "Interior of the aqueduct of the fontana di Trevi, Rome," watercolor, 6 3/8 × 12 3/8 in. (17.1 × 31.4 cm.). Inscribed on the verso in Ramsay's hand: "The aqueduct of the Fontana di Trevi with the inscription of Claudius after a drawing of Clerisseau by A. R. 1755."
  IV. D. 3773, "The Temple of the Sybil at Tivoli," pencil, 13 3/8 × 8 1/8 in. (13.9 × 20.6 cm.). Inscribed on verso with title and date: "Sept. 29, 1755."

V. D. 3774, "Part of the Colosseum, Rome," watercolor, 14 3/4 × 10 3/8 in. (37.4 × 26.4 cm.). Inscribed on the verso in Ramsay's hand: "by A. R. in the Colliseo 1755."
  VI. D. 3775, "Part of the Colosseum, Rome," watercolor, 14 5/8 × 10 3/4 in. (37.2 × 27.4 cm.). Inscribed on verso in Ramsay's hand: "Drawn in the coliseum by A. R. in Summer 1755."

40. See note 39, no. III.

41. Hermitage, no. 2365, pen and gouache, 7 11/16 × 11 7/8 in. (19.5 × 30.2 cm.). Inscribed on mat: "Vue de La Fontainne de Treve a Rome."

42. Penicuik House, Midlothian, Sir John Clerk Collection, "192 Views," no. 77, "Acqua Vergine in via del Nazareno, Rome," pen, brown ink, gray and brown wash, 8 × 12 3/8 in. (20.3 × 31.4 cm.); no. 106, "Acqua Vergine in via del Nazareno, Rome," pen, brown ink, gray and brown wash, 8 × 12 3/8 in. (20.3 × 31.4 cm.).

43. Fleming, "Italian Sketchbook," 190, 192.

44. See note 39, no. II: Hermitage, no. 2581, "Le temple de Venus et de Rome," pen and gouache, 16 1/4 × 23 1/8 in. (41.2 × 58.7 cm.).

45. See note 39, nos. I, IV, V, and VI.

46. Edinburgh, Register House, Clerk of Penicuik Papers, no. 4808, Robert Adam to William, May 29, 1756; Fleming, "Ramsay and Adam," 78–84.

47. Fleming, "Ramsay and Adam," 78.

48. The drawings by Robert Adam of Tivoli, now at Blair Adam are:
  I. B/5673, "Ruins of Hadrian's Villa at Tivoli," pencil, gray and brown wash, 10 1/8 × 12 1/8 in. (25.7 × 30.7 cm.).
  II. B/5705, "Ruins of Hadrian's Villa at Tivoli," pencil, gray and brown wash, 10 1/8 × 12 1/8 in. (26.7 × 30.7 cm.).
  III. B/5673, "Ruins of Hadrian's Villa at Tivoli," pencil, gray and brown wash, 10 1/8 × 12 1/8 in. (25.7 × 30.7 cm.).

49. See note 48, no. II: Hermitage, no. 2564, "Exterieur d'un temple a la ville Adrienne proche de Rome," pen, brown ink, gray and brown wash, gouache, 16 1/4 × 23 in. (41.2 × 58.3 cm.). Title inscribed on verso.

50. London, Royal Institute of British Architects Drawings Collection, "Adam Works," a sketchbook containing nine drawings, L 12/5 (5), "Hadrian's Villa at Tivoli," black and gray washes, 5 1/4 × 9 1/4 in. (13.3 × 23.5 cm.).

51. London, Royal Institute of British Architects Drawings Collection, "Adam Works," L 12/5 (7). "Scene at Hadrian's Villa," black and gray washes, 8 1/4 × 7 1/4 in. (20.9 × 18.4 cm.); Cambridge, Fitzwilliam Museum, no. 3666, "Hadrian's Villa at Tivoli," gouache, 22 1/8 × 16 3/8 in. (56.2 × 41.6 cm.), signed, inscribed on verso: "a villa adriene proche de Rome," T. McCormick, "An Unknown Collection of Drawings by Charles-Louis Clérisseau," *Journal of the Society of Architectural Historians*, XXII, Oct. 1963, 126.

52. Norton, MA, McCormick Collection. "A Prospect of the Ruins of the Temple of Jupiter Capitolinus in the Campo Vacino at Rome." "Clerrisseau (*sic*) pinx (lower left) M. Morin sculp (lower right) Published as the Act directs. April 19th 1756 by T. Major at the Golden head in Chandois Street London," 10 × 15 in. (25.3 × 38.0 cm.). I have been unable to find any trace of an M. Morin either in England or France. Perhaps, as David Alexander has suggested, Major, who returned from Paris in 1753, kept connections there and the plate may have been engraved in France. The misspelling of Chandos Street would seem to confirm this. An engraved broadside published by Major in 1760 listing all the engravings he has for purchase includes "The Temple of Jupiter" at o. 1. o. For Thomas Major (1720–99) see *The Dictionary of National Biography*, London, 1917, XII, 833–34. I am indebted to Patrick Noon of the Yale Center for British Art for his help in obtaining a copy of the broadside.

53. Penicuik House, Midlothian, Sir John Clerk Collection, "192 Views," no. 8, "The Interior of the Pantheon," pen, brown ink, and gray wash, 11 3/8 × 10 7/16 in. (29 × 26.5 cm.); Fleming, "Italian Album," 192; Hermitage, no. 2328, "Interieur du Panthéon a Rome," pen and gouache, 11 × 10 7/16 in. (27.8 × 26.5 cm.), so inscribed on mat. Inscribed on drawing: "interno del Panteone."

54. Penicuik House, Midlothian, Sir John Clerk Collection, "192 Views," no. 37, "Arch of the Goldsmiths," pen, brown ink, gray and brown wash, 12 × 16 in. (30.5 × 40.6 cm.); Hermitage, no. 2397, "Arch of the Goldsmiths," ink and gouache, 7 5/8 × 12 1/16 in. (19.5 × 30.7 cm.); Fleming, "Italian Album," 188, suggests a parallel to Hermitage, no. 2565, but no. 2397 is much closer.

55. Penicuik House, Midlothian, Sir John Clerk Collection, "192 Views," no. 29, "The Basilica of Maxentius," pen, ink, and wash, 8 1/2 × 15 1/4 in. (21.6 × 38.7 cm.); Norton, MA, McCormick Collection, "The Basilica of Maxentius," pen, ink, and gouache, 7 × 15 in. (17.8 × 38 cm.). Inscribed lower left: "Clerisau." Illustrated in H. Hawley, *Neo-classicism Style and Motif*, Cleveland, 1964, 24.

56. Penicuik House, Midlothian, Sir John Clerk Collection, "192 Views," no. 43, "The Forum of Trajan," pen and wash, 13 1/2 × 16 1/4 in. (34.2 × 41.2 cm.); Hermitage, no. 2563, "Forum of Trajan," pen and gouache, 16 5/8 × 23 3/16 in. (41.5 × 59 cm.).

57. Penicuik House, Midlothian, Sir John Clerk Collection, "192 Views," no. 46, "Grotto of Egeria," pen, ink, and wash, 12 1/4 × 14 1/2 in. (31.1 × 36.7 cm.); Hermitage, no. 2569, "Vue de l'interieur de la grotte de la nimphe Egérie à Rome," so inscribed on verso, pen and gouache, 16 5/16 × 23 3/16 in. (41.5 × 58.7 cm.).

58. Penicuik House, Midlothian, Sir John Clerk Collection, "192 Views," no. 1, "Entry to the Farnese Palace, The architecture of Michelangelo Di Buonarotti Done at Rome 1756," so inscribed above drawing, pen, ink, and wash, 16³/₄ × 24¹/₈ in. (42.6 × 61.3 cm.).

59. Fleming, "Italian Album," 186–94, does not comment on or give a specific attribution for this most important drawing; Hermitage, no. 2589, "Interieur d'un vestibule au Palais Maxime à Rome," so inscribed on verso, pen and gouache, 18⁵/₈ × 14⁵/₈ in. (97.2 × 37 cm.).

60. London, Soane Museum, "Miscellaneous Sketches and Drawings by Robert Adam and Others," no. 41, "Imaginary Landscape," brown ink and gray wash, 15¹/₄ × 22 in. (38.7 × 55.8 cm.), inscribed lower left: "Rome 1756."

61. A. Bolton, *The Architecture of Robert and James Adam,* London, 1922, I, 77–79; A. Bolton, "The Classical and Romantic Compositions of Robert Adam," *The Architectural Review,* LVII, Jan. 1925, 28.

62. I am indebted to Sir John Summerson for confirming my views on this matter.

63. New York, Pierpont Morgan Library, "Album of Landscape Sketches by Robert Adam," 39 drawings, no. 18, "Fantastic Building in a Landscape," pen and wash heightened with white, 10³/₄ × 16⁵/₈ in. (27.3 × 42.2 cm.).

64. Edinburgh, Register House, Clerk of Penicuik Papers, no. 4777, Robert Adam to James, July 4, 1755.

65. Florence, Uffizi, San. 11790, attributed to Lerussou, "Fantastic Building in Landscape," pen and ink, 8 × 11¹/₈ in. (20.3 × 28.2 cm.). I am indebted to the late Professor Ulrich Middeldorf of the Kunsthistorisches Institut, Florence, for telling me about this drawing which he thought was by Clérisseau, as indeed it is. It came to the Uffizi as part of the Santarelli collection in 1866, so that it cannot be one of the Clérisseau drawings which had belonged to Hugford mentioned in note 1.

66. London, Victoria and Albert Museum, no. 3436. 18r. "Fantastic Scene," pen, ink, and wash, 7¹/₂ × 10 in. (10 × 25.4 cm.); London, Victoria and Albert Museum, no. 34. 36. 18V. "Plan and Façade of Palace," pencil, pen, and ink, 7¹/₂ × 10 in. (19.2 × 25.5 cm.), inscribed above: "J'aprouve cette project fait a rome an de grace Mille Sept Cent Cinquante Sept-Clery." I am indebted to John Fleming for bringing this drawing to my attention. See also A. Rowan, *Robert Adam, Catalogues of Architectural Drawings in the Victoria and Albert Museum,* London, 1988, 33–35, nos. 6 and 15. Rowan's suggestion in one of his unpublished Slade Lectures at Oxford in 1989 that Clérisseau's note and the great flourish of his signature was meant to be taken humorously is completely out of character for the architect.

67. Hermitage, no. 2453, "Maison Antique," pen, ink, and wash, 6¹/₂ × 9¹/₁₆ in. (16.5 × 23 cm.). This is not the famous Roman house Clérisseau designed for Catherine the Great in 1773, which will be discussed in Chapter VII. Hermitage, no. 2403, "Intérieur de la Chambre Sépulcrale de ma Composition," pen, ink, and gouache, 8³/₄ × 117/16 in. (22.1 × 29 cm.).

68. London, Soane Museum, "Miscellaneous Sketches," no. 145, "Reconstruction Based on the Roman Baths," pen, ink, and wash, 11 × 15³/₄ in. (27.8 × 40 cm.).

69. Edinburgh, Register House, Clerk of Penicuik Papers, no. 4811, Robert Adam to James, July 24, 1756.

70. Edinburgh, Register House, Clerk of Penicuik Papers, no. 4817, Robert Adam to James, Sept. 11, 1756.

71. Edinburgh, Register House, Clerk of Penicuik Papers, no. 4817, Robert Adam to James, Sept. 11, 1756. Clérisseau's plan of Hadrian's Villa and the drawings for the Roman bath publication mentioned at the beginning

of this long excerpt were in the sale after his death, *Catalogue des livres . . . du cabinet . . . Clérisseau . . . 11 . . . 16 Décembre 1820 . . . l'hotel de Bullion,* 44, no. 17; 45, no. 20. Agostino Brunias was active from 1752 to 1810, and the "Liegois" was Laurent-Benoît Dewez (1731–1812). For both see Fleming passim. For Brunias, see also E. Croft-Murray, *Decorative Painting in Britain,* London, 1970, II, 177. The publications of Xavier Duquenne, particularly his *Le Chateau de Seneffe,* Brussels, 1978, 103–14, are basic for Dewez.

72. Edinburgh, Register House, Clerk of Penicuik Papers, no. 4823, Robert Adam to Nelly, Oct. 23, 1756.

73. See Chapter I.

74. Edinburgh, Register House, Clerk of Penicuik Papers, no. 4811, Robert Adam to James, July 24, 1756.

75. Edinburgh, Register House, Clerk of Penicuik Papers, no. 4823, Robert Adam to Nelly, Oct. 23, 1756.

76. Edinburgh, Register House, Clerk of Penicuik Papers, no. 4833, Robert Adam to Jenny, Mar. 30, 1757.

77. Edinburgh, Register House, Clerk of Penicuik Papers, no. 4837, Robert Adam to Mother, May 16, 1757. Adam made a drawing of the theater at Terento, six miles away from Viterbo, on that date. It is labeled in French and is now in the drawing collection of the Royal Institute of British Architects, London, no. B4/1 A, black and gray washes, 7¼ × 14¼ in. (18.3 × 36.2 cm.).

78. Fleming, *Adam,* 234. Count Francesco Algarotti (1712–64), was a well-known critic. J. G. Links, *Canaletto and his Patrons,* New York, 1977, 81–82.

79. Brunias and Dewez: R. Adam, *Ruins of the Palace of the Emperor Diocletian at Spalatro in Dalmatia,* London, 1764, 2.

Chapter III

1. J. Fleming, "The Journey to Spalatro," *The Architectural Review,* 123, Feb. 1958, 102–107 is still the best discussion. Three of the drawings illustrated in this article were discovered by the present writer; Hermitage, no. 2348, "Church in Piran," gouache, 7⅞ × 11¾ in. (20 × 30 cm.), inscribed on rear: "Vue de Parenzo in Istria." I have used the eighteenth-century place names throughout for clarity. However, I prefer the usual "Spalato" for Adam's "Spalatro."

2. Edinburgh, Register House, Clerk of Penicuik Papers, no. 4811, Robert Adam to James, July 24, 1757.

3. London, Royal Institute of British Architects Library, no. L 12/7r, "Dimensions of the Amphitheatre at Pola in Istria measured on the spot July 1757" and "Dimensions of the Triumphal Arch at Pola in Istria measured July 1757," so inscribed, pen and sepia, 16 × 12 in. (45 × 35 cm.). The Temple of Diana is the building now identified as the Temple of Augustus. Attilio Krizmanić, Director, Zavod za Urbanizm i Stambeno Kamunaline Poslove, Pula, showed me these monuments and discussed them with me.

4. Views of Pola by Clérisseau.
   I. Present whereabouts unknown. Photograph in Witt Library. "Temple of Augustus, Pola" from the left, ink and wash, 6½ × 11½ in. (16.5 × 29 cm.). Exhibited as Panini at Ferault, Paris, 1928 no. 76, pl. 38. Possibly done on the spot in 1757.
   II. "Temple of Augustus, Pola," from left, gouache, 14½ × 18 in. (36.2 × 45.8 cm.) signed and dated "Clerisseau f à Vènise 1760," Drumlanrig Castle, Dumfriesshire, Collection of the Duke of Buccleuch and Queensberry, no. 77. Lorna MacEchern provided invaluable help in my study of the works at Drumlanrig.
   III. "Temple of Augustus, Pola," from left, gouache, 15⅜ × 18⅞ in. (39.1 × 47.9 cm.), signed and dated "Clérisseau f à Venise 1760," Pretoria, South Africa, Collection E. Bernardi. Almost identical to II except for figures.

IV. "Temple of Augustus, Pola," from left with part of façade cut off, gouache, 16 × 21 3/4 in. (40.7 × 55.3 cm.) signed, London, Soane Museum, no. 136.

V. "Temple of Augustus, Pola" from left with part of façade cut off, pen, ink, and gouache, 9 7/8 × 15 in. (24.9 × 38 cm.), Hermitage, no. N 11671.

VI. "Temple of Augustus," from opposite side, pen, ink, and gouache, 15 15/16 × 23 11/16 in. (40.5 × 60.2 cm.), Hermitage, no. 16917. The Cunego engraving of this temple, called "The Temple of Pola in Istria," after Clérisseau, is probably based on this drawing. Thomas Girtin also made a drawing, now in the British Museum, no. 104, after the engraving.

VII. "Rear of the Temples of Augustus and Diana," pen, brown ink, and brown wash, 7 3/4 × 13 in. (19.6 × 38 cm.). Present whereabouts unknown. Sold, Christie's, London, May 4, 1965, no. 126 as "Antique Ruins" by Hubert Robert with added signature of "H. Robert Roma." Possibly done on the spot in 1757. The second temple is sometimes identified as the Temple of Poseidon.

VIII. "Rear of the Temples of Augustus and Diana," gouache, 14 1/2 × 18 1/4 in. (36.8 × 46.4 cm.), signed and dated "Clérisseau f à Venise 1760," Drumlanrig Castle, Dumfriesshire, Collection of the Duke of Buccleuch and Queensberry, no. 79.

IX. "Rear of the Temples of Augustus and Diana," from left, gouache, 16 × 21 3/4 in. (40.7 × 55.2 cm.), London, Soane Museum, no. 115.

X. "Rear of the Temples of Augustus and Diana," from left, gouache, 24 3/8 × 36 1/4 in. (62 × 92 cm.), signed and dated 1790. Wörlitz, Staatlichen Schlosser und Garten, no. 73.

XI. "Rear of the Temple of Augustus and Diana," from right, pen, ink, and gouache, 10 × 14 3/4 in. (25.4 × 37.4 cm.), Hermitage, no. N 11672.

XII. "Amphitheatre, Pola," gouache, 14 1/2 × 18 1/4 in. (36.8 × 46.4 cm.), signed, Drumlanrig Castle, Dumfriesshire, Collection of the Duke of Buccleuch and Queensberry, no. 76.

XIII. "Amphitheatre, Pola," gouache, 8 11/16 × 12 3/4 in. (22 × 32.3 cm.). Hermitage, no. N 11676.

XIV. "Amphitheatre, Pola," showing corner, gouache, 9 7/8 × 15 in. (25 × 38 cm.), Hermitage, no. N 11675.

XV. "Arch of the Sergie, Pola," from right, gouache, 17 3/8 × 24 in. (44 × 61 cm.), Hermitage, no. 16914, the Cunego engraving after Clérisseau of the scene is related to this version. J. G. Links has suggested that a *capriccio* of the Arch by Canaletto is based on a Clérisseau drawing such as this one. (Links, *Canaletto and his Patrons*, new 1977, 82.)

XVI. "Arch of the Sergie, Pola," from right, gouache, 18 × 24 in. (45.8 × 59.8 cm.), sold Christie's, London, July 4, 1984, no. 105. Inscribed "Arc de Pola en Istrie," lower left, signed lower right, and dated 1753. This date is surely impossible. The drawing appears from a photograph to be almost identical with XV and the Cunego engraving.

XVII. "Arch of the Sergie, Pola," gouache, 14 13/16 × 18 13/16 in. (37.6 × 47.8 cm.), signed and dated "Clérisseau f à Venise 1760," Pretoria, South Africa, Collection E. Bernardi. The flanking buildings differ from XV. T. McCormick, "Painter of Classical Ruins," *Country Life*, CXLII, no. 3736, Aug. 17, 1967, 355.

XVIII. "Arch of the Sergie, Pola," from right, gouache, 14 1/2 × 18 in. (36.8 × 45.7 cm.), signed, Drumlanrig Castle, Dumfriesshire, Collection of the Duke of Buccleuch and Queensbury, no. 81. Identical except for figures with XVII.

XIX. "Arch of the Sergie, Pola," from right, gouache, 16 3/8 × 23 5/16 in. (41.6 × 59.3 cm.), Ottawa, National Gallery of Canada. Almost identical with XVIII.

XX. "Arch of the Sergie, Pola," from left, gouache, 12 1/16 × 10 3/8 in. (30.7 × 26.3 cm.), Hermitage, no. N 11668.

XXI. "Arch of the Sergie, Pola," from end, gouache, 9 7/16 × 15 in. (24.1 × 38 cm.), Hermitage, no. N 11669.

XXII. "Greek capital from Pola in Istria," gouache, 3⁷/₈ × 5³/₄ in. (9.9 × 14.6 cm.), inscribed: "Chapiteau Grec a Pola en Istria," Hermitage, no. N 2775.

XXIII. "Three Byzantine Churches, Pola," gouache, 9¹/₈ × 14⁷/₁₆ in. (23.2 × 36.8 cm.), inscribed: "Pola," Hermitage, no. 11674.

XXIV. "Apse of Ruined Byzantine Church, Pola," gouache, 9⁷/₈ × 14⁵/₈ in. (25.2 × 37.2 cm.), inscribed: "Pola," Hermitage, no. 11620. This is the Church of S. Maria Formosa o del Canetto.

XXV. "Byzantine Fortress from Water," gouache, 7⁷/₈ × 11⁹/₁₆ in. (20 × 29.4 cm.), Hermitage, no. 11616.

I do not accept the drawing in the Victoria and Albert Museum, 3436.51, "Temple of Pola, Istria," pen and wash, 8 × 10³/₄ in. (20.3 × 27.3 cm.). It is thought to be a study by Clérisseau for the engraving, but I think it is a reduced copy after the engraving by an unknown artist. For a general survey of artists' views of Pola from the sixteenth to the nineteenth centuries, see Duško Kečkemet, "Antički Spomenci Pule na Slikama i u opisima stranih autora od XVI do XIX stoljeca," *Jadranski Zbornik prilozi za povijest Istre, Rijeke, Hrvatskog primorja i gorskog Kotara,* VII, 1966–69, 549–90 (with English summary). However, this does not include all of the views by Clérisseau.

5. J. Fleming, *Robert Adam and His Circle in Edinburgh and Rome,* London, 1962, 273.

6. See note 4, nos. II, III, VIII, and XVII.

7. Edinburgh, Register House, Clerk of Penicuik Papers, no. 4868, James Adam to Robert, Aug. 13, 1760.

8. See note 4, nos. VI and XV.

9. The engravings are part of a series of fourteen by Cunego after drawings by Clérisseau which were published by J. Brett as *The Architectural Beauties of Ancient Rome.* Complete sets, lacking title pages, are in the Royal Institute of British Architects Library, the Victoria and Albert Museum, and in the Feldberg Library at Dartmouth College, Hanover,

New Hampshire. Recently, a set with the title page dated 1766 appeared on the London art market (information kindly communicated by David Alexander). Sets of six of the prints (including "The Arch of the Sergie") were offered for sale in the *Public Advertiser* beginning on Dec. 12, 1766. The same year impressions of several of them were painted over and sold as original drawings. See Chapter IV. Many of these engravings are listed in the first Adam sale of 1773, second day, Feb. 26, nos. 67–72, and third day, Feb. 27, nos. 71–77 (A. Bolton, *The Architecture of Robert and James Adam,* London, 1922, II, 326–27). Much later, probably in 1823, a book list of Priestley and Weale included a second edition as "Shortly to be published"—"Architectural Remains in Rome, Pola and Naples, from drawings made by Clérisseau under the direction of the late Robert Adam Esq., F. R. S., Architect to the King." The book list was published by A. Bolton, "Robert Adam, F. R. S., F. S. A., Architect to King George III and to Queen Charlotte, as a Bibliographer; Publisher and Designer of Libraries," *Transactions of the Bibliographical Society,* XIV, 1915–17, 306. In 1825 Priestley and Weale published *Bibliotheca Architectonica: A Catalogue of Books on the Fine Arts,* in which the fourteen prints are listed individually.

10. See note 4, no. VII. Considering the high quality of the drawing, it is not surprising that it was sold in 1965 with a false Hubert Robert signature. For another sketch showing the façade of the Temple of Augustus probably also done on the spot, see no. I.

11. Gouache and body color are often used interchangeably but I prefer the former term.

12. See note 4, nos. XIII and XIV.

13. See note 4, no. XII.

14. Fleming, *Adam,* 237.

15. See note 14, no. XXIII.

16. Edinburgh, Register House, Clerk of Penicuik Papers, no. 4841, Robert Adam to James, Aug. 6, 1757.

17. Hermitage, no. 2350, inscribed on mat "Zbenigo en Dalmathie," inscribed on verso: "Vue de Zébénigo en Dalmatie," ink and wash, 6³/₈ × 11⁷/₈ in. (16.8 × 30.2 cm.).

18. On the basis of the photograph of the drawing provided by the present author for the exhibition "Robert Adam i Dioklecijanova Palača u Splitu," Mūzej Grada Splita, Split, Yugoslavia, Dec. 1964–Jan. 1965, Milan Ivanišević wrote an article "Porušena Kula-zvonik Šibenske Stolne Crkve," *Prilozi povijesti umjetnosti u Dalmaciji*, 15, 1963 (printed 1965), pp. 84–110 (with French summary). T. Jackson, *Dalmatia, the Quarnero and Istria*, Oxford, 1887, I, Pl. XV, illustrates the cathedral after the removal of St. Roch but before the destruction of the tower.

19. Hermitage, no. 2350, inscribed on mat: "Traou in Dalmatie," verso, "Vue de Traou en Dalmatie," pen, ink, and wash, 6¹¹/₁₆ × 10¹/₄ in. (17 × 26 cm.). I am indebted to Tomislav Marasović for the identification and significance of this church.

20. Tomislav Marasović has published this drawing with my permission. "Izvorni izgled ranosrednjovjekovne crkve Sv. Marije u Trogiru," Slovenska Akademija Znanosti in Umetnosti [Academia Scientiarum et Artium Slovenica] Razred za Zgodovinske in Družbene Vede [Classis I: Historia et Sociologia] Razprave [Dissertationes], V, Hauptmannov Zbornik, Ljubljana, 1966, 101–108. See also Jackson, *Dalmatia*, II, 144–45.

21. Edinburgh, Register House, Clerk of Penicuik Papers, no. 4841, Robert Adam to James, Aug. 6, 1757.

22. R. Adam, *Ruins of the Palace of the Emperor Diocletian at Spalatro in Dalmatia*, London, 1764, 3.

23. Edinburgh, Register House, Clerk of Penicuik Papers, no. 4841, Robert Adam to James, Aug. 6, 1757.

24. Adam, *Spalatro*, 3.

25. Edinburgh, Register House, Clerk of Penicuik Papers, no. 4843, Robert Adam to James, Nov. 1, 1757.

26. Edinburgh, Register House, Clerk of Penicuik Papers, no. 18/4953, Mss. of Robert Adam, introduction to *Spalatro*. Duško Kečkemet brought this document to my attention.

27. Adam, *Spalatro*, 2.

28. Adam, *Spalatro*, xi. The idea of including Clérisseau's name on a sarcophagus was probably inspired by Piranesi's putting the names of Robert Adam and Allan Ramsay on two tombs shown in the frontispiece of his *Antichità romane* in 1756. (Fleming, *Adam*, 207).

29. Fleming, "Spalatro," 107, suggests that the delay was to allow time for the acclaim given Stuart and Revett's *Antiquities of Athens* to subside.

30. Edinburgh, Register House, Clerk of Penicuik Papers, no. 4844, Robert Adam to Betty, Nov. 17, 1757.

31. Edinburgh, Register House, Clerk of Penicuik Papers, no. 4848, Robert Adam to James, June 17, 1758.

32. Edinburgh, Register House, Clerk of Penicuik Papers, no. 4849, James Adam to Robert, June 25, 1758.

33. C.-L. Clérisseau, *Antiquités de la France: Première Partie, Monumens de Nisme*, Paris, 1778, xiii. I believe that many of the large drawings by Clérisseau now in the Hermitage were made for this proposed edition.

34. Edinburgh, Register House, Clerk of Penicuik Papers, no. 4852, Robert Adam to James, Sept. 5, 1758. Several early proofs have survived and will be discussed later in this chapter.

35. Fleming, "Spalatro," 106.

36. Edinburgh, Register House, Clerk of Penicuik Papers, no. 4853, Robert Adam to James, Nov. 10, 1758. On December 14, 1757, Messrs. Innes and Clark were informed by Messrs. Adam to honor about eight or nine monthly drafts from Clérisseau (Guildhall Library, Innes and Clark Mss., 3070).

37. Edinburgh, Register House, Clerk of Penicuik Papers, no. 4861, James Adam to Robert, June 25, 1760.

38. Edinburgh, Register House, Clerk of Penicuik Papers, no. 4861, James Adam to Robert, June 25, 1760.

39. Edinburgh, Register House, Clerk of Penicuik Papers, no. 4862, James Adam to Jenny, July 2, 1760.

40. Edinburgh, Register House, Clerk of Penicuik Papers, no. 4866, Robert Adam to James, July 24, 1760. "Smith" is Joseph Smith (c. 1675–1770), the British Consul in Venice and famous art collector. The drawings of Pola sent to Lord Brudenell are the four drawings, two of which are dated 1760, described in note 4, nos. II, VII, XII, and XVIII. These drawings plus two others signed and dated 1759 are now in the Collection of the Duke of Buccleuch and Queensberry. The sister of Lord Brudenell (1735–70) married Henry, third Duke of Buccleuch, and on Lord Brudenell's death his possessions passed to the Buccleuch family. The drawings were at Queensberry House, Richmond, Surrey, by the last quarter of the nineteenth century when they were transferred to Drumlanrig Castle, Dumfriesshire, where they now are. I am grateful to the eighth Duke and Duchess of Buccleuch Queensbury and to Miss Lorna MacEchern for their help, and for allowing me to study the drawings. For Lord Brudenell see J. Fleming, "Lord Brudenell and His Bear Leader," *English Miscellany*, IX, 1958, 127–41. "Mr. Blackfriars" refers to Robert Mylne (1734–81), Scottish architect and rival of Robert Adam, who built Blackfriars' Bridge, London, 1760–69.

41. Edinburgh, Register House, Clerk of Penicuik Papers, no. 4869, James Adam to Robert, Aug. 20, 1760.

42. Edinburgh, Register House, Clerk of Penicuik Papers, no. 4869, James Adam to Robert, Aug. 20, 1760.

43. Edinburgh, Register House, Clerk of Penicuik Papers, no. 4872, James Adam to Betty, Sept. 17, 1760.

44. Edinburgh, Register House, Clerk of Penicuik Papers, no. 4868, James Adam to Robert, Aug. 13, 1760.

45. See Chapter II.

46. Edinburgh, Register House, Clerk of Penicuik Papers, no. 4868, James Adam to Robert, Aug. 13, 1760.

47. Fleming, *Adam,* 284–85. The Clérisseau sale after his death included "Un Volume, contenant les plans, coupes, élévations des Thermes de Dioclétian, de Caracalla et de Titus, mesurés et dessinés par M.. Clérisseau," *Catalogue des livres . . . du cabinet . . . Clérisseau . . . 11 . . . 16 Décembre 1820 . . . l'hôtel de Bullion,* 44, no. 17.

48. Edinburgh, Register House, Clerk of Penicuik Papers, no. 4866, Robert Adam to James, July 24, 1760.

49. Edinburgh, Register House, Clerk of Penicuik Papers, no. 4867, James Adam to Robert, Aug. 5, 1760.

50. Edinburgh, Register House, Clerk of Penicuik Papers, no. 4873, James Adam to Margaret, Sept. 24, 1760.

51. Edinburgh, Register House, Clerk of Penicuik Papers, no. 4871, James Adam to Nelly, Sept. 2, 1760.

52. R. Adam, "Journal of a Tour in Italy," *Library of the Fine Arts,* II, Oct. 1831, 165–78; Nov. 1831, 135–45. This is actually James Adam's journal. For a more detailed and colorful version of these journeys, see Fleming, *Adam,* 268–94. In his quotations Fleming rarely gives the specific source. Unless otherwise noted, the information—but not the spelling—which follows comes from the journal. Footnotes are cited only in the case of long quotations.

53. Presumably concerning the Spalato book. However, J. Swarbrick, *Robert Adam and His Brothers, Their Lives, Work and Influence on English Architecture, Decoration and Furniture*, London, 1915, 118–19, states that arrangements were made for the engravings of Clérisseau's drawings by Cunego. A series of fourteen was issued (See note 9), but this set eventually included sites not yet visited by James and Clérisseau.

54. The Hermitage contains drawings of Bologna and Florence by Clérisseau which may have been done at this time. I believe it more probable that they were done earlier, when Clérisseau was living there before he met Robert Adam.

55. Adam, "Journal," 175.

56. I am indebted to Sir Brinsley Ford for this reference. It is quoted with the incorrect date of 1761 in Bolton, *Architecture*, I, 39. Hayward's list has now been fully published by Lindsay Stainton in the *Walpole Society*, XLIX, 1983.

57. Fleming, *Adam*, 280.

58. Adam, "Journal," 237–38.

59. Lockerbie, Dumfriesshire, Hope-Johnstone Collection, B/7846, "Ancient Sepulchre near Pozzuoli," pen and gouache, 17 1/2 × 23 in. (44.2 × 58.4 cm.). This is one of a group of drawings commissioned in 1763, which I shall discuss in Chapter IV. However, this particular drawing might have been executed earlier. I suspect that the original or an earlier version might have been done in 1761. There is also a Cunego engraving, which is one of the series discussed in note 9, closely related to this drawing. The Hope-Johnstone drawings have recently gone to Percy Hope-Johnstone's heir, the Earl of Annandale.

60. I believe Clérisseau's drawings of Capua, Pozzuoli, Cuma, Beneventum, and Baia were made at this time, but recognize that he could have done them on earlier trips. At present there is no way of precisely dating them.

61. Adam, "Journal," 241.

62. These buildings are now recognized as nymphia; Hermitage, no. 11491, inscribed on verso: "Baja terme (Temple de Mercure)," pen, ink, black and brown wash, and gouache, 16 9/16 × 23 1/4 in. (42.2 × 59.1 cm.). The Morgan Library has recently purchased a smaller version which has an additional figure.

63. I identify this "operation" as Clérisseau's finishing drawings of the buildings or their details or taking measurements of the Temple of Serapis which he and James had started to investigate on October 25. The latter idea is more likely.

64. Adam, "Journal," 243.

65. Hermitage, no. 16921, "The Ruins of the Temple of Poseidon at Paestum," ink, body color, and gouache, 16 3/16 × 22 3/4 in. (41.2 × 57.7 cm.). The Fitzwilliam Museum has a drawing of perhaps the same temple, no. 3604, pen, ink, black chalk, and gouache, 12 1/4 × 16 1/4 in. (31 × 41.2 cm.), inscribed on verso: "à Pesto." See T. McCormick, "An Unknown Collection of Drawings by Charles-Louis Clérisseau," *Journal of the Society of Architectural Historians*, XXII, Oct. 1963, 126.

66. J. Winckelmann, *Briefe*, H. Diepolder and W. Rehn, eds., Berlin, 1952–57, II, 255. Winckelmann to Mengs about the sale of the Albani drawings identifies the agent as "Adam d'Edinburgo, il fratello minore di quello che avete consciuto voi."

67. Fleming, "Spalatro," 106.

68. Edinburgh, Register House, Clerk of Penicuik Papers, no. 4926, Robert Adam to James, Feb. 8, 1762.

69. Adam, *Spalatro*, 30.

70. Edinburgh, Register House, Clerk of Penicuik Papers, no. 4926, Robert Adam to James, Feb. 8, 1762.

71. Edinburgh, Register House, Clerk of Penicuik Papers, no. 4907, James Adam to Robert, Aug. 14, 1761.

72. J. Summerson, *Architecture in Britain 1530 to 1830*, 4th ed. rev. and enl., Harmondsworth, 1963, 250.

73. The eighteen items will be described as they are discussed. However, there is one other drawing which has been called a view of the palace and attributed to Clérisseau, though it has nothing to do with either. This drawing is in the Witt Collection of the Courtauld Institute of Art, London, n. 3186, said to be by Clérisseau and entitled "View of the Palace of Diocletian, Split" (*Handlist of the Drawings in the Witt Collection,* London, 1956, 136). I attribute this drawing to James Bruce of Kinnaird (1730-84) or Luigi Balugami (1737-70) on the basis of comparison with similar drawings at Windsor Castle (see A. P. Oppé, *English Drawings of the Stuart and Georgian Periods in the Royal Library at Windsor Castle,* London, 1950, 30, no. 94, and Plates 35-37). I wish to thank Philip Trautman, formerly Curator of the Courtauld Institute of Art Galleries, for facilitating my study of this drawing.

74. Engraving, "Plan Exact de ce qui existe du Palais de Diocletian à Spalatro." This reads: «C. L. Clérisseau inv.» (lower left) and «Desmaisons del.» (lower right). L. F. Cassas and J. Lavallée, *Voyage pittoresque et historique de l'Istrie et de la Dalmatie . . . ,* Paris, 1802, 167, and Pl. 54 bis. Clérisseau is listed as a subscriber on page iii and his son-in-law, J. G. Legrand, as an honorary subscriber on page v. Tomislav Marasović of the Town Planning Institute of Split not only criticized what follows but also allowed me to read his unpublished essay on Diocletian's Palace as a major monument of Dalmatian art.

75. Cassas and Lavallée, *Voyage,* Pl. 54 bis, "Les Teintes noires indiquent ce qui reste de visible, les pale ce qui est détruit mais dont il y a des traces sensibles." The importance of Clérisseau's original plan has been recognized by some of the later scholars who have studied the palace. It is published in E. Hébard and J. Zeiller, *Spalato: Le Palais de Dioclétian,* Paris, 1912, 17.

76. Adam mentions these underground rooms, but does not say they appear in his plan (Adam, *Spalatro,* 16). Professor Sheila McNally suggests that the group entered what is now called Room 4A (which Hébard calls 9) through an opening from a street above. She also thinks they got into 4B (which Hébard calls 10) through the window in the north wall of the superstructure, but did not get into rooms west of 4A.

77. J. Marasović and T. Marasović. "Pregled rodova Urbanistickog biroa na istrzivanju, zastiti i uredenju Diokecijanove palače," *Urbs,* IV, 1961-62, (Split 1965), 23-54, is the most thorough discussion of the excavations and discoveries up to 1965. It is supplemented by T. Marasović, "Gli appartamenti dell'Imperatore Diocleziano nel suo Palazzo a Split," *Acta Institutum Romanum Norvegiae,* IV, 1969, 33-40., J. Marasović and T. Marasović, *Diocletian Palace,* Zagreb, 1970, (first published in Serbo-Croatian, 1968), and J. Marasović, T. Marasović, S. McNally, J. Wilkes, *Diocletian's Palace, Report on the Joint Excavations in Southeast Quarter, Part One,* Split, 1972. The latest study by S. McNally, J. Marasović, T. Marasović, *Diocletian's Palace, Report on Joint Excavations, Part Two,* Split, 1976, 15, states that the basement rooms were mainly unused and had no apparent function other than to support the walls above and therefore reflect the plan of the upper or main floor. I am indebted to Jerko Marasović for discussing this matter with me.

78. J. Marasović and T. Marasović, *Urbs,* IV, 27.

79. This portion was first studied by the Town Planning Institute in 1959; see J. Marasović and T. Marasović, *Diocletian Palace,* Fig. 34 transparency; and McNally, J. Marasović, T. Marasović, *Report, Part Two,* 53, Pl. 26a and Fig. 24.

80. Hébard and Zeiller, *Spalato,* 11, realized that Adam was wrong in his symmetrical reconstruction of the residential section, although none of the southeast basement had been excavated at that time. J. Marasović and T. Marasović, *Urbs,* IV, 24-30.

81. McNally, J. Marasović, T. Marasović, *Report, Part Two*, 62.

82. Hermitage, no. 2566, inscribed on verso: "Court du palais de l'empereur Diocletian en Dalmatie," pen, brown and black ink, gouache, 16 × 17¹³/₁₆ in. (40.7 × 45.1 cm.).

83. The figures at the right in the engraving appear in a reversed form in a Clérisseau drawing in the Fitzwilliam Museum, no. 3618, which is inscribed on the reverse: "Figures by Bartolozzi." For the Fitzwilliam drawing see T. McCormick, "An Unknown Collection of Drawings by Charles-Louis Clérisseau," *Journal of the Society of Architectural Historians*, XXII, Oct. 1963, 126.

84. Two sets of the Spalato drawings were made, so that this may be one from the second set, J. Fleming, "Spalatro," 104.

85. Hermitage, no. 2491, inscribed on verso, "Interieur de la Palais," pen and gouache, 11⁷/₁₆ × 13³/₄ in. (29 × 35 cm.), inscribed lower left: "Spalatro."

86. Cassas and Lavallée, *Voyage*, Pl. 41. The watercolor now in the Victoria and Albert Museum, London, is discussed and illustrated in D. Kečkemet, "Louis-François Cassas et ses illustrations de L'Istrie et de la Dalmatie (1782)," *Annales de L'Institut de Zagreb*, 2ème. ser. no. 22–23, 1970–71, 45–53.

87. The sculptural group, possibly from the studio of Nicolo Ferentino, is now in the Town Museum, Split. Duško Kečkemet kindly located it for me.

88. Hermitage, no. 2456, ink and wash, 8¹/₈ × 10¹/₄ in. (20.5 × 26 cm.), inscribed on verso: "Composition Architecturale."

89. To avoid confusion, the present identification of the various buildings will be used.

90. Hermitage, no. 11670, "Interior of the Vestibule," gouache, 11³/₁₆ × 9¹/₂ in. (28.4 × 24.2 cm.).

91. Hermitage, no. 11615, "Side of the Mausoleum," gouache, 11⁹/₁₆ × 10¹/₄ in. (29.7 × 26 cm.).

92. Reproduced in *Apollo*, CI, Mar. 1975, 26. I wish to thank Mr. Links for discussing this drawing with me. It was lot 21 in the sale of March 19. See also, J. G. Links, *Canaletto and His Patrons*, London, 1977, 82, Pl. 122; W. G. Constable and J. G. Links, *Canaletto, Giovanni Antonio Canale 1697–1768*, Oxford, 2nd ed., I, 807, 848, and 856; II, 603, 620, and 622; Kruno Prijatelj, "Canalettor Crtez Dioklecyanova Mauzoleja U Splitu," *Jugoslavenska Akademija Znanosti Poseban otisak iq Zbornika za narodni zivot i obicaje Juznih Slavena*, 49, 505–13, based on photographs provided by the present writer.

93. While it may seem odd for Canaletto at this late date in his career to copy a drawing by a lesser-known younger artist, there are other examples of this, such as those of the Quirinale and the Piazza Navona (Constable and Links, II, 396, no. 394, 401, no. 485), which are copies of engravings. Mr. Links kindly brought these to my attention. Canaletto did three drawings of the monuments of Pola although he had never been there. Links suggests these are probably after Adam drawings (Links, 823). They are not after any known Clérisseaus. Canaletto was not the only prominent artist to copy Clérisseau's drawings of the mausoleum or prints after them. The Huntington Library and Art Gallery, San Marino, CA, has a sketchbook of Thomas Rowlandson that includes a copy of Adam's Pl. XXVII. See Robert Wark, *Drawings of Thomas Rowlandson in the Huntington Collection*, San Marino, 1975, no. X, "An Architectural Capriccio in the Manner of Clérisseau," 37–38, Pl. IX. See also note 97 for Hubert Robert copies.

94. Hermitage, no. 2351, inscribed on verso: "Dans le palais de Diocletian se trouve le temple de Jupiter a Spalatre in Dalmatie," ink and wash, 9¹/₄ × 9⁷/₁₆ in. (23.5 × 24 cm.), inscribed in lower left: "Spalatro Tempeio."

95. Duško Kečkemet and Jerko Marasović provided helpful comments on this drawing.

96. Hermitage, no. 16920, inscribed on verso: "Vue du temple de Baccus situe dans l'interieur du Palais de Diocletien en Dalmate," pen, black and brown ink, gouache, 16 × 22⁷/₁₆ in. (43.2 × 59.5 cm.). The verso also has a drawing of a profile of a molding.

97. In 1766 Hubert Robert produced in pen and aquarelle a paraphrase of the Adam engraving of the temple. The drawing is similar in its depiction of the building, but Robert made several changes. He reduced the number of stairs, rearranged the projecting wall and the stone in the pediment, added a window on the side, and even changed the end-relief of the sarcophagus. The figures have been transformed, so that a mother and child mount the stairs instead of a Turk. Robert moves the Turkish figures to the right of the temple and adds a group of antiquarians, one classically dressed, admiring an inscription containing Robert's signature. The greatest change, however, is the addition at the left of an arched structure with Corinthian columns and surmounted by statues—this is an invention of Robert perhaps inspired by the interior of the mausoleum. This drawing and another also by Robert and freely based on Pl. LXI "The Aqueduct of Salona," are now in a private collection. They were in the exhibition *Autour du Neoclassicisme, peintures, dessins, sculpture*, Paris, Galerie Cailleux, Mar. 1973, nos. 37 and 38, illustrated in catalogue.

98. Cassas and Lavallée, *Voyage*, Pl. 53.

99. London, Victoria and Albert Museum, no. 3436.10, Robert Adam, "Temple of Aesculapius," gray ink and wash, 9⁷/₈ × 14¹/₈ in. (25 × 35.8 cm.). A. Rowan, *Robert Adam, Catalogues of Architectural Drawings in the Victoria and Albert Museum*, London, 1988, implies it is by Clérisseau, no. 14, 35.

100. Other copies after the Spalato plates are known. The Cooper-Hewitt Museum has an even cruder copy of Pl. XLII, and also ones of Pls. XII, XXVII, XXXIII, and XLI, accession nos. 1938–88 7313 to 1938–88 7317.

101. Gouache, 11⁷/₈ × 16¹¹/₁₆ in. (29.2 × 42.5 cm.), Hermitage, no. N 11506.

102. Sir Albert Richardson Collection, "Temple of Aesculapius," pen and sepia wash, 11 × 15¹/₂ in. (27.9 × 29.3 cm.). Prof. John Wilton-Ely brought the drawing to my attention and gave me a photograph. It was shown in the exhibition "Architectural Drawings from the Collection of Sir Albert Richardson" at the University of Nottingham, Apr. 24–May 11, 1968, no. 12, illustrated in the catalogue as Pl. IV.

103. Hermitage, no. N 2438, ink and gouache, 8 × 11³/₈ in. (20.2 × 29 cm.).

104. Hermitage, no. N 11160, gouache, 9³/₄ × 7⁹/₁₆ in. (24.8 × 19.2 cm.). Hermitage, no. N 11594, gouache, 11¹/₁₆ × 8³/₈ in. (28 × 21.2 cm.).

105. T. J. McCormick, "An Unknown Collection of Drawings by Charles-Louis Clérisseau," *Journal of the Society of Architectural Historians*, XXII, no. 3, Oct. 1963, 119–26; 3624, "A Fountain in Front of Ruins," gouache, 10¹/₂ × 16⁵/₈ in. (26.7 × 42.2 cm.); 1677, "Ruined Classical Doorway," pencil, pen, and sepia ink with gray wash, 10¹/₄ × 7⁵/₁₆ in. (26 × 18.5 cm.).

106. Letters from David Scrase. Sept. 8 and 9 and Oct. 25, 1977.

107. Hermitage, no. 2600, "Porta Ferrea," pen and gouache, 16 × 23 in. (40.6 × 58.4 cm.), inscribed on verso: "Petit Palais de Diocletian à Spalato."

108. Duško Kečkemet answered numerous questions about eighteenth-century Split.

109. L. F. Cassas's watercolor of this gate, made about 1782 and now in the Victoria and Albert Museum, London, and the engraving made from it in 1802, pushed the bell tower further to the left in order to expose a second niche as well. See Cassas and Lavallée, *Voyage*, Pl. 41.

110. London, Royal Institute of British Architects Library, B/41. "The Porta Aurea," pen and wash, 18 × 15 in. (45.7 × 38 cm.).

111. Heinz Kähler proposed that the five original statues represented the four tetrarchs with Jupiter in the middle. H. Kähler, "Split i Piazza Armerina, residencije dvaju careva tetrarha." *Urbs*, IV, 1961–62, 106–107, Figs. 4 and 5. I am greatly indebted to John Riely for bringing it to my attention, and Ben Weinreb, London, for allowing me to study at length this unique copy formerly in his possession and now in the National Library of Scotland. Dr. Iain G. Brown, Assistant Keeper, Department of Manuscripts has helped immeasurably. While it lacks much of the final text and many of the final plates, it is an invaluable record of the making of the book as it contains notes throughout by Robert or possibly James Adam on corrections to be made in the text and captions. For example there is a note written in James's handwriting on Table 23 (now Pl. XXII) "Clérisseau believes that this temple is built of free stone the entablature of capitals of marble and the columns of granite. The window in the front is a modern alteration, the temples of the anc'ts being allways dark." Robert's comments on the building material were also mentioned in his letter to James of Feb. 8, 1762. See above.

112. New York, Cooper-Hewitt Museum, 1962-47-12, "An Oblique View of a Section of a Ruined Building," pencil, pen, and bistre ink with gray wash, 11 5/8 × 5 11/16 in. (29.5 × 14.5 cm.), signed "Clérisseau." This drawing appeared in sales catalogue no. 730 of Joseph Baer and Company, Frankfurt-am-Main, 1922, no. 142, reproduced, Pl. XXV, as by G. B. Piranesi.

113. I wish to thank Duško Kečkemet for discussing this matter with me.

114. Conversation with Jerko Marasović.

Chapter IV

1. A copy of Piranesi's *Lettere di giustificazione scritte a Milord Charlemont e a di lui agenti di Roma*, Rome, 1757, belonging to the late James G. Vanderpool of New York, contains a handwritten list of people to whom Piranesi planned to send a copy of the *Lettere*. I share Vanderpool's considered opinion that the first name on the list is Clérisseau's. The relationship with the Adam family continued. Clérisseau's letter of Mar. 28, 1764, to Baynes and Adam in London (principally William Adam) mentions works to be undertaken for them and that he is looking forward to meeting William in Rome. This letter was sold at Sotheby's on June 28, 1977, no. 5023, and is now in the collection of the Fondation Custodia, (coll. F. Lugt), Institut Neerlandais, Paris, which kindly provided a copy.

2. Vienna, Osterreichisches Staatsarchiv, Haus-Hof und Staatsarchiv: Mann-Albani correspondence, fazc. 161, Mann to Albani, Feb. 21, 1755. The Osterreichisches Staatsarchiv supplied a microfilm of the relevant drafts of the Mann letters and Albani's originals. The letters are summarized in F. Noack, "Des Kardinals Albani Beziehungen zu Kunstlern," *Der Cicerone*, XVI, May 1924, 402–13, 451–59, and in Lesley Lewis, whose book, *Connoisseurs and Secret Agents in Eighteenth Century Rome*, London, 1961, *passim*, illuminates this whole matter. Horace Mann (1706–86) is best known today for his voluminous correspondence with Horace Walpole. This particular correspondence does not mention Clérisseau, as Warren Smith, Associate Editor of the Yale Edition of Horace Walpole's Correspondence, informed me.

3. Vienna, Haus-Hof und Staatsarchiv, Mann-Albani correspondence, fazc. 161, Albani to Mann, Mar. 22, 1755.

4. Vienna, Haus-Hof und Staatsarchiv, Mann-Albani correspondence, fazc. 169, Mann to Albani, Sept. 27, 1757.

5. Vienna, Haus-Hof und Staatsarchiv, Mann-Albani correspondence, fazc. 169, Albani to Mann, Oct. 1, 1757.

6. J. Winckelmann, *Briefe*, H. Diepolder and W. Rehn, eds., Berlin, 1952–57, I, 267, no. 167, Winckelmann to Berendis, Jan. 29, 1757. "Ein einziger Französischen Architekt ist mein guter Bekannter; aber er hat sich seiner Nation abgesondert, um nicht lächerlick zu werden."

7. Winckelmann, *Briefe*, I, 566.

8. See Chapter I.

9. J. Locquin, *La Peinture d'histoire en France de 1747 a 1785*, Paris, 1912, 104. The late Professor Walther Rehn confirmed in a letter to me that he had found no evidence of such a journey.

10. J. Winckelmann, *Remarques sur l'architecture des ancienes*, Paris, 1783, ii. First edition, 1762. I have been unable to discover whether this quotation occurs in the first German edition of 1762; Winckelmann, *Briefe*, II, 238, no. 491, Winckelmann to Volkmann, June 18, 1762.

11. Winckelmann, *Briefe*, II, 356, no. 608, Winckelmann to Caspar Füssli, Nov. 26, 1763. Rehn interprets this as referring to Clérisseau on the basis of unpublished letters from Reiffenstein to Füssli (Winckelmann, *Briefe*, II, 514). I agree.

12. "Ich habe den Card. vermocht, unserem Clerisseau, welchen. er zweymahl mit mir besuchet hat, und zuletzt in Gesellsch. der Prinzessin Albani, die Anlage und Ausziehrung eines Saals zu uberlasen, welcher kunstigen Monat angefangen wird und 60 palmen lang ist," Winckelmann, *Briefe*, III, 57, no. 673, Winckelmann to Füssli, Sept. 22, 1764.

13. "Es werden dazu alle schone Bilder aus dem Alterthume gesucht und die mehresten Stucke werden auf Kupfer gemahlet. Herr Clerisseau welcher Ihnen bekannt seyn sollte, regieret dieses Werk, und wird die grossen Stucke von Landschaften un Alterthumern in Dalmatien und bey Baja mahlen," Winckelmann, *Briefe*, III, 65, no. 683,

Winckelmann to von Stosch, Dec. 7, 1764. This is summarized in C. Justi, *Winckelmann und Seine Zeitgenossen*, W. Rehn, ed., 5th ed., Cologne, 1956, II, 393. Baron Phillip von Stosch (1691–1757) was a collector and British agent. See L. Lewis, "Phillip von Stosch," *Apollo*, LXXXV, May 1967, 320–27.

14. Lewis, *Connoisseurs*, 202.

15. J. Lalande, *Voyage d'un français en Italie fait dans les années 1765–66*, Paris, 1769, III, 166; Ramdohr, *Uber Mahlerei und Bildhauer Arbeit in Rom*, Leipzig, 1787, II, 51. Platner, Bunsen, Gerhard and Roestell, *Beschreibung der Stadt Rom*, Stuttgart, 1838, III, 540, mentions only the Lapiccola paintings, and Nibby, *Roma nell anno MDCCCXXXVIII*, Rome, 1840, 900, does likewise. The late Hannelore Glasser of Wells College was helpful in this matter.

16. M. Whinney, *Sculpture in Britain 1530 to 1830*, Harmondsworth, 1964, 267, no. 7, mentions a 1785 edition which I have been unable to find.

17. Morcelli, Fea and Visconti, *Déscription de la Villa Albani aujourd'hui Torlonia*, Imola, 1870, 98.

18. Justi, *Winckelmann*, I, x–xii. The first edition appeared in 1866–72; "Annesi fuhrte diese Landschaftchen und Marinen aus; in demselben Saal hat der Calabrese Niccola Lapiccola das Bacchanal des Giulio Romano nach der kleinen kolorierten Zeichnung in der Albanischen Galerie an die Decke gemalt. Sonst sorgte fur die Dekoration der Zimmer durch Veduten, Ruinenlandschaften, Szenen antiker Villeggiaturen, Chiaroscuri nach Reliefs Anton Bicchierari, fast der letzte, der noch romische Kirchen im alten Stil Fresko gemalte," Justi, *Winckelmann*, II, 393.

19. L. Callari, *La ville di Rome*, 2nd ed., Rome, 1943, 317; P. Pecchiai, "La Villa delle Rose," *L'Urbe*, XVI–XVII, 1933, 23–33; J. Veysset, "Les Merveilles cachées de la Villa Albani," *Connaissance des Arts*, Mar. 1960, 37–42; Isa Belli Barsali *Ville di Roma*, Lazio I. Milan, 1970, "Villa Albani," 315.

20. A. Clark, "Four Decorative Panels by Unterberger," *Worcester Art Museum Annual,* IX, 1961, 10, no. 10.

21. Veysset, "Les Merveilles," 3, 7.

22. F. Noack, *Das Deutsches Rom,* Rome, 1912, 82.

23. Lewis, *Connoisseurs,* 172, suggests that they may not have been executed. This would not be unusual. In her correspondence, Mrs. Lewis mentions commissions from Albani to Richard Wilson which were never carried out. Joachim Gaus, in *Carlo Marchionni: Ein Beitrag zur Romischen Architektur des Settecento,* Cologne, 1967, 31, also suggests that the decorations were never executed.

24. Lewis, *Connoisseurs,* 202. The late Wolfgang Lotz, Director of the Bibliotheca Hertziana, Rome, kindly checked the files of his vast library for references to Clérisseau and the Villa Albani, but he found none.

25. Winckelmann, *Briefe,* III, 344–49, no. 925, Winckelmann to Clérisseau, 1767. This is a series of excerpts from letters dating from the summer of 1767 to Dec. 1767.

26. Hermitage, no. 2604, "Roman House Project Interior Elevation," ink and gouache, $32^{7/16} \times 54^{1/2}$ in. (95.1 × 138.5 cm.).

27. See Appendix B. L. Hautecoeur, *L'Architecture classique à Saint-Pétersbourg,* Paris, 1912, 44–46, includes a brief description of some of the portfolios. These are discussed in more detail in my College Art Association of America talk referred to in Chapter I.

28. F. Noack, *Deutsches Leben in Rom 1700 bis 1900,* Stuttgart, 1907, 414.

29. John Fleming and I have published a study of this commission. The discussion that follows is an expansion and revision of the earlier article, "A Ruin Room by Clérisseau," *The Connoisseur,* CXLIX, Apr. 1962, 239–43.

30. Winckelmann, *Briefe,* II, 79, no. 355, Winckelmann to von Stosch, Feb. 9, 1760; 291, no. 540, Winckelmann to Ustieri, Feb. 20, 1763; 346, no. 594, Winckelmann to Barthélemy, Sept. 30, 1763.

31. Winckelmann, *Briefe,* III, 349, no. 925, Winckelmann to Clérisseau, 1767. See note 26. These excerpts were first published by H. Janson as early as 1781 (*Lettres familières de M. Winckelmann,* H. Janson, ed., Yverdon, 1784, II, 234). "Cette chambre qui est une des curiosités de Rome, représente l'intérieur d'un temple antique ruiné, dans lequel on suppose qu'un Hermite a fixé son domicile. M. Clérisseau n'en a point exécuté ici dans ce style, peu connu en France," Winckelmann, *Lettres familières,* II, 234, no. 1.

32. Lalande, *Voyage,* IV, 24.

33. J. Casanova, *Mémoires de Jacques Casanova di Seingall,* Brussels, 1863, I, 312.

34. J. W. Goethe, *Italienische Reise,* Weimar, 1903, I, 262–63; F. Noack, "Aus Goethe's Römische Reise," *Goethe Jahrbuch,* XXVI, 1905, 181.

35. "Clérisseau venait de transformer en une ruine pittoresque la cellule du *Père Le Sueur,* son ami, célèbre mathématicien au couvent de *la Trinité du Mont, Le Père Jacquier Minime* non moins savent, lui a succédé dans cette habitation singulière, l'une des curiosités de Rome.

"On croyait en y entrant, voir la cella d'un temple enrichie de fragmens antiques échapés aux ravages du tems la voûte et quelques pans de murailles en partie écroulées, soutenues par de mauvaises charpentes laissaient percer le ciel à travers et semblaient donner passage aux rayons du soleil, ces effets rendus avec savoir et vérité produisaient une illusion complète. Pour y aider mieux encore, tous les meubles participaient à ce caractère. Le lit était une vasque richement ornée, la cheminée une réunion de divers fragmens, le secrétaire un antique sarcophage mutilé, la table et les sièges un fragmens de corniche, et des chapiteaux renversés, et jusqu'au chien gardien fidèle de ces meubles d'un nouveau genre, était logé dans les débris d'un vase," J. G. Legrand, "Notice historique sur la vie et sur les Ouvrages de J. B. Piranesi," Paris, Bibliothèque Nationale, nouv. acq. fr. 5968, 146r.

36. This article was written in Russian, signed A. T., and entitled in French and Russian. I give here the French titles: "Documents pour servir à l'histoire des collections impériales, IV: Clérisseau," *Starye Gody,* July–Sept. 1913, 43–52. The late Professor Helen Muchnic of Smith College kindly translated this article for me.

37. Hermitage, no. 2598, Portfolio N 18 (115), "Ruin Room," pen, black ink, brown wash, and gouache, 14⁷/₁₆ × 20¹⁵/₁₆ in. (36.6 × 53.1 cm.). The Fitzwilliam Museum, Cambridge, has a replica of this drawing, no. 3607, which is inscribed on the back by an unknown hand: "Chambre Exécutée par le Sieur Clerisseau aux Minimes dans l'infermerie de la Trinité à Rome." It is executed in gouache, pen, ink, and black chalk, 14³/₈ × 21 in. (36.6 × 53.4 cm.). See T. McCormick, "An Unknown collection of Drawings by Charles-Louis Clérisseau," *Journal of the Society of Architectural Historians,* XXII, Oct. 1963, 125–26, Fig. 9.

38. Hermitage, no. 2597, "Ruin Room," pen, black ink, brown wash, watercolor, and gouache, 14⁷/₁₆ × 20⁷/₈ in. (36.6 × 53 cm.), inscribed: "Vue d'une chambre composée et peinte à Rome par Clérisseau pour le père le Sueur mathématicien, habitée presentement par le père Jacquet. Cette chambre représente le débris d'un temple antique dont on suppose qu'un hermite a voulu faire son habitation. Les sièges sont en forme de differens fragmens, le secrétaire représente un sarcophage, ainsi des autres meubles."

39. Prof. J. Douglas Stewart of Queen's University, Kingston, Canada, in a letter of March 22, 1980, advanced the idea that the parrot, often a symbol of the virgin birth of Christ, might have a religious significance in this interior. Though the idea is fascinating, I suspect the parrot was added for its bright color or to provide an exotic note, as I believe was often the case in the portraits of Van Dyck cited by Stewart. Professor John R. Martin of Princeton University, generously shared his opinion on this matter.

40. Nantes, Musée des Beaux Arts, "Portrait of Père Le Sueur and Père Jacquier," oil on canvas, 55 × 39¹/₄ in. (139.7 × 100 cm.), signed and dated 1772.

Caricatures of the two men were made by Ghezzi: Rome, Bibl. Vat. Ottob. Lat. 3118 f. 34v, "Le P. François Jaquier"; Rome, Bibl. Vat. Ottob. Lat. 3118 f. 35, "Le Père Le Sueur." Both have detailed inscriptions beneath; both are dated "20 avril 1747." See Archives de France et Musées de Rome, "Les Français à Rome, Residents et Voyageurs dans la Ville Eternelle de la Renaissance aux débuts du Romantisme," Paris, Hôtel de Rohan, Feb.–Apr. 1961, 218, no. 673 and 219, no. 675 (with mistakes in date and accession number).

41. This is the opinion of M. Luc Benoist, Director of the Museum at Nantes.

42. J. J. Barthélémy, *Travels in Italy,* London, 1802, 136; *Riflessioni dei Padri Tommaso Le Sueur, Francesco Jacquier . . . e Ruggiero Giuseppe Boscovich . . . sopra alaine difficoltà spettanti i danni, Risarcimenti della cupola di S. Pietro, Prosposte nella congregazione tenutasi nel Quirinale al 20 Gennaro 1743,* Rome, 1743. For a fuller discussion of these two men, see Bonnard Fourier, *Histoire du couvent de la Trinité du Mont Pincio à Rome,* Rome, 1933, 178, 186.

43. Marcello Miccert, of the Pieux Etablissemente de la France à Rome, and the Most Reverend Mother Superior of the Convento Istituto delle Dame de S. Cuòre (Convent at Trinità dei Monti) graciously permitted me to visit the room.

44. M. Gothein, *A History of Garden Art*, London, 1928, II, 235; P. Zucker, *Fascination of Decay, Ruins: Relic-Symbol-Ornament*, Ridgewood, N.J., 1968, 244, 245 illus. *Balthasar Neumann in Baden-Wurttemberg, Bruchsalm Karlsruhe*, Stuttgart, 1975, 38–47. Alastair Laing informed me that the ceiling was destroyed in 1945. The rest of the building has been remodeled.

45. McCormick, "Unknown Collection," 126.

46. Hautecoeur, *Histoire de l'architecture classique en France*, Paris, 1950, III, 398; F. Boyer, "Catalogue raisonné de l'oeuvre de Charles Natoire," *Archives de l'art français*, nouvelle période, XXI, 1946–49, 59; *Mercure de France*, Juillet 1750, 167; L. Duclaux, "La Decoration de la Chapelle de L'Hospice des Enfants-Trouvés à Paris," *Revue de L'Art*, 14, 1971, 45–50.

47. A. de Montaiglon and J. Guiffrey, *Correspondance des Directeurs de L'Académie de France à Rome avec les Surintendants des Bâtiments*, Paris, 1901, XI, 416, no. 4926, Vandières à Natoire; Hautecoeur, *Histoire*, III, 398; *Germain Boffrand 1667–1759, L'aventure d'un architecte independant*. Délégation à L'Action Artistique de La Ville de Paris, 1986, 112, 255–91.

48. *Boffrand*, 63–69.

49. Legrand, "Notice historique," 146r.

50. London, Victoria and Albert Museum, 3436–60, "Une cote du Temple Ruiné et restoré avec les fragmens antiques," pen and ink, 9^1/$_4$ × 7^1/$_4$ in. (23.7 × 190 cm.); London, Victoria and Albert Museum, 3436–59, "Un autre temple frequenté par un Hermit et par [ou il est converté à] Chappelle," pen and ink, 8^1/$_4$ × 7^1/$_4$ in. (21.6 × 18.6 cm.). The inscriptions in brackets are crossed out and corrected in Clérisseau's hand to read "e par lui changé en." A. Rowan, *Robert Adam, Catalogues of Architectural Drawings in the Victoria and Albert Museum*, London, 1988, 33. nos 7 and 8 and 52 no. 61.

51. "Cette fantaisie d'artiste eut du succès; le *Bailli de Breteuil* seigneur français ambassadeur de Malthe à Rome voulut aussi faire décorer sa maison dans un style pittoresque, et employa quelques années après les talens des peintres Lavallée Poussin et Robert si connu en France par la grâce de ses compositions, la fécondité de son imagination et son étonnante rapidité d'exécution. L'architecte romain *Barberi* actuellement à Paris, dirigeait les travaux, les conseils de *Piranesi* ne leur étaient point inutiles et il résulta du concours de ces artistes un lieu des plus agréables que les étrangers s'empressaient de visiter, et qui retinrent le nom de *Jardins de Malthe*.

"La *Marquise Boccapaduli Gentili* suivit cet exemple et fit également décorer dans ce genre ses maisons de ville et de ce campagne," Legrand, "Notice historique," 146–47.

52. P. Pecchiai, "La Villa della Rose," *L'Urbe*, XVI–XVII, 1938, 23–33; H. Focillon, *Giovanni Battista Piranesi*, new ed., Paris, 1928, 116.

53. "Piranesi dirigeait tous les travaux du Prieuré de Malthe, Clérisseau s'occupait des jardins et faisait des ruines; Piranesi aidé de la Vallée Poussin, d'Hubert Robert et de l'architecte Barbier décorait l'intérieur," M. J. Ballot, *Etienne de la Vallée Poussin, peintre d'histoire et décorateur (1735–1802)*, Rouen, 1927, 55. I am indebted to the late Sybille Pantazzi of the Art Gallery of Ontario for bringing this practically unknown book to my attention. Mlle. Madeleine Barbin of the Bibliothèque Nationale, Paris, discovered that the Bailli de Breteuil owned a nine-panel tapestry after designs by Clérisseau.

Three of these represented ruins such as the Temple of Peace (Basilica of Maxentius and Constantine) and the Pyramid of Cestius. It was item 297 in the Breteuil sale. He also owned a gouache by Clérisseau done in 1764 representing a triumphal arch and other monuments with a frame encrusted with three cameos (no. 31 in his sale).

54. Barsali, *Villa di Roma*, "Villa Chigi," 334–35 with illustrations.

55. ". . . c'est M. l'Abbé Farcetti; il craint que vous n'abandonniez le magnifique projet dont il vous a chargé. Il s'imagine que c'est à Rome seulement qu'il est possible de composer dans ce style vraiment antique, qu'il dit que vous avez dérobé aux Anciens. Je suis là-dessus fort de son avis; et le superbe dessin que vous lui avez remis de la *Spina antica*, qui fait partie de son projet, m'a paru plutôt le portrait d'un monument de l'antiquité qu'une composition dans le même genre. Je souhaite beaucoup pour vous et pour lui que l'air contagieux du moderne que vous allez respirer ne s'imprime point sur vos nouvelles productions . . .

"Je revois toujours avec un nouveau plaisir et même avec illusion le grand modèle de la ruine qui sera le point de vue de sa maison. Il est d'une vérité parfaite, et votre Polichinel Napolitain a mis dans son exécution une précision et un esprit admirables. L'Abbé Farcetti en est enchanté. Il me charge de vous recommander encore de poursuivre un projet si bien commencé, et de lui envoyer le plutôt possible la route consulaire et le pont triomphal qui y conduit. Vous avez sans doute reçu le plan général de son territoire qu'il vous a adressé. Il brûle de mettre le tout à exécution, et vous ne pourrez vous dispenser d'y veiller vous-meme; il y compte beaucoup," Winckelmann, *Briefe*, III, 345, no. 925, Winckelmann to Clérisseau, 1767; also Winckelmann,

Lettres familières, II, 222–25. The Neapolitan model maker was almost certainly Giovanni Altieri, who was in Rome about 1767 (see R. Rowland Pierce, "Thomas Jenkins in Rome," *The Antiquarian Journal*, XLV, part 2, 1965, 200–29). Thomas Hardwick and Sir John Soane also employed Altieri.

56. "Ce projet devoit s'exécuter à Sala dans le territoire de Venise. M. l'Abbé Farcetti vouloit que son jardin, d'une grande ètendue, représentât les débris de l'habitation d'un Empereur Romain, dans le style de la villa Adrienne aux environs de Rome. La grande route qui passoit effectivement au milieu de son terrain, auroit représenté les restes d'une route antique consulaire, ornée de tous les monumens qui avoient coutume de les avoisiner, tels que fontaines, statues, inscriptions, et un grand nombre de sépultures et de sarcophages. Cette route étoit bordée dans une partie, par un canal de deux cent toises de longueur sur lequel auroit été placé le pont triomphal.

"Le *Spina antica* étoit un Stylobate continu de quatre-vingt toises de longueur terminé par deux obélisques; une fontaine occupoit le milieu, et le reste étoit garni de statues, vases, trepieds, autels et autres fragmens antiques.

"La ruine qui terminoit le point de vue de sa maison à deux cents quatre-vingt toises d'éloignement, et dont le modele fut exécuté en liége de quinze pieds de longueur, représentoit les débris d'un monument triomphal immense, enrichi de fragmens antiques, figures, bas-reliefs etc. Sa masse étoit de quarante toises de largeur sur près de cent pieds de hauteur. A quelques distance de ce monument se trouvoient une naumachie et un amphithéatre. Le principal de sa maison devoit former un superbe Museum," Winckelmann, *Lettres familières*, II, 223–24, no. 1.

57. De Montaiglon and Guiffrey, *Correspondance*, X, 442, no. 4946, Natoire à Vandiéres, 3 mars 1753.

58. "Clérisseau après avoir beaucoup travaillé pour l'abbe Farsetti, qui lui demanda des projects de bâtiment, dont l'exécution étoit au dessus des forces d'un particulier, à juger par les dessins que Clérisseau m'en a fait voir, ce dernier se determina à revenir en France," P. J. Mariette, *Abécédario*, Ph. de Chennevières and A. de Montaiglon, eds., Paris, 1851–53, 379.

59. Lalande, *Voyage*, VIII, 298–99, describes in detail the exotic fruits and flowers but makes no mention of any of the antique features. Ettore Vio, *La Villa Farsetti a Santa Maria di Sala*, Venice, 1967, 8, quotes P. Gradenigo "Notatori Museo Correr, Venice" of Sept. 30, 1762, on various antique statues, and cites letters of 1765–74 about botanical matters which mention nothing of interest; the same is true of an inventory of 1767 which he also quotes. Emilio de Tipaldo, *Descrizione della deliziosa Villa di Sala di proprieta del seg. Demetrio Mircovich*, Venice, 1833, 9–10; G. Mazzotti, *Le Ville Venete*, 3rd ed., Treviso, 1954, 133, illus. 90. Professor Francis Haskell of Oxford University helped me in this matter.

60. E. R. Riesenfeld, *Erdmannsdorff der Baumeister des Herzogs Leopold Friedrich Franz von Anhalt-Dessau*, Berlin, 1913, 32. David Watkin and Tilman Mellinghoff, *German Architecture and the Classical Ideal*, Cambridge 1987, 29.

61. Winckelmann, *Briefe*, III, 556, note to no. 916.

62. Winckelmann, *Briefe*, III, 345–48, no. 925, Winckelmann to Clérisseau, 1767.

63. Winckelmann, *Briefe*, III, 345, no. 925, Winckelmann to Clérisseau, 1767.

64. Winckelmann, *Briefe*, III, 346–47, no. 925, Winckelmann to Clérisseau, 1767; Winckelmann, *Briefe*, III, 363–64, no. 934. Winckelmann to Clérisseau, Feb. 3, 1768.

65. Olivier Michel has generously provided me with copies of the relevant marriage documents, including a certificate from Charles Natoire certifying that Clérisseau had entered the French Academy in Rome in Aug. 1749, and the interrogation by the notary Nicolo Ferri on Nov. 23 of Michele Petit and Pierre L'Estache (Not. Ferri, Liber matrimoniorum, 1763 [363] Fol. 614, and the "position" [Le dossier] of Dec. 1 which dispensed with the publication of banns. 'Archivo del Vicento di Roma, Notzio Nicolo Ferri, Positiones Matromizles, l Decembre 1763).

66. For L'Estache, see Robert Enggass. *Early Eighteenth-Century Sculpture in Rome*, University Park, PA, 1976, I, 211–16.

67. Winckelmann, *Briefe*, III, 333.

68. Clérisseau's retainer fee from the Adam brothers was last paid from Drummonds Bank, Adams account, in Dec. 1766. Quoted in G. Beard, *Georgian Craftsmen and Their Work*, London, 1966, 69.

69. Winckelmann, *Briefe*, III, 356, no. 608, Winckelmann to Caspar Füssli.

70. "Nons fîmes la connaissance de Mr. Clérisseau excellent dessinateur en fait d'architecture . . . Il a fait des voyages par l'Italie, la Dalmatie et l'Istrie, dont il a fait en quelque façon la description par une suite de vues, qu'il a pris partout après nature. Ses desseins finis sont un lavis de différentes couleurs. Les restes majestueux de l'antiquité, ou ses idées formées sur ces grand modèles, y sont ornées des paysages et de figures touchées avec esprit . . . Son travail est estimé en Angleterre," quoted in Riesenfeld, *Erdmannsdorff*, 32.

71. Riesenfeld, *Erdmannsdorff*, 32.

72. H.-J. Kadatz, *Friedrich Wilhelm von Erdmannsdorff, Wegbereiter des deutschen Frühklassizismus in Anhalt-Dessau*, Berlin, 1986, 52–55, drawings reproduced in Figs. 64–72; M. L. Harksen, *Erdmannsdorff und seine Bauten in Wörlitz*, Worlitz, 1973, 10, Fig. 2; Riesenfeld, *Erdmannsdorff*, 33, 133–34, no. 24.

73. A. Rode, *Leben des Herrn Friedrich Wilhelm von Erdmannsdorf,* Dessau, 1801, 13. The Wörlitz palace is illustrated and discussed in Kadatz, 62–85.

74. This plate is "Restes d'un Pilaster très orné (Villa Medicis) aggrandissement de la corniche; colonne trouvee dans l'ile Tiberne," from *Vasi, canelabri, cippi, sarcophagi, tripodi, luverne ed ornamenti antichi, diseonati ed incisi par cav. Gio. Batt. Piranesi.* H. Focillon, *Giovanni-Battista Piranesi: Essai de catalogue raisonné de son catalogue,* Paris, 1927, 45, no. 638.

75. Edinburgh, Register House, Clerk of Penicuik Papers, no. 4817, Robert Adam to James, Sept. 11, 1756.

76. E. Edwards, *Anecdotes of Painters Who Have Resided or Been Born in England with Critical Remarks on Their Productions,* London, 1808, 73. Edwards added that Clérisseau was "so much affected by his exertion that he felt the impression for weeks after."

77. London, formerly Ralph Edwards Collection, "The Colosseum and Meta Sudans," gouache, 16 × 22⅝ in. (40.6 × 57.4 cm.), signed lower left, 1765. Mr. Naimaster, formerly of the Walker Gallery provided me with a photograph.

78. B. Skinner, "Nineteen Drawings by C. L. Clérisseau," *The Burlington Magazine,* CV, no. 721, Apr. 1963, 162. The late Edgar Wind first brought these drawings to my attention.

79. Skinner, "Nineteen Drawings," 162. Basil Skinner of the University of Edinburgh arranged for me to study these drawings then in the possession of the Marquess of Linlithgow and Major Percy Hope-Johnstone.

80. Hopetoun House, West Lothian, Marquess of Linlithgow, B 7671, "The Ponto Rotto," gouache, 17½ × 23 in. (44.4 × 58.4 cm.), signed lower left, "Clérisseau 1766."

81. Hopetoun House, West Lothian, Marquess of Linlithgow, B 7676, "The Arch of the Goldsmiths," gouache, 17½ × 23 in. (44.4 × 58.4 cm.), signed lower right, "Clérisseau 1766."; Skinner, "Nineteen Drawings," 162. See Chapter III, note 9 for a discussion of the engravings after Clérisseau. It was common practice for eighteenth-century artists to paint over outlines as well as over complete engravings.

82. Drumlanrig Castle, Dumfriesshire, Duke of Buccleuch and Queensberry, no. 78, gouache and watercolor, 18½ × 23½ in. (47 × 59.6 cm.), signed lower right center, "Clérisseau f. 1759." See Chapter III, note 40 for the history of this drawing. The Hermitage has an almost identical version of this drawing, although it lacks figures, N11625, 9⅛ × 11⁷/₁₆ in. (23.2 × 29 cm.).

83. Aurora, NY, Wells College, pen and ink, brown wash, green and white gouache, 10¼ × 14⅜ in. (26 × 36.5 cm.). The Hermitage has a very similar drawing, N11587, 10¹³/₁₆ × 15³/₁₆ in. (27.5 × 38.5 cm.).

84. Private Collection, France, gouache on paper, 18⅛ × 23¼ in. (46 × 59 cm.), signed and dated 1759. Reproduced in Jeanne Lejeaux, "Charles-Louis Clérisseau architecte et peintre de ruines 1721–1820, II, Son Oeuvre," *La Revue de l'Art,* LIV, Oct. 1928, 130. An almost identical drawing, also signed and dated 1759, was sold at the Palais Galleria, Paris, June 10, 1965. no. 29 *bis* (reproduced in catalogue), with the same dimensions. The drawing was purchased by a Roman art dealer and its present location is unknown.

85. Paris, Louvre, 25242, gouache, 23⅛ × 18¼ in. (58.7 × 46.4 cm.), signed "Clérisseau 1762." See J. Guiffrey and P. Mareil, *Inventaire général des desseins du Musée du Louvre et du Musée de Versailles,* Paris, 1909, III, 68, no. 2273.

86. London, Soane Museum, no. 129, "Interior of an Ancient Chamber," gouache, 18¼ × 13¼ in. (46.3 × 33.2 cm.), signed lower right, "Clérisseau Rom 1763."

87. Paris, Augier, "Roman Capriccio," gouache, 23⅛ × 18⅛ in. (58.8 × 46.2 cm.), signed and dated 1764. This drawing was sold at Sotheby's, London,

March 13, 1975, no 25; Hopetoun House, West Lothian, Marquess of Linlithgow, B 7674, "Ruins of an Arch," gouache, 23 × 17¹/₄ in. (585 × 43.9 cm.) signed "Clérisseau 1766." See Skinner, "Nineteen Drawings," 162.

88. London, Brinsley Ford Collection, "Architectural Capriccio," watercolor and gouache, 23¹/₄ × 17³/₄ in. (59 × 45.1 cm.), signed and dated "Clérisseau 1764 [or 5]." Sir Brinsley allowed me to study his drawing.

89. Windsor Castle Royal Library, Her Majesty Queen Elizabeth II, RL 13027 "A Roman Bath," watercolor and gouache, 19 × 13⁹/₁₆ in. (48.3 × 35.1 cm.) signed lower left, "Clérisseau f. Roma 1763."

90. Burlington, VT, Robert Hull Fleming Museum, "Bathers in a Ruined Roman Bath," gouache, 23¹/₂ × 18¹/₈ in. (59.7 × 46.1 cm.), signed and dated lower right, "Clérisseau 1764."; Paris, Louvre, 25243, "Un Bain Antique," gouache, 23 × 18¹/₄ in. (58.4 × 46.3 cm.), signed "Clérisseau 1765," Guiffrey and Mareil, *Inventaire*, 68, no. 2272.

91. C. L. Clérisseau, *Antiquités de la France; Première Partie, Monumens de Nismes*, Paris, 1778, xii.

92. London, Soane Museum, 64, "Interior of a Vaulted Hall," gouache, 24 × 18¹/₄ in. (61 × 46.4 cm.), signed and dated "Clérisseau 1764." The Soane also has a drawing of 1765 "Architectural Ruins" (no. 110) which shows a ruined vaulted interior with a vista to a columned interior. It is almost identical, even to the figures, to a signed version formerly in the collection of Ralph Holland (sold Sotheby's, May 29, 1975, no. 95) and with one in the Hermitage (N 16927) dated 1781.

93. Hermitage, no. 1860, "Ceiling Sketch," pen and watercolor, 13 × 9¹¹/₁₆ in. (33 × 24.5 cm.), inscribed: "Ritrovata in un cava fatta di feb. 1766 nel monte Celio vicino alla curia ostilea." The other N 1859 and has the same inscription. The inscriptions are in Italian, which is most unusual.

94. Such as the design for the Lansdowne Drawing Room ceiling of 1767. See D. Stillman, *The Decorative Work of Robert Adam,* London, 1966, Pls. 134 and 135.

95. Drumlanrig Castle, Dumfriesshire, Duke of Buccleuch and Queensberry, no. 80, mistakenly called "Bridge and Temple." Its correct title was recognized by the present writer, gouache and watercolor, 18¹/₂ × 23¹/₂ in. (47 × 59.7 cm.), signed lower left, "Clérisseau 1759." See Chapter III, note 40, for the history of this drawing. A Clérisseau drawing of the temple in the British Museum no. L.B. 4 1877.1013.942, mistakenly called "Ruins of a Temple possibly in Dalmatia," watercolor, 17¹/₂ × 22¹/₂ in. (44.5 × 57.2 cm.), also lacks the large arched bridge and is related to the Hermitage sketch. See chapter II. A drawing, probably by Robert Adam, in the Italian sketchbook discussed in Chapter II, no. 164, pen, brown ink, and gray and brown wash, 9¹/₁₆ × 14⁹/₁₆ in. (23 × 37 cm.), shows the temple from another point of view but omits any sort of bridge. See J. Fleming, "An Italian Sketchbook by Robert Adam and Others," *The Connoisseur,* CXLVI, no. 589, Dec. 1960, Fig. 9. A drawing in the Albertina, Vienna, 12449, pen and wash, 10⁵/₈ × 14³/₈ in. (27 × 36.5 cm.), depicts the bridge in the form of the Buccleuch drawing but is far less dramatic. I am indebted to Konrad Oberhuber for his help in obtaining information about the Clérisseau drawings in Vienna which are not included in any Albertina catalogue.

96. The picture is not as dramatic as the black-and-white photograph makes it appear. The colors are intense blues, yellows, and greens, but nowhere near as dark as they appear here.

97. A. Hind, *Giovanni Battista Piranesi, A Critical Study with a List of His Published Works and Detailed Catalogues of the Prisons and the Views of Rome,* London, 1922, 75, states that the print was done between 1743 and 1748; H. Focillon, *Catalogue,* 15, no. 68.

98. Hermitage, no. 2467, "Initials," pen and watercolor, each 4⁵/₁₆ × 5³/₁₆ in. (11 × 3.2 cm.); Focillon, *Catalogue*, 63, no. 930. Piranesi first used an initial with an ancient background in the third issue of the first printing of the *Prima Parte* at the beginning of the Dedication. See A. Robison, *Piranesi, Early Architecural Fantasies, a Catalogue Raisonné of Etchings,* Chicago, 1986, 98.

99. Hermitage, no. 2269, Portfolio N 7 (104), "Frieze," pen and watercolor, 6⁷/₁₆ × 11 in. (16.4 × 28 cm.), inscribed: "après l'antique." Focillon, *Catalogue*, 47, no. 681, "Fregio che si vede nella Villa Borghese fuori di Porta Pinciana." See McCormick, "Piranesi and Clérisseau's vision of Classical Antiquity," *Piranèse et Les Français 1740–1790* (Académie de France à Rome II), George Brunel, ed., Rome, 1978, 308, Figs. 14–17.

100. Hermitage, Portfolio N 15 (112); Hermitage, no. 2497, (112), "Maison de la campagne," gouache, 12 × 17 in. (30.5 × 43.1 cm.); Focillon, *Catalogue*, 33, no. 402, II, "Del Castello dell'Acqua Giulia." McCormick, "Piranesi and Clérisseau" 308, Figs. 18 and 19.

101. Hermitage, Portfolios N 2 (99), N 3 (100), and N 4 (101); Focillon, *Catalogue*, 18, 43.

102. Hermitage, no. 1959, "Helmets," pen and gouache, 7⁷/₈ × 11 in. (20 × 27.9 cm.); no. 2038, "Candelabra," pen and gouache, 7¹⁵/₁₆ × 11¹/₄ in. (17.6 × 28.6 cm.), Focillon, *Catalogue*, 48, 700. There are also parallels between Clérisseau's drawings of trophy reliefs and Piranesi's from the column of Trajan.

103. Cambridge, Fitzwilliam Museum, no. 3660, "Ruined Coffered Dome," pen, ink, and gouache, 14¹/₄ × 11³/₁₆ in. (36.2 × 28.4 cm.). McCormick, "Unknown Collection," 126.

104. Montreal, Russell Collection, "Ruin," pen, ink, and gouache, 26¹/₂ × 20⁷/₈ in. (67 × 53 cm.). The Witt Library of the Courtauld Institute, University of London, supplied a photograph of this drawing.

105. Geneva, C. A. Mincieux Collection, "Ruines romaines." I have no further information about the drawing. The Witt Library provided a photograph, on which my discussion is based.

106. Cambridge, Fitzwilliam Museum, no. 3659, "Ruined Coffered Dome," pen, ink, and gouache, 14¹/₄ × 11 in. (36.1 × 27.9 cm.).

107. These are catalogued in F. Boyer, "Catalogue raisonné de l'oeuvre de Charles Natoire," *Archives de l'art français, n.p., XXI, 1949*, 97–105: Boyer, "Natoire," 100, no. 625, Montpellier, Coll. Atger, no. 40, 11, pen, watercolor, and wash, 14³/₄ × 11⁵/₈ in. (37.4 × 29.5 cm.), signed lower right, "C. Natoire." From album M 43. See also J. Claparède, "Les Dessins Romains de Charles Natoire, Musée Atger, Faculté de Médecine Montpellier," *Journées médicales de Montpellier, 1957*, no. 4 and Pl. 4, who relates it to a Piranesi etching "Tempio antico inventato e desegnato alla maniera di quelli che si fabbricavano in onore della Dea Vesta" (F. 17 from *Prima parte di architetture e prospettive* of 1743). I fail to see any close relationship between the two, aside from the fact that both depict a dome and rotunda.

108. The unpublished manuscript diary of Pierre Adrien Pâris (1745–1819) who was in Italy from 1771–74, 1783–84, and 1806–1807 (now preserved in the Municipal Library, Besançon), states that students at the Academy were constantly exchanging counterproofs and copying each other's works. This reference is cited by J. F. Méjanès in "A Spontaneous Feeling For Nature, French 18th Century Landscape Drawings," *Apollo,* 104, Nov. 1976, 143.

It has recently been suggested that the figures in the Natoire drawing are by another artist (exhibition catalogue *Charles-Joseph Natoire (Nîmes, 1700-Castel Gandolfo 1777) peintures, dessins, estampes et tapisseries des collections publiques françaises* (Troyes, Nîmes, Rome 1977), 177.

Chapter V

1. J. Winckelmann, *Briefe,* N. Diepolder and W. Rehn, eds., Berlin, 1952–56, III, 340–45, no. 925, Winckelmann to Clérisseau, 1767. He and James Adam had considered such a publication.

2. Clérisseau, *Antiquités de la France: Première Partie, Monumens de Nismes,* Paris, 1778, vii, viii.

3. See J. Balty, *Etudes sur la Maison Carrée de Nîmes,* Paris, 1960, 10–13, for a summary of the history of the literature on this monument. See also R. Amy and P. Gros, *La Maison Carrée de Nîmes (XXXVIII) supplément à Gallia,* Paris, 1979.

4. A second revised edition published in collaboration with Clérisseau's son-in-law, J. G. Legrand, appeared in 1804.

5. Clérisseau, *Antiquités,* xx. It is interesting to compare this statement with the advice given to him by Winckelmann to seek the truth and refute the works of others (quoted above in Chapter IV).

6. Clérisseau, *Antiquités,* vii.

7. Clérisseau, *Antiquités,* viii.

8. Clérisseau, *Antiquités,* xii. "Apprenons donc des Anciens Les règles auxquelles nous devons soumettre nos operations: apprenons d'eux aussi à soumettre les règles mêmes au génie. Effaçons cette empreinte de servitude et d'imitation froide qui déparent nos productions."

9. Winckelmann, *Briefe,* III, 346–47, no. 925, Winckelmann to Clérisseau, 1767.

10. Winckelmann, *Briefe,* III, 349.

11. Winckelmann, *Briefe,* III, 345.

12. Winckelmann, *Briefe,* III, 347.

13. Winckelmann, *Briefe,* III, 346.

14. Winckelmann, *Briefe,* III, 347.

15. For example, two drawings in the Huntington Art Gallery, San Marino, CA, one of which is signed and dated 1771, are identified as "The Temple of Diana at Nîmes." They have nothing to do with the temple and are imaginary compositions.

16. De Belder Collection, Essen, Belgium, ink and gouache, 36 3/8 × 34 1/4 in. (92.5 × 87 cm.), inscribed on stone in lower right: "Vue de l'arc d'Orange, mesuré et dessiné en 1768 par Clérisseau." Sold Sotheby's, June 17, 1976, no. 185. Daniel and Diane de Belder kindly allowed me to study the drawing at length.

17. Number 20 in the drawing section included the "L'Arc d'Orange, mesuré et dessiné par M. Clérisseau," *Catalogue des livres . . . du cabinet . . . Clérisseau . . . 11 . . . 16 Décembre 1820 . . . l'hotel de Bullion,* 45.

18. Winckelmann, *Briefe,* III, 347. London, Victoria and Albert Museum, E 5151–1910, "The Triumphal Arch at St. Rémy," gouache, 16 3/4 × 23 1/4 in. (42.5 × 59 cm.), signed and inscribed: "Arc de Triomphe à St. Rémy en Provence Clérisseau 1769." A second version, signed and dated 1754, a clearly impossible date, was sold at Christie's, July 4, 1984, and is now in a private collection. Its dimensions, 15 3/4 × 23 1/4 in. (40 × 59 cm.), are nearly the same as those of the one in the Victoria and Albert Museum. There are slight differences: The vegetation varies, there are no shadows on the left side of the tomb, one of the drums of the columns on the left side of the arch is different, and there is also more open space on the left side. A third version, signed, but undated and the subject formerly unidentified, was in the collection of the late J. Knapp-Fisher, London, sold Christie's, March 30, 1976, no. 145, now in the collection of the Canadian Centre for Architecture, Montreal. I am indebted to Mr. J. Byam Shaw and Mr. J. Knapp-Fisher for allowing me to study this drawing.

19. Hermitage, Portfolio N 10 (107), statement at the beginning of the portfolio.

20. London, Royal Institute of British Architects Library, Hardwick Note-books, IV, 9, inscribed "Dessaux de L'Archivolte de L'Arc de St. Remi."

21. Cambridge, Fitzwilliam Museum, no. 3664, "Side of a large Wall," pen, ink, and gouache, 15 5/8 × 24 1/16 in. (39 × 61.1 cm.). For the history of the drawings in the Fitzwilliam, see T.

McCormick, "An Unknown collection of Drawings by Charles-Louis Clérisseau," *Journal of the Society of Architectural Historians,* XXII, Oct. 1963, 119–26. Number 3664 is listed there under "Unidentified Views and Fantasies of Roman Scenes." I have since identified it as the theater at Orange.

22. This is the reason given by Baron Grimm in 1779. L. Réau, "Correspondance artistique de Grimm avec Catherine II," *Archives de l'art français,* XVIII, 1932, 44. Mlle Marie-Félicie Perez presented a paper, "A Propos de la Publication des 'Antiquités de La France' par Clérisseau (1778)," at the Seventh Enlightenment Congress in Budapest, in July 1987, in which she discusses the book in relation to earlier projects.

23. C.-L. Clérisseau, *Antiquités de la France, Le texte historique et déscriptif par J. G. Legrand,* Paris, 1804.

24. See P. Collins, *Changing Ideals in Modern Architecture 1750–1950,* London, 1965, 74.

25. L. Lagrange, "Musées de Provence: Le Chateau Borély à Marseille," *Gazette des Beaux-Arts,* I, VI, no. 3, May 1860, 155.

26. Marseille, Musée Borély, "Façade," pen and wash, 14 9/16 × 25 3/16 in. (37 × 64 cm.).

27. Hermitage, no. 2274, 7, "Deux Fragments de la Villa Adriani à Tivoli," pen and gouache, 3 5/8 × 10 1/4 in. (9.2 × 26 cm.). The relief, shown (or one very similar to it), is illustrated in P. Gusman, *L'art décoratif de Rome de la fin de la république au IVe siècle,* Paris, 1908–14, Pl. 143.

28. The cupid-and-garland motif is based on the Clérisseau drawing. I relate it to the Piranesi etching. See Chapter IV.

29. A. Saurel, *Notice historique sur le Château-Borély avec une vue et un plan,* Marseille, 1876, 16 and 18. Much of Saurel's information is based on the Lagrange article cited in note 25. Michel Gallet helped me find a copy of this book.

30. Fernand Benoit, "L'Oeuvre du Peintre Louis Chaix au Château Borély, *La Revue Marseille,* 1964, 29, 32.

31. Saurel, *Borély,* 16–17; *Monographie du Palais Borély à Marseille,* Paris, 1908, table of contents (unpaginated).

32. R. P. Classements, "Le Château Borély à Marseille," *Monuments historiques de la France,* 1936, 160.

33. "The drawing has been preserved but fortunately for the chateau . . . it was not executed. . . . Clérisseau amassed in it useless features of the worst taste, such as statues on the balconies of the windows, so-called antique friezes above the casement windows, busts in round niches. Finally he hid the attic behind an enormous pediment decorated with three statues holding the arms of the Borély family and their motto *Altiora vincit.* Of this bizarre project le Brun preserved only the pediment reduced to two statues, but he placed it over the attic. On the facade there are no bas-reliefs, no busts, and no pilasters. The simplest lines were sufficient for him to make a building of great elegance."

"Ce dessin a été conservé; mais heureusement pour le château-il n'a pas suivi. . . Clérisseau y accumulait les inutilités de plus mauvais goût, telles que des statues sur le balcon d'appui des fenêtres, des frises soi-disant antiques au-dessus des croisées, des bustes dans des niches rondes. Enfin il dissimulait l'attique derrière un immense fronton décoré de trois statues qui soutenaient les armes des Borély et leur devise: *Altiora vincit.* De ce projet bizarre Brun n'a conservé que le fronton réduit à deux statues; mais il l'a placé au-dessus de l'attique; sur la façade ni bas-reliefs, ni bustes, ni pilastres. Les lignes les plus simples lui ont suffi pour faire un édifice plein d'élégance," Lagrange, "Borély," 155–56.

34. *Monographie du Palais Borély, passim;* Fernand Benoit, "L'oéuvre du Peintre Louis Chaix au Château Borély," *La Revue Marseille,* 1964, 29–35; E. Berckenhagen, *Die Französischen Zeichnungen der Kunstbibliothek Berlin,* Berlin, 1970, 393–96.

35. T. Jefferson, "Notes of a tour into the southern part of France in the year 1787," in *The Papers of Thomas Jefferson*, Julian Boyd, ed., Princeton, XI, 1955, 429; XV, 321–24.

36. P. Mariette, *Abécédario*, Ph. de Chennevières and A. de Montaiglon, eds., Paris, 1853, 380.

37. "J'ay vu M. Clarisseau, et il me confirme dans l'idée que j'avais de ses talents et de ses trauvaux. Il lui faudrait un Mécène et où le trouver? Tout le monde louera ses connaissances, son zèle, ses projets et personne ne les secondera; je le vois avec regret; *mais le goût de la nation porté d'un autre coté*, il ne trouvera dans sa patrie que des élonges et point d'encouragement," J. J. Barthélémy, letter to unknown correspondent, now in the Bibliothèque Royale, Brussels, Mss. II, 2249, published in Henri Glaesener, "Quelques aspects de la situation des artistes sous le regne de Louis XV," *Revue étude historique*, CVI, 1939, 42.

38. "M. Clérisseau P. *agrée* (3, 27) *Réception de M. Clérisseau — Le Sr. Charles Clérisseau*, Peintre d'architecture, né à Paris, a présenté de ses ouvrages. L'Académie, après avoir pris les voix à l'ordinaire et reconnu sa capacité, a agréé sa présentation, et, s'étant trouvé, dans le nombre de ses ouvrages qu'il a présentés, deux tableaux dont il pouvoit disposer, l'Académie, sans tirer à conséquence, les a acceptés pour sa réception," A. de Montaiglon, *Procès-Verbaux de L'Académie Royale de Peinture et de Sculpture*, Paris, 1888, VIII, 22; Hubert Robert was among those present. D. Diderot, *Salons, 1769, 1771, 1775, 1781*, J. Seznec, ed., Oxford, 1967, IV, 3; "Notice sur la vie et les trauvaux de Charles Dewailly par le citoyen Andrieux, secretaire," *Mémoires de l'Institut national des sciences et des arts: Littérature et beaux-arts*, 3, Paris an IX (1801), 39, cites the precedent of Clérisseau.

39. J. Lejeaux, "Charles-Louis Clérisseau, architecte et peintre des ruines 1721–1820, I, Sa Vie," *La Revue de l'Art*, LIII, no. 295, Apr. 1928, 229; Diderot, *Salons*, IV, 4.

40. "Les gouaches de M. Clérisseau, agrée et reçu en même tems, ne doivent point être regardées comme des desseins de fantaisie et de pur agrément, ce sont des tableaux d'une belle couleur et surtout d'un grand mérite pour l'exactitude de la perspective, les figures cependant y sont inférieures à l'architecture, et la touche en est si différente, qu'on soupçonneroit qu'elles sont d'une autre main," *Mercure de France*, 1320, Oct. 1766, 198–99.

41. London, Soane Museum, no. 68, "Architectural Ruins," gouache, 16 × 23 in. (40.5 × 58.4 cm.), signed and dated "Clérisseau 1771"; Hopetoun House, West Lothian, Marquis of Linlithgow, B 7672, "Ancient Gateway," gouache, 17 1/2 × 23 in. (44.5 × 58.4 cm.). The drawings commissioned by the Hopes are discussed in Chapter IV.

42. London, formerly Frank T. Sabin, "Architectural Scene," gouache, 23 3/4 × 18 1/4 in. (60.3 × 46.3 cm.), signed and dated "C. L. Clérisseau 1769."

43. Cambridge, Fitzwilliam Museum, no. 3629, verso, "Drawing of Architectural Interior," pencil and ink, 10 1/8 × 15 3/4 in. (25.7 × 40 cm.).

44. See Chapter IV.

45. The annotated copy of the La Livre de Jully sales catalogue is in the Johnson Collection of the Philadelphia Museum of Art, and the de Guiche one is in the Bibliothèque d'Art et d'Archéologie, Paris where the Rubens was lot 19.

46. I am indebted to Burton B. Fredericksen of the Getty Provenance Index for helping me with this matter. W. Adler, *Landscapes and Hunting Scenes (Corpus Rubenianum Ludwig Burchard, pt. XVIII)*, London, 1982, 80, no. 19, following Rooses mistakenly believes that the original version belonging to Sir Robert Walpole, sold to Catherine the Great in 1779 and now in the Hermitage, was in the de Guiche sale. The Harcourt painting was sold at Christie's on July 11, 1948, but was bought in so is still at Stanton Harcourt.

Chapter VI

1. "En 1771, il a passé en Angleterre, et c'est ce qu'il pouvait faire de mieux. Il ne restera pas, comme à Paris, les bras croisés," P. J. Mariette, *Abécédario*, Ph. de Chennevières and A. de Montaiglon, eds., Paris, 1851–53, 380.

2. Mariette, *Abécédario*, 380.

3. E. Edwards, *Anecdotes of Painters Who Have Resided or Been Born in England with Critical Remarks on Their Productions*, London, 1808, 73.

4. Mariette stated that many of the figures in Clérisseau's pictures were by Zucchi (Mariette, *Abécédario*, 380); see Chapter III.

5. London, Soane Museum (Adam Drawings), vol. XXXIX, no. 58.

6. D. Stillman, *The Decorative Work of Robert Adam*, London, 1966, 69.

7. London, Royal Institute of British Architects Drawing Collection. James Palmes and Prunella Fraser helped me with these drawings.

8. For Manocchi see J. Harris, "Some English Architectural and Decorative Drawings in the Museum's Collection," *Metropolitan Museum of Art Bulletin*, XXI, Feb. 1963, 220, and Fig. 11.

9. London, Royal Institute of British Architects Drawing Collection, IV, 55b, "Frieze, Temple of Antoninus and Faustina," ink and gouache, inscribed: "Clérisseau fin."

10. Hermitage, no. 2212, "Decorative Design," inscribed below: "au Temple de Faustine a Rome," pen, gouache heightened with white, 6 1/6 × 11 3/4 in. (11.5 × 29.9 cm.). There are other parallels.

11. London, Soane Museum, vol. 26, no. 28, "Decorative Designs," ink, 17 1/2 × 11 1/2 in. (44.5 × 29.2 cm.); vol. 26, no. 95, "Ceiling Design after Ancient Examples," pen, ink, and watercolor, 14 1/2 × 15 3/4 in. (36.8 × 40 cm.).

12. Hermitage, no. 2197, "Decorative details," pen, ink, and wash, 10 5/8 × 10 in. (27 × 25.4 cm.); Hermitage, no. 2263, "Bain delinié au palais des empereurs," pen, and watercolor, 7 3/4 × 8 in. (19.7 × 20.3 cm.).

13. Lansdowne purchased it with the understanding that Adam finish it at Bute's expense. The discussion of the library which follows is based largely on D. Stillman, "The Gallery for Lansdowne House: International Neoclassical Architecture and Decoration in Microcosm," *The Art Bulletin*, LII, 1970, 75–80. Throughout the discussion I refer to the Earl of Shelburne by his later and better-known title of the Marquess of Lansdowne, which he assumed in 1784; the building is better known as Lansdowne House.

14. *Catalogue of the Celebrated Collection of Ancient Marbles, the Property of the Most Honourable the Marquess of Lansdowne, M.V.O., D.S.O., sold at Auction Messrs. Christie, Manson and Woods, London, Wednesday, March 5, 1930*, London, 1930, 80.

15. Bowood House Archives, Clérisseau to Lord Lansdowne, May 27, 1771.

16. Christie's, *Catalogue*, 85.

17. London, Soane Museum, drawer LXVIII, set 5, no. 2, 17 × 19 in. (43.2 × 48.3 cm.); no. 3, 17 × 28 in. (43.3 × 71.2 cm.), signed "Clérisseau 1774"; no. 4, 7 × 11 3/8 in. (17.8 × 28.2 cm.).

18. Stillman, "Gallery," 78.

19. Stillman, "Gallery," 78.

20. P. du Prey, *Sir John Soane, Catalogues of the Architectural Drawings in the Victoria and Albert Museum*, London, 1985, 27. no. 2, Pl. 1. In another hand "Soane" is written in pencil. I am indebted to Pierre du Prey for bringing this drawing to my attention.

21. Letter to present writer July 6, 1977. However, du Prey identifies the Soane inscription as being after 1800.

22. Christie's, *Catalogue*, 97. Sir Francis Watson first brought this reference to my attention.

23. Christie's, *Catalogue*, 62, no. 2 in the collection, lot 93 in the sale. See also A. Bolton, *The Architecture of Robert and James Adam*, London, 1922, II, 5.

24. R. and J. Adam, *The Works in Architecture of Robert and James Adam*, London, 1778-1822, II, fasc. III, Pl. viiii; London, Soane Museum, vol. 22, no. 116, executed as designed.

25. I wish to thank A. H. Paine, Acting Secretary of the Lansdowne Club, for allowing me to tour the house before its destruction.

26. C. L. Clérisseau, *Antiquités de la France: Première Partie, Monumens de Nismes*, Paris, 1778, xxiv.

27. Royal Academy Catalogue, 1772, 7. The Clérisseau entries are 49-52. Walpole's R.A. catalogues are now at Dalmeny House, East Lothian, Scotland. John Sunderland arranged for me to study the microfilm copy at the Witt Library. I am indebted to Warren Hunting Smith, John Riely, and Catherine Jestin for their help.

28. L. Réau, "Correspondance artistique de Grimm avec Catherine II," *Archives de l'art français*, XVI, 1932, 43-44, no. 32, Grimm à Catherine II, 2 février 1779.

29. *Dictionary of National Biography*. . . . Sir Leslie Stephen and Sir Sidney Lee, eds., London, 1937, VIII, 1209; E.W. Harcourt, *Harcourt Papers*, Oxford, 1880-1905, III, 102. George III wrote Harcourt in 1770 that he had given up collecting pictures, "at least for the present."

30. Windsor Castle. Royal Library. Her Majesty Queen Elizabeth II. The late Anthony Blunt, as Surveyor of the Queen's Pictures, first told me of this cabinet. Sir Francis Watson, formerly Surveyor of the Queen's Works of Art, and Sir Geoffrey de Bellaigue, present Surveyor, arranged to have this cabinet photographed and for me to see it. It is not known when the cabinet was acquired (it first appears in an 1825 inventory of Buckingham House) or exactly when the mirrors were replaced.

31. Sold Christie's, Nov. 29, 1984, no. 119, now in a private collection. See Chapter III for a discussion of the print.

32. M. Hardie, *Watercolour Painting in Great Britain*, Dudley Snelgrove, ed., with Jonathan Mayne and Basil Taylor, London, 1966, I, 110-111: J. Fleming, "The Journey to Spalatro," *The Architectural Review*, CXXIII, Feb. 1958, 105.

33. J. L. Roget, *A History of the "Old Water Colour Society" Now the royal Society of Painters in Watercolours*, London, 1891, I, 3, 31. The only prints I have been able to find by Sandby after Clérisseau are two in the Victoria and Albert Museum: no. 28231.1, "Triumphal Arch at Fano Built in Honour of Constantine published as the Act Directs, St. George's Row Oxford Turnpike, 1778, Clérisseau Pinx . . . Paul Sandby fecit 1777," and no. 2831.2, "Sepulchre of King Theoderic at Ravenna, published as the Act Directs, St. George's Row Oxford Turnpike 1778, Clérisseau Pinx . . . Paul Sandby fecit 1778." The British Museum also owns impressions of these two prints, nos. 1872.7.13.462 and 1872.7.13.463. The Robertson and Sandby prints consisted of two series: views in the Bay of Naples and views in other parts of the kingdom of Naples. It is not known if any of the others are after Clérisseau.

34. Norton, MA, McCormick Collection, "Santa Costanza," ink and wash, 6 1/8 × 9 15/16 in. (15.5 × 25.3 cm.), signed lower right, with collector's mark of Paul Sandby lower left (Lugt 2112). Inscribed on back of mount: "Temple of Bacchus, vol. 2, p. 676 appendix." E. Edwards, *Anecdotes*, 73, states that Paul Sandby owned several Clérisseau drawings given to him by the Hon. Charles Greville, who had obtained them in Rome. For Greville see Chapter X.

35. See note 27.

36. Burney Collection of Newspapers, British Museum.

37. London, Soane Museum, no. 119, "Interior of a Sepulchral Chamber," gouache and watercolor, 16 3/4 × 22 1/2 in. (42.5 × 57.2 cm.), signed and dated lower left, 1772; Private Collection, France "Sepulchre," gouache, 18 × 23 5/8 in. (45.8 × 59.9 cm.), signed and

dated 1771, reproduced in *La Revue de l'art*, LIV, Oct. 1928, 127.

38. A. Graves, *The Society of Artists of Great Britain 1760–1791, The Free Society of Artists 1761–1783, A Complete Dictionary of Contributors and Their Work from the Foundations of the Societies to 1791*, London, 1907, 58. Clérisseau probably started exhibiting at the Society of Artists because his pictures for the annual exhibition at the Royal Academy of Arts were rejected for "being sent out of time." (Royal Academy of Arts Library: Council Minutes I, 198, Exhibition Rooms, Pall Mall, April 17, 1775).

39. Graves, *Society*, 58.

40. T. McCormick, "An Unknown collection of Drawings by Charles-Louis Clérisseau," *Journal of the Society of Architectural Historians*, XXII, Oct. 1963, 119–25.

41. Cambridge, Fitzwilliam Museum, no. 3669, gouache heightened with white, 16 ¹/₂ × 23 in. (41.2 × 58.5 cm.), signed and dated lower right, "Clérisseau 1774." Inscribed on verso in ink: "Nimphé à Castel Gandolfo a 15 mille de rome."

42. Hermitage, no. 2585, gouache, 16 × 22 in. (41.9 × 55.9 cm.).

43. Burton Constable, gouache, 16 ¹/₂ × 22 ¹/₂ in. (41.2 × 57.1 cm.), signed and dated 1774, listed in the catalogue as a gift of Brown; no. 76 in exhibition and catalogue, Ferens Art Gallery, Kingston upon Hull, Jan. 27–Feb. 22, 1970.

44. Hermitage, no. N 2582, gouache, 13 ³/₄ × 21 ¹/₁₆ in. (35 × 53.5 cm.).

45. Munich, Collection Peter Pröschel, "The Arch of Constantine," gouache, 20 ¹/₈ × 26 ¹/₈ in. (51 × 67 cm.), signed and dated 1771. The 1732 restoration is based on an entry in Pietro Bracci's diary. See M. Wegner, *Arch. Anz.*, 53, 1938, col. 172, for the most recent discussion. I am indebted to Richard Brilliant for his help on this matter.

46. E. McParland, *James Gandon, Vitruvius Hibernicus*, London, 1985, 20–23.

Chapter VII

1. A. Graves, *The Society of Artists of Great Britain 1760–1791, The Free Society of Artists 1761–1783, A complete Dictionary of contributors and Their Work from the Foundation of the societies to 1791*, London, 1907, 58.

2. *Livret des Salons*, 1773, quoted by J. Lejeaux, "Charles-Louis Clérisseau architecte et peintre de ruines 1721–1820, I, Sa Vie," *La Revue de l'Art*, LIII, Apr. 1928, 228, no. 3. This exhibition is also described in the *Mercure de France* of Oct. 1, 1773, no. 1384, 174, which I have been unable to consult.

Clérisseau may already have been back in Paris by this time, because Edward Edwards says he "returned to France when his patron, Robert Adams [*sic*], ran into financial difficulty," E. Edwards, *Anecdotes*, London, 1808, 73. This difficulty would be the Adelphi disaster of 1772–73.

3. D. Diderot, *Oeuvres complètes*, J. Assezat, ed., Paris, 1876, XII, 19. See also D. Diderot, *Salons, 1768, 1773, 1775, 1781*, J. Seznec, ed., Oxford, 1967, IV, 252, 288.

4. De Bachaumont, *Mémoires secret pour servir à l'histoire de la republique des lettres en France depuis 1762 jusqu' à nos jours*, London, 1780, VII, 206.

5. Formerly Orléans, Musée Fourché, "Ruin Scene," gouache, 23 × 18 in. (58.4 × 45.7 cm.). The Frick Art Reference Library supplied a photograph.

6. *Archives de l'art français*, 2eme série, XXI, 1905, 75.

7. L. Réau, "La Décoration de l'Hôtel Grimod de la Reynière d'après les dessins de l'architecte polonais Kamsetzer," *Bulletin de la Société de l'histoire de l'art français*, 1937, 7–16. C. Bauchal, *Nouveau dictionnaire biographique et critique des architectes français*, Paris, 1887, 626. 1772 to 1775 has been suggested by Svend Eriksen, 1775 by Fiske Kimball, 1777 by Edward Croft-Murray, about 1775–77 by Damie Stillman, and 1780 by Serge Grandjean. To some extent each date

has been proposed to substantiate the writers' arguments concerning the question of English or French priority in the use of arabesques in decoration. Much of the following discussion has been included, with my permission, in Pierre Rosenberg's and Udolpho van de Sandt's *Pierre Peyron, 1774–1814,* Neuilly-sur-Seine, 1983, 73–78. Mr. van de Sandt has generously allowed me to cite archival documents he discovered. S. Eriksen, *Early Neo-Classicism in France,* London, 1974, 310–11; F. Kimball, "Les Influences anglaises dans la formation du style Louis XVI," *Gazette des Beaux-Arts,* VI per., V, 1931, 238; E. Croft-Murray, "The Hôtel Grimod de la Reynière: the Salon Decorations," *Apollo,* LXXVII, no. 21, Nov. 1966, 84; D. Stillman, *The Decorative Work of Robert Adam,* London, 1966, 84; S. Grandjean, *Empire Furniture 1800–1820,* New York, 1966, 23.

8. J. Lejeaux, "Clérisseau," 229.

9. "Mais nous avons de lui deux sallons qu'il a décorés régulièrement en arabesques pour M. de la Reynière, directeur genéral des postes. Le premier dans son ancienne maison, rue Grange-Batelière; la peinture d'histoire est de M. Peiron, pensionnaire du roi. La second dans sa nouvelle maison sur les Champs Elisées, dont la peinture d'histoire est de M. le Chevalier Poussin," (J. Winckelmann, *Lettres familières,* H. Janson, ed., Amsterdam, 1781, II, 215, no. 1). It is interesting that Diepolder and Rehn's edition of the Winckelmann correspondence does not publish this part of the Janson notes. In a letter to me, Colin Bailey has suggested that Clérisseau may have first met Grimod de la Reynière at a sale held on Feb. 10, 1773. This sale had been organized by Grimod de la Reynière and M. Donjeaux. Clérisseau purchased a gem (no. 97, une double tête antique, bronze, 292 livres); Grimod de la Reynière was also a purchaser.

10. " . . . on trouve à gauche de la rue Grange-Batelière, occupée par de beaux hotels; . . . celui qui fût, bâti par Carpentier, Architect du Roi, pour le Sr M. Bouret, a appartenu depuis à M. de la Borde, puis à M. de la Reynière, et en dernier à le Sr M. le Duc de Choiseul. On doit y remarquer un sallon carré, formant sallon de compagnie, décoré d'un ordre corinthien en boiserie, dont les portes et la voute sont décorées dans le style antique. La partie historique de la décoration, consistant en bas-reliefs et plafond, a été traitée par M. Perron, Peintre du Roi: toute la décoration de cette pièce a été composée et exécutée sur les dessins de M. Clérisseau, Peintre du Roi. Cet Artiste a été assujetti aux arcades et aux pilastres antérieurement faits," (L. V. Thiéry, *Guide des amateurs et des étrangers voyageurs à Paris . . . ,* Paris, 1787, I, 186).

11. G. Desnoiresterres, *Grimod de la Reynière et son groupe d'après les documents entièrement inedits,* Paris, 1877, 21. The most recent account of Laurent Grimod de la Reynière is in Yves Durand, *Les Fermiers Généraux au XVIIIe Siècle,* Paris, 1971, 258, 541–42; unfortunately Horace Walpole's 1765 description of the Hôtel Laborde does not include the salon remodeled by Clérisseau, *Horace Walpole's Correspondence with Madame Du Deffand and Wiart,* W.S. Lewis and Warren Hunting Smith, eds., New Haven, 1939, V, 280 (Paris Journals December 1765); and *Horace Walpole's Correspondence with Hannah More . . . Lady Suffolk . . . ,* W.S. Lewis, Robert A. Smith and Charles H. Bennett, eds., New Haven, 1961, 80, to Lady Suffolk, Dec. 5, 1765).

12. Archives de la Seine, DQ^{10}1621 (see also boxes DQ^{10}1622 and DQ^{10}1623). These contain all the notary deeds and sale contracts of the building from 1761 to 1812. J. Hillairet, *Dictionnaire Historique des Rues de Paris,* Paris, 5th ed., 1963, I, 442.

13. Desnoiresterres, *Grimod de la Reynière,* 21 and n. 4, Archives de la Seine, DQ^{10}1621.

14. E. Bellier de la Chavignerie and L. Auvray, *Dictionnaire général des artistes de l'école française,* Paris, 1882; J. Locquin, *Le Peinture d'histoire en France de 1747 à 1785,* Paris, 1912, 215; *Biographie universelle (Michaud) ancienne et moderne,* new ed., Paris, 1840, XXXII, 645; L. Courajod, *L'Ecole royale des élèves protégés,* Paris, 1874, 185; A. de Montaiglon and J. de Guiffrey, *Correspondance des Directeurs de L'Académie de France à Rome avec les Surintendants des Bâtiments,* Paris, 1903, XIII, 123; De Montaiglon and Guiffrey, *Correspondance,* XIII, 1903, 171. A letter from Vien to d'Anguiller of Dec. 13, 1775, states that Peiron [sic] is in Marseille and will arrive. P. Rosenberg and U. van de Sandt, *Pierre Peyron 1744–1814,* 8, 23. I share Sir Francis Watson's opinion that such a young artist might well have been employed.

15. *Catalogue des livres . . . du cabinet . . . Clérisseau . . . 11 . . . 16 Décembre 1820 . . . l'hôtel de Bullion,* 44, no. 15.

16. Thiéry, *Guide,* I, 187.

17. Archives Nationals, Minutier Central, Etude XVIII, liasse 791, "La Boiserie du Sallon, composée de seize Pilastres peints en gris, rechampis et quatre tableaux dessus de porte, peints sur toille." A copy of this deed is in the Archives de la Seine, DQ¹⁰1621.

18. E. Fournier, *Paris démoli,* new ed., Paris, 1883, 380.

19. Archives de la Seine, DQ¹⁰1621, document dated 2 frimaire au XIV (November 23, 1805).

20. Archives de la Seine DQ¹⁰1623; Comte D'Aucourt, *Les Anciens Hôtels de Paris,* new ed., Paris, 1890, 22.

21. Jules Bertaux, "L'Ancien Opéra de la rue Le Peletier," *Le Correspondant,* n.s., 264, Aug. 25, 1925, 615.

22. D'Aucourt, 22.

23. A. de Champeaux, *L'Art Décoratif dans le Vieux Paris,* 1898, 329.

24. The delays were caused by Gabriel's insistence that the new building match his Hôtel. Grimod found this impossible, with the result that Soufflot intervened and a compromise was found. The relevant documents are cited in M. Dumolin, "Signalement de la vente de l'Hôtel de la Reynière. . . . *Ville de Paris Commission municipale du Vieux Paris, Procès-Verbaux* (Année 1926), Paris, 1930, 143–44 and June 30, 1928, 138–39.

25. Archives Nationales, Minutier Central, Etude XVIII, liasse 790. A copy of this notarial deed, as well as all the others of the sale of the building, is in the Archives de la Seine, 31 DQ¹⁰1621.

26. See note 9.

27. "A l'entrée de la rue des Champs-Elysées, vous verrez la Maison de M. Grimod de la Reynière, Administrateur général des Postes, bâtie par M. Barré, Architecte, dans laquelle vous remarquerez un salon de forme quarrée, décoré sur les dessins de M. Clérisseau, Peintre du Roi, et Premier Architecte de l'Impératrice de Russie. Ce salon, dans le style arabesque, est orné de beaucoup de sculptures et de dorures. Les peintures d'histoire ont été exécutées par M. de la Vallée, surnommé le Chevalier Poussin," (Thièry, *Guide,* I, 103).

28. Réau, "Grimod," 7–16. I am indebted to the late Professor Réau for his help. The late Jan Bialostocki of the National Museum, Warsaw, Professor Stanislawa Sawicka, former keeper of Prints and Drawings at the University of Warsaw Library, and Professor Adam Milobędzki helped me obtain photographs of the drawings and a microfilm of the text. Professor Milobędski also provided a copy of the article on these drawings by Zygmunt Batowscy Podroze, "Artystyczne Jana Chrystjana Kamsetzera W. Latach 1776–1777 i 1780–1782," *Prace Komisji Historji Sztucki,* VI, 1934–35, 192–208. See also Natalia and Sygmunt Batowscy, Marekd Kwiatkowski, *Jan Chrystian Kamsetzer, Architect Stanislawa Augusta,* Warsaw, 1978, 79–80.

29. Warsaw, University Library [Accession Number] z T. 173, no. 246, Pl. 1, J. C. Kamsetzer [Plan], pen, ink, and watercolor, 11 1/16 × 17 1/4 in (28 × 44 cm.), also z T. 173, no. 247.

30. Warsaw, University Library [General Accession Number] z T. 173, nos. 246–52, "Description de la maison de M. de la Reynière," 1–2, " . . . *La Grande Salle,* ou le Sallon, qui fait le principal de ornement la maison, est entre l'appartement de Mr. et Mad. on en voit l'élévation *planche* III et IV.

"Elle est decorée des arabesques peintes en couleurs d'un fond blanc sur un chassis posé en toile; ces arabesques sont rangées en récadres, entourées de bordures riches dorées, de même que les grandes glaces placeés vis à vis les fenêtres.

"Les battans des portes sont en *bois de rose,* et ont des panneaux d'un bois gris avec des Trophées en rélief appliquées la-dessus. Une frise surmontée d'une cimaise, forme la Corniche, sur la-quelle frise sont des festons reliefs de fleurs et de feuiles.

"Le Plat-font, *planche* V, forme un grand ovale avec une bordure d'un feston de fruits en relief; le tableau qui s'y trouve représente les trois heures du jour; au pour tour de la vossure, il-y-a un ornement de figures et verseaux en demi-coloris." Réau, "Grimod," 7–16, gives part of the above description of the wall decoration, but leaves out several essential details. He summarizes the descriptions of the ceiling and the rest of the room. This shortened version is also quoted by Croft-Murray, "Grimod," 377–83.

31. Warsaw, University Library, "Description," 2.

32. Croft-Murray, "Grimod," 379–80.

33. Hillairet, *Evocation de vieux Paris;* II, 544–46.

34. Réau, "Grimod," 11.

35. Hillairet, *Evocation du vieux Paris; II,* 545–46: Russian Embassy, 1828; Turkish Embassy, 1842; Cercle Impérial, 1854; Cercle des Champs-Elysées, 1872; Cercle de l'Union Artistique ou de l'Epatant, 1887; Comte D'Aucourt, *Les Anciens Hôtels de Paris,* Paris, nov. ed., 1890, 39.

36. Croft-Murray, "Grimod," 377–83.

37. Croft-Murray, "Grimod," 383, does not mention that behind the canvas panels, as installed at Ashburnham Place, there was "stated to be a flock paper of a green, red, and white pattern which may be of c. 1800": (C. Hussey, "Ashburnham Place, Sussex III," *Country Life,* Apr. 30, 1953, 1335).

38. Warsaw, University Library, [Accession Number] x T. 173, no. 248, J.C. Kamsetzer, Pl. III, "Décoration du Salon du côté de la Cheminée," ink, watercolor, and gouache, 10 15/16 × 17 1/4 in. (27.7 × 43.8 cm.), and z T. 173, no. 249, J. C. Kamsetzer, Pl. IV, "Décoration du Salon du côté de la Porte," ink, watercolor, and gouache, 10 15/16 × 17 1/16 in. (27.7 × 43.2 cm.).

39. Croft-Murray, "Grimod," 377, mentions an overmantel and two other pilasters by another hand, so clearly not part of the set. These were needed to fill out the space in Ashburnham Place, as can be seen in the illustrations of Hussey's article ("Ashburnham Place," 1336, Figs. 5, 6). The original paintings now in the Victoria and Albert Museum include: twelve pilasters, each 144 × 18 in. (165.8 × 45.7 cm.); four panels, each 144 × 49 1/6 in. (165.8 × 124.6 cm.); two panels, each 144 × 47 3/4 in. (165.8 × 121.3 cm.); two panels, each 144 × 42 7/16 in. (165.8 × 100.8 cm.). The four matching panels were probably on the end walls flanking the doors, while the narrowest pair would have flanked the fireplace; the other pair would have been on the window wall. The Victoria and Albert Museum provided the dimensions.

40. The scene of "Achilles Dipped by His Mother Thetis in the Styx" appears to be the painting shown to the right of the door in the Kamsetzer drawing of the end of the wall (see Fig. 140).

41. A. de Champeaux, 297–98. The de Comondo sale took place in Paris on Feb. 1–3, 1893 (Lugt 51324). The panels, lot 34, which brought 12,000 francs, are reproduced in the catalogue, a copy of which is in the library of the Victoria and Albert Museum. Photocopies are in the Witt Library, London.

42. M.J. Ballot, *Etienne de La Vallée Poussin, peintre d'histoire et décoration 1735–1802*, Rouen, 1927, 70.

43. Ballot, *La Vallée Poussin*, 69, for dimensions.

44. Warsaw, University Library, "Description," 3; Ballot, *La Vallée Poussin*, 68.

45. Ballot, *La Vallée Poussin*, 70.

46. Henri Carrée, *La noblesse en France et l'opinion publique au XVIIIe siecle*, Paris, 1920, 47–49 as quoted in Durand, *Les Fermiers Généraux*, 542. The best recent summary of the life of Madame de Genlis is in Ann Sutherland Harris and Linda Nochlin, *Women Artists: 1550–1950,* New York, 1976, 186–87.

47. Ballot, *La Vallée Poussin*, 70.

48. Jean Baptiste Le Brun. *Almanach historique et raisonné des architectes, peintres, sculpteurs, graveurs et ciseliers année 1777,* Geneva, 1972.

49. Croft-Murray, "Grimod," 379–80. Long ago, however, C. Gabillot correctly identified the *Almanach* passage as referring to the first salon (*Hubert Robert et son temps,* Paris, 1895, 32–33).

50. *Livre-Journal de Lazare Duvaux Marchand Bijoutier,* L. Courajod, ed., Paris, 1873, I, ccci.

51. *"Le salon de M. de La Reynière nouvellement décoré par M. Clérisseau.* Le genre agréable et nouveau que cet artiste a employé dans l'ordonnance de ce sallon, le rend des plus beaux et des plus distingués. Le style noble dans lequel il est traité répond très-bien à la grandeur de cette pièce qui a 38 pieds de long sur 28 de large et de haut: aussi le spectateur éprouve-t-il en y entrant une satisfaction qui augment à mesure qu'il en examine les différentes parties. Leur liaison et leur accord entre elles produisent un tout harmonieux qu'on est forcé d'admirer, et l'étonnement redouble lorsqu'on s'aperçoit que l'artiste a été assujetti à un ordre déjà exécuté et à plusieurs autres parties défectueuses qu'il a été obligé de conserver. Il a su tellement les changer, en ôtant les ornemens de mauvais gôut qui le couvroient et en substituant d'autres de meilleur choix, qu'il est impossible de s'apercevoir, sans être prévenu, que cet ouvrage est une restauration.

"La cheminée qu'on y voit est d'un marbre précieux, revêtu de bronze, dont l'application est très-bien entendue. Elle se lie parfaitement avec les quatre candélabres dorés qui ornent les angles du sallon où ils sont placés sur des piédestaux du même marbre. Ces candélabres, dont le travail est très-soigné, ont été exécutés par M. Duplessis, fameux ciseleur de Paris.

"Le plafond a 8 pieds de hauteur du dessus de la corniche, et 42 pieds de développement sur sa longeur. Il est entièrement de la composition de cet Architecte et a une parfaite analogie avec le reste de la décoration. Les quatre portes sont traitées d'une manière fort intéressante; la peinture qui en orne les panneaux et le couronnement s'accorde avec celle du plafond, et les ornemens qui entourent cette pièce sont d'une composition très agréable et d'une exécution précieuse. . . .

"Les glaces, dont les effets sont très séduisans lorsqu'elles ont à réfléchir et multiplier des objets intéressans, comme dans le salon de M. de La Reynière, ... Enfin, ce beau sallon, que nous citons comme un modele à suivre, fait également honneur au bon gout du propriétaire et aux talens de l'artiste. . . . ," Le Brun, *Almanach,* 84–86.

52. Thiéry, *Guide,* I, 187.

53. Archives Nationales minutier Centrale, Etude XVIII, laisse 790.

54. De Montaiglon and Guiffrey, *Correspondance,* XIII, 175, lists the date as Sept. 16, 1775. On page 315 the same information is repeated with the date as Sept. 16, 1777, which must be correct as it fits into the context of later letters. Hautecoeur, *Histoire de l'architecture classique en France,* Paris, 1952, IV, 483, gives the 1775 date. Ballot, *La Vallée Poussin,* 62, gives the date as 1778, following Piranesi's death.

55. Archives de la Seine, DQ¹⁰1621.

56. The 1780 *Almanach de Paris* lists Grimod as still on the rue de la Grange-Batelière. Kamsetzer mentions that Madame Grimod's salon was not yet finished in 1782, but one assumes that this smaller room would have been left until after the main salon was completed.

57. De Bachaumont, *Mémoires secrets pour servir à l'histoire de la république des lettres en France depuis 1762 jusqu'à nos jours,* Londres, 1783, XXI, 4–5; Le Comte Léonce de Montbrison, *Mémoires de la Barrone d'Oberkirch,* Paris, 1869, I, 286–88; L. Réau, "Correspondance artistique de Grimm avec Catherine II," *Archives de l'art français,* XVII, 1932, 142–44.

58. L. Hautecoeur, *Histoire,* IV, 483–84; Réau, "Grimod," 7–16.

59. See also Damie Stillman, "Robert Adam and Piranesi," *Essays in the History of Architecture presented to Rudolf Wittkover,* D. Fraser, H. Hibbard, and M. Lewine, eds., New York, 1967, 197–206.

60. W. G. Kalnein and M. Levey, *Art and Architecture of the Eighteenth Century in France,* Harmondsworth, 1972, 327.

61. Stern, J., A. *L'Ombre de Sophie Arnould, François Joseph Bélanger Architect de Menus-Plaisirs, premier architecte du Comte D'Artois,* Paris, 1930, I, 19–20; Deshairs, Leon, "Recherches sur le sculpteur Lhuillier," *Bulletin de la Société de l'histoire de l'art français,* 1907, 66–71.

62. Stillman, *Decorative Work,* 84, Figs. 9, 12.

63. Hermitage, no. 2114, "Arabesque," pen and gouache, 12 1/2 × 7 ¹¹/₁₆ in. (31.8 × 19.4 cm.).

64. Hermitage, statement at beginning of Portfolio N 6 (103).

65. Marie-Catherine Sahut, *Le Louvre d'Hubert Robert* (Les dossiers du département des peintures), Paris, 1979, 20, 57.

66. Archives Nationales, O¹ 1670, 123, 124.

67. Two letters of 1776 and 1778 are concerned with the presentation of a copy of the volume to the Academy. Institut de France, Archives de l'Académie des Beaux-Arts. Lettres de Charles-Louis Clérisseau, July 29, 1776; Nov. 23, 1778.

68. He purchased from Paillet 194 Bouchardon drawings that he sent to Russia. Paillet had purchased them at the Mariette sale of 1775, no. 1147 (Henri Cohen, *Guide de l'amateur Livres a Gravures de XVIII siècle,* Paris, 6th ed., 1912, 683). He also bought at the Natoire sale, Dec. 14, 1778, no. 101, Natoire's study of the head of the Virgin for one of the paintings in Boffrand's Chapelle des Enfants-Trouvés (*Germain Boffrand 1667–1759,* 290, n. 17c).

Chapter VIII

1. " . . . distribuée intérieurement à l'antique, toutes les chambres ornées de meme selon leurs diverses destinations et tous les meubles dessinés selon le costume, la maison ni trop grande ni trop petite. . . . ," L. Réau, ed., *Correspondance de Falconet avec Catherine II 1767–1778,* Paris, 1921, 216, no. 168, Catherine II à Falconet, 2 septembre 1773. The Falconet and other correspondence were published in fragmentary form in Ch. de Larivière, "Une Impératrice et son premier architecte, Catherine II et Clérisseau," *Souvenirs et Memoires,* VI, Apr. 1901, 193–226 and 315–38, and in A. T., "Documents pour servir à l'histoire des collections impériales: Clérisseau," *Starye Gody,* July–Sept. 1913, 43–52.

2. Réau, *Falconet,* 217, no. 169, Falconet à Catherine II, 2 septembre 1773; 227, no. 180, Falconet à Catherine II, 11 novembre 1773.

3. Réau, *Falconet,* 229, no. 182, Falconet à Catherine II, 6 décembre 1773.

4. Falconet also wrote about Catherine's views to Prince Galitzin and Cochin, and tried to absolve himself of all blame. Copies of all these letters are included in Réau, *Falconet,* 231–32, no. 184, Falconet à Catherine II, 24 decembre 1773. The criticism that the design was impractical for Russia does not seem to agree with Clérisseau's comments; see Appendix A.

5. It is possible that the elaborate finished drawings now in the Hermitage were not sent at this time, or were sent back as Prince Paul saw them in Paris in 1778 or 1779. In any case they went to Russia in 1779 when Catherine purchased Clérisseau's collection of drawings. L. Hautecoeur, *L'Architecture classique à Saint Pétersbourg à la fin du XVIIIe siècle,* Paris, 1912, 42–43, states that Clérisseau went ahead with the drawings. Hautecoeur gives the best summary of the Clérisseau-Catherine relationship.

6. Hermitage, Portfolio N 19. See Appendix A.

7. Hermitage, no. 2603, "Plan of the Roman House," pen and wash, 34 $^1/_8$ × 45 $^1/_2$ in. (86.8 × 113.2 cm.).

8. See Appendix A.

9. Hermitage, no. 2609, "The Roman House Project, Interior Elevation," ink and gouache, 14 $^3/_{16}$ × 15 $^3/_4$ in. (36.2 × 40.3 cm.).

10. Hermitage, no. 2610, "The Roman House Project, Interior Elevation," ink and gouache, 12 $^5/_8$ × 20 $^1/_4$ in. (32.4 × 40.3 cm.).

11. See Chapter VI.

12. Hermitage, no. 2604, "Project for House," ink and gouache, 32 $^5/_{16}$ × 20 $^1/_{16}$ in. (82.2 × 50.9 cm.). Closely related to this drawing are two, now joined as one, "Design for Salon," 7 $^1/_2$ × 12 $^{13}/_{16}$ in. (19 × 32.5 cm.), formerly attributed to Lavallée-Poussin, sold at Sotheby's, June 25, 1970, as part of lot 123 and now in the McCormick collection. It depicts the window and door walls of a salon, in which the division of the wall panels into arabesques, medallions, and Classical scenes is almost identical with that of the Clérisseau design. Furthermore, the two largest inset scenes are based on known views by Clérisseau, of which only one was engraved. While Clérisseau's Russian design is in his usual grays and tans, the unattributed one adds blue, yellow, green, and pink watercolor. The drawing was exhibited as a Clérisseau in "The Spirit of Antiquity: Piranesi, Adam and Clérisseau," Washington University Art Gallery, St. Louis, Oct.–Dec. 1984, no. 25, illus. Fig. 17, but the level of execution is below his usual standard. This suggests another hand, perhaps a pupil of Clérisseau, obviously familiar with the Russian design and his ruin scenes. Two other drawings in Sotheby's lot 123 (now in the collection of Terry Friedman) are probably by the same hand for the handwriting on the scale beneath the drawing is identical in all three works. If these drawings are by one

artist and executed at the same time, the Clérisseau-inspired one is *retardataire* and the two others—the Friedman drawings which show walls of a salon of about 1800 decorated with large eagles—are more advanced in style.

13. Hermitage, no. 2607, "The Roman House Project, Interior Elevation," ink and gouache, 17 3/4 × 15 in. (44.9 × 37.7 cm.).

14. Hermitage, no. 2612, "Roman House Project, Arabesque Panels," ink and gouache, each 23 1/4 × 7 1/8 in. (59.7 × 17.7 cm.); Hermitage, no. 2617, "The Roman House Project, Decorative Panels," pen and gouache, each 5 15/16 × 21 1/4 in. (15 × 64.3 cm.).

15. P. Gusman, *L'Art Décoratif de Rome de la fin de la république au IVe Siècle,* Paris, 1908–14, II, 105.

16. C. Tatham, *Etchings Representing the Best Examples of Ancient Ornamental Architecture in Rome and other Parts of Italy during the years 1794, 1795, 1796,* London, 3rd ed., 1810, Pl. 12.

17. Réau, *Falconet,* 233, no. 185, Falconet à Catherine II, 22 février 1774; 234, no. 186, Catherine II à Falconet, 23 février 1774; 235, no. 187, Falconet à Catherine II, 5 mai 1774.

18. Réau, *Falconet,* 243, no. 192, Falconet à Catherine II, 14 août 1774.

19. Réau, "Correspondance artistique de Grimm avec Catherine II," *Archives de l'art français,* XVI, 1932, 38–39, no. 31, Catherine II à Grimm, 17 décembre 1778.

20. Réau, "Grimm," 41–48, no. 32, Grimm à Catherine II, 2 février 1779.

21. Hautecoeur, *St. Petersbourg,* 44; Réau, "Grimm," 41–71, no. 32–49, correspondence between Catherine and Grimm, 2 février–7 décembre 1779.

22. Réau, "Grimm," 38, no. 31, Catherine II à Grimm, 17 décembre 1778.

23. A. T., "Documents," 46 and 51, no. 33.

24. Réau, "Grimm," 90, no. 63, Catherine II à Grimm, 7 novembre 1780. The best recent summaries of Cameron's career are the two essays by Tamara Talbot Rice and A. A. Tait, published in the Arts Council exhibition catalogue, "Charles Cameron c. 1740–1820," London, 1967–68. See also the review of the exhibition by Larissa Salmina-Haskell in *The Burlington Magazine,* CX, Jan. 1968, 51–52. Two monographs, *Charles Cameron,* by V. N. Taleporovski, Moscow, 1939 (in Russian), and *Charles Cameron (1740–1820), An Illustrated Monograph on His Life and Work in Russia, Particularly at Tsarskoe Selo and Pavlovsk, in Architecture, Interior Decoration, Furniture Design and Landscape Architecture,* by Georges Loukomski, London, 1943, are superseded by the Arts Council Catalogue. Isabel Rae's *Charles Cameron, Architect to the Court of Russia,* London, 1971, while based on the 1967–68 exhibition, adds very little.

25. Réau, "Grimm," 101, no. 68, Grimm à Catherine II, 4 mai 1781; 102–103, no. 69, Catherine II à Grimm, 23 juin 1781; 106, no. 72, Grimm à Catherine II, 17 juin 1781; 110, no. 74, Grimm à Catherine II, 26 juin 1781; 114, no. 77, Catherine II à Grimm, 10 juillet 1781 and 12 juillet; 116, no. 79, Catherine II à Grimm, 27 septembre 1781.

26. Hermitage, no. 40406, "Plan Général d'une Porte Triomphale projetée en 1781 par Charles Clérisseau," pen and watercolor, 39 11/16 × 23 7/16 in. (109 × 59.5 cm.), signed and dated; no. 40407, "Plan au res-de-Chausée," pen and watercolor, 23 5/16 × 38 9/16 in. (59.2 × 97.9 cm.); no. 40408, "Façade Principale," pen and watercolor, 23 5/16 × 38 15/16 in. (59.2 × 98.9 cm.); no. 4049, "Coupe sur le grand axe du percé intérieur," pen and watercolor, 23 5/16 × 38 15/16 in. (59.2 × 98.9 cm.); no. 40410, "Coupe sur l'axe des Massifs" and "Coupe sur l'axe des Petites portes," pen and watercolor, 23 3/16 × 38 15/16 in. (58.9 × 98.9 cm.); no. 40411, "Plan des Plafonds," pen and watercolor, 23 3/16 × 38 15/16 in. (58.9 × 98.9 cm.); A wooden model of

the arch was in the sale of Clérisseau's effects after his death, *Catalogue des livres . . . du cabinet . . . Clérisseau . . . I . . . 16 Décembre 1820 . . . l'hôtel de Bullion*, 47, no. 52. This is probably the one now in Leningrad.

27. A. T., "Documents," 46 and 51, no. 34.

28. Réau, "Grimm," 102, no. 69, Catherine II à Grimm, 23 juin 1781.

29. Réau, "Grimm," 142–44, no. 98, Grimm à Catherine II, 4 novembre 1782.

30. Le Comte Léonce de Montbrison, *Mémoires de la Baronne d'Oberkirch*, Paris, 1869, I, 286–88.

31. De Bachaumont, *Mémoires secrets pour servir à l'histoire de la république des lettres en France depuis 1762 jusqu'à nos jours*, London, 1783, XXI, 4–5.

32. Réau, "Grimm," 115, no. 77, Catherine II à Grimm, 12 juillet 1781.

33. Hermitage, no. 11551, "Architectural Fantasy," gouache, 24 1/4 × 35 11/16 in. (61.7 × 90.7 cm.), signed and dated *Clérisseau 1784*. The Hermitage has five other drawings dated 1781, five dated 1782, and one each from 1783 and 1784. All are large, brightly colored gouaches.

34. Réau, "Grimm," 173, no. 133, Catherine II à Grimm, 1 janvier 1787.

Chapter IX

1. The best general account of the building is Henry-Russell Hitchcock and William Seale, *Temples of Democracy, the State Capitols of the USA*, New York, 1976, 28–35. See also the present author's entries on the Jefferson drawings and the model for the Capitol in the exhibition catalogue *The Eye of Thomas Jefferson*, William Howard Adams, ed., National Gallery of Art, Washington, 1976, 225–29, nos. 393–99. James Buchanan and William Hay to Thomas Jefferson, Richmond, March 20, 1785, *The Papers of Thomas Jefferson*, Julian Boyd, ed., Princeton 1953, VIII, 48–49.

2. Jefferson to James Buchanan and William Hay, Paris, Aug. 13, 1785, *Papers*, VIII, 366.

3. Thomas Jefferson to James Madison, Paris, Sept. 2, 1785, *Papers*, VIII, 534.

4. Thomas Jefferson to James Buchanan and William Hay, Paris, Jan. 26, 1786, *Papers*, 1954, IX, 220–21.

5. *Memoirs, Correspondence and Private Papers of Thomas Jefferson Late President of the United States Now First Published From the Original Manuscript*, Thomas Jefferson Randolph, ed., London, 1829, I, "Autobiography," 39. Jefferson's work is dated Jan. 6, 1821.

6. Thomas Jefferson to James Buchanan and William Hay, Paris, Jan. 26, 1786, *Papers*, IX, 221.

7. Thomas Jefferson to James Buchanan and William Hay, Paris, Dec. 26, 1786, *Papers*, X, 632.

8. Jefferson, "Autobiography," 39. Jefferson does not mention the model maker's name. There has been confusion over his name as both "Bloquet" and "Fouquet" are listed in the related documents. It has often been thought that the name Bloquet might be a misreading of Fouquet. In "Instructions of Unpacking the Model of the Virginia Capitol with Invoice," the invoice is

signed "Bloquet" as follows: "Je reconnais avoir recu du Meur. Petit la somme de 84 de la part of Meur. Jefferson ce 6 juillet 1786. Bloquet" (*Papers*, IX, 637–38). The payment of 84 livres is confirmed by Jefferson's account book in which, under the date of July 1, 1786, he notes a payment of 84 livres to Petit (his maître d'hôtel and occasional errand boy) "for the Stuccateur packing Model of Capitol for Sta. Virga." However, Jefferson's account book has an earlier entry of May 22, which reads: "pd. Fouquet for the state of Virginia for model of the Capitol in plaister 372 f." The late Howard C. Rice provided the account book material in letters of May 12, 1975, and May 21, 1977.

Fouquet's name as the model maker is also given in the sale catalogue of Clérisseau's possessions after his death: In it, lot 53 is described as "Modèle en plâtre de la Maison carrée, exécuté par Fouquet, d'après les dessins de M. Clérisseau," *Catalogue des livres . . . du cabinet . . . Clérisseau . . . 11 . . . 16 Decembre 1820 . . . l'hotel de Bullion*, 47. Fouquet was undoubtedly the name of the model maker and Bloquet must have been one of the assistants. See also H. C. Rice, *Thomas Jefferson's Paris*, Princeton, 1976, 26–27 and 120, no. 13. See now Geneviève Cuisset, "Jean-Pierre et François Fouquet Artistes Modeleurs," *Gazette des Beaux-Arts*, VI per., CXV, Mai–Juin 1990, 227–40.

9. F. Kimball, "Thomas Jefferson and the First Monument of the Classical Revival in America" [III], *Journal of the American Institute of Architects*, III, Nov. 1915, 475.

10. Edmund Randolph to Thomas Jefferson, Richmond, July 12, 1786, *Papers*, X, 133.

11. Kimball, "Jefferson" [III], 479.

12. Kimball, "Jefferson" [III], 484.

13. Thomas Jefferson to James Buchanan and William Hay, Paris, Aug. 13, 1785, *Papers*, VIII, 366.

14. In both the engraving and the model the steps shown on the side of the building and parallel to it may be the original temporary ones. They were later replaced by permanent ones at right angles to the building as seen in a photograph before 1906 and in a drawing by Albert Lybrock, made in 1858, which is reproduced in Kimball, "Jefferson" [III], 478, Fig. 14, and 480.

15. In the early nineteenth-century view (see Fig. 158), only one small window is shown. The three curved top windows shown in the photograph were inserted before May 1865 when they first appear in a photograph of that date reproduced in William Gaines, Jr., "From Bullets to Ballots," *Virginia Cavalcade*, I, winter 1953, 12.

16. F. Kimball, *Thomas Jefferson Architect*, Boston, 1916, 142–48, and Kimball, "Jefferson" [I], [II], [III], Sept., Oct., Nov. 1915, *passim*.

17. F. Kimball, "Jefferson and the Public Buildings of Virginia, II: Richmond 1779–1780," *The Huntington Library Quarterly*, XII, no. 3, May 1949, 307–10 and Figs. 10–11. San Marino, CA, Henry E. Huntington Library, no. 9373, "First Floor of Capitol," ink, 14 3/4 × 9 1/4 in. (37.4 × 23.4 cm.).

18. M. Kimball, *Jefferson: The Scene of Europe 1784 to 1789*, New York, 1950, 74. San Marino, CA, Henry E. Huntington Library, no. 9374, "Notices explicatives des plans du Capitole pour l'etat de la Virginie." See also F. Nichols, *Thomas Jefferson's Architectural Drawings, Compiled with a Commentary and Check List*, Boston and Charlottesville, rev. and enl. 2nd ed., 1961, 37, no. 271.

19. Richmond, Virginia State Library, Mss. This is in Clérisseau's hand and addressed to "rue Peri [Berry] a la grille de chajot," *Papers,* 1954, IX, 603–604. The prison plans, which have disappeared, were drawn by Clérisseau after the work of Pierre-Gabriel Bugniet of Lyon. See H. C. Rice, Jr., "A French Source of Jefferson's Plan for the Prison in Richmond," *Journal of the Society of Architectural Historians,* XII, Dec. 1953, 28–30. Clérisseau's statement that the drawings had to be done twice would seem to bear out his great concern for accuracy, which the Adam brothers had doubted. I wish to thank the officials of the Virginia State Library for making this document available to me.

20. Jefferson, *Papers,* IX, 604 n.

21. Richmond, Virginia State Library, Clérisseau to Thomas Jefferson, June 2, 1786, endorsed by Jefferson "Clérisseau 28tt" (received on June 28).

22. Kimball, "Jefferson" [I], 381. The late Julian P. Boyd has kindly provided me with a copy of the invoice of June 3, 1789, which is now in the Virginia State Library, Richmond. The present whereabouts of the urn are not known, but it may have resembled one by Jacques-Louis-Auguste Lequay owned by Jefferson and now at Monticello. Jefferson made a drawing (now in the collection of the Massachusetts Historical Society) of that urn, which may have been a model for the one given to Clérisseau. According to the annotated copy of the sale catalogue of Clérisseau's possessions (in the British Library), Odiot was the purchaser of lot 53, the model of the Maison Carrée. Earlier, Jefferson had considered giving Clérisseau a silver copy of a Roman askos unearthed near the Maison Carrée. See *Papers,* 1958, XV, xxvii–xxxii; Julian P. Boyd, "Thomas Jefferson and the Roman Askos of Nîmes," *Antiques,* CIV, no. 1, July 1973, 116–24; and *The Eye of Thomas Jefferson,* Washington, 1976, 96, nos. 151–53, and 306–307, nos. 527–28.

23. Kimball, "Jefferson" [II], 430–31.

24. Kimball, *Jefferson Architect,* 147. Boston, Massachusetts Historical Society, no. 116, Thomas Jefferson and Charles-Louis Clérisseau, "Study Front Elevation, Virginia State Capitol," ca. 1785, pencil, 19 × 25 in. (48.3 × 63.5 cm.); no. 115, Thomas Jefferson and Charles-Louis Clérisseau, "Study Side Elevation, Virginia State Capitol," ca. 1785, pencil 19 × 25 in. (48.3 × 63.5 cm.); Kimball, *Jefferson Architect,* 147.

25. Jefferson, "Autobiography," 39. Kimball points out, however, that the columns on the model are Roman Palladian Ionic, and presumably those on the final drawings were also in this form. The capitals were actually carried out in the Ionic of Scamozzi, presumably by the builder Samuel Dobie. See Kimball, "Jefferson" [II], 430; [III], 483.

26. Kimball, "Jefferson" [III], 484. Kimball's argument that Latrobe may have been called in seems unlikely. I believe that the simplifications were strictly the result of a need for economy.

27. Boston, Massachusetts Historical Society, no. 110, Thomas Jefferson, "Early Plan Virginia State Capitol," ca. 1785, pencil, 8 × 12 in. (20.4 × 30.5 cm.).

28. Prof. Frederick D. Nichols, the foremost authority on Jefferson's architecture, gave me his appraisal of the present interior in a letter of May 29, 1970.

29. Thomas Jefferson to William Short, Eppington, Dec. 14, 1789, *Papers,* 1961, XVI, 26.

Chapter X

1. F. Noack, "Clérisseau," *Allegemeines Lexikon der Bildenden Künstler*, U. Thieme and F. Becker, eds., Leipzig, 1912, VII, 91, gives the date of the commission as 1776. The drawings are dated 1778.

2. Lejeaux, "Charles-Louis Clérisseau, architecte et peintre de ruines (1721–1820), I, Sa Vie," *La Revue de l'Art*, LIII, no. 295, Apr. 1928, 230. One of the drawings is inscribed "laissé à Metz par M. Clérisseau, l'avant-vielle de son départ pour Paris, en 1778." I am greatly indebted to Studio Remi Villaggi, Metz, for photographing the building and drawings for me.

3. Also spelled "Lemasson." His brother Louis Lemasson (1743–1829) was a pupil of Clérisseau, according to Michel Gallet, *Demeures parisiennes de l'époque de Louis XVI*, Paris, 1964, 190.

4. J. Lejeaux, "Charles-Louis Clérisseau, architecte, [28 août 1721–19 janvier 1820] *L'Architecture* XLI, no. 4, 1928, 120."

5. "Ce bâtiment, très considérable, porte un caractère de grandeur et de simplicité qui tient beaucoup de l'antique," J. Winckelmann, *Lettres familières*, H. Janson, ed., Yverdon, 1784, II, 235.

6. Hermitage, Portfolio 4.

7. A. Doebber, "Das Schloss in Weimar, seine geschichte vom Brande 1774 bis zur Wiederherstellung 1804," *Zeitschrift des Vereins für thüringische Geschichte und Altertumskunde*, n. f., 3rd supp., 1911, 33–34.

8. Doebber, "Schloss," 33–35. Only one of the drawings is known to me and it has not been possible to obtain any information about the others, which are in East Germany.

9. Doebber, "Schloss," 3; D. Watkin and T. Mellinghoff, *German Architecture and the Classical Ideal*. Cambridge, 1987, 261–62.

10. D. Diderot, *Correspondance, littéraire, philosophique, et critique*, Maurice Tourneux, ed., Paris, 1880, XIII, 436.

11. A. Graves, *The Society of Artists of Great Britain 1760–1791, the Free Society of Artists 1761–1783. A Complete Dictionary of Contributors and Their Work from the Foundation of the Society to 1791*, London, 1907, 58.

12. M. L. Karten, *Schloss und Park Wörlitz*, Barg B. M., 1939, 185; L. Grote, *De Park zu Wörlitz*, Berlin, 1944, 64–65; *Charles-Louis Clérisseau 1722–1820 Ruinenmalerei*, Staatliche Schlösser und Gärten Wörlitz, Oranienbaum, Luisium (Wörlitz 1984) with text by Burkhard Gäbler. Gäbler gives a description of the drawings, illustrating all thirteen of them in color (and two drawings from another source, which I believe are not by Clérisseau). He also illustrates the room in the Villa Hamilton where the Clérisseaus hang (Fig. 15). Gäbler also includes an excellent summary of Clérisseau's career with a complete bibliography; Watkin and Mellinghoff, 31–32.

13. Norton, MA, T. J. and M. D. McCormick, "Charles-Louis Clérisseau," black crayon, 8 1/4 in. diameter (21 cm.); and Wörlitz, Schloss Bibliothek, "Portrait of Clérisseau" by Johann Fischer, fresco, 16 11/16 × 12 9/16 in. (42.5 × 32 cm.), illus. Gäbler, *Clérisseau Ruinmalerei*, Fig. 16, where it's dated 1772, see Chapter I, no. 71, IV. The drawing and the fresco based on it depict a man who could be seventy-one. Clérisseau certainly appears older here than in the probable portrait drawing by Angelica Kauffmann of 1761–66, also described in Chapter I, no. 71, IV. A view of the library is reproduced in H.-J. Kadatz, *Friedrich Wilhelm von Erdmannsdorff, Wegbereiter des deutschen Früh Klassizismus in Anhalt-Dessau*, Berlin, 1986, 77, Fig. 128.

14. "Ruins of an Imaginary Palace," gouache, 24 3/4 × 37 in. (63 × 93 cm.), signed lower left, "Clérisseau 1793." The basic composition is almost identical with that of a smaller drawing in the Fitzwilliam Museum, no. 3655, 12 × 17 15/16 in. (30.5 × 45.5 cm.), that lacks figures and differs in other details.

15. Examples include one dated 1800, in a private collection, and two dated 1801, formerly Paul Prouté S.A. (see *Dessins originaux anciens et modernes . . . 1973*, no. 3). In the Platt Collection of Photographs in the Department of Art and Archaeology, Princeton University, is a picture of a ruin scene signed and dated "Clérisseau 1798," which appeared in *Parson's Book Catalogue,* New York, 1934, no. 50. From the reproduction the work does not appear to be by Clérisseau, and I suspect the signature and date were later additions.

16. Paris, Paul Prouté S.A. (*Dessins originaux anciens et moderne. . . .* Automne 1986, nos. 4–17, 5 $^{1}/_{2}$ × 7 $^{1}/_{2}$ in. (14 × 19 cm.). All of the drawings are now dispersed. Hubert Prouté kindly provided me with photographs.

17. Jean-Marie Pérouse de Montclos, *Etienne-Louis Boullée (1728–1799) de l'architecture classique à l'architecture révolutionnaire,* Paris, 1967, 253; Jean Ziegler, "Françoise Baudelaire (1759–1827) Peintre et Amateur d'art," *Gazette des Beaux-Arts* VI per. XCIII, Mar. 1979, III.

18. London, British Museum, 40714 folio 247, Clérisseau to Charles Greville, April 1788.

19. Paris, Archives Nationales Procès Verbal de la Visite des trois Maisons D'Auteuil le 20 frimaire on 2 (Dec. 10, 1793) J.-B.-P. LeBrun mandaté par la Commision des Arts.

20. "Notice sur les artistes candidats à la Classe de beaux-arts de l'Institut (23 fructidor an VIII)," *Archives de l'art français* nouvelle periode IV, fascicule II, 1910, 244.

21. C.-L. Clérisseau, *Antiquités de la France, Le Texte historique et descriptif par J.G. Legrand,* Paris, 1804. While this edition contains much of Clérisseau's original text, Legrand added considerably to it; further, nearly all of the illustrations are new.

22. Paris, Archives Nationales, A F IV, 184.

23. *La Grande Encyclopédié,* Paris, 1856, VI, 653.

24. See Chapter I, no. 71, II.

25. Paris, Grande Chancellerie de la Légion d'honneur, dossier Clérisseau.

26. Déclaration de succession de Ch.-L. Clérisseau, is juillet 1820. Bureau de L'Enregistremend de Neuilly.

27. *Catalogue des livres . . . du cabinet . . . Clérisseau . . . 11 . . . 16 Décembre 1820 . . . l'hotel de Bullion.* Clérisseau's collection is briefly described in a report to the Commission by Lebrun on 20 frimaire l'an 2, 178 (Archives Nationals, F^{17a}1231, doss. 4, 7 L).

Index